D1565455

Disability

Recent Titles in the
CONTEMPORARY WORLD ISSUES
Series

Books in the **Contemporary World Issues** series address vital issues in today's society such as genetic engineering, pollution, and biodiversity. Written by professional writers, scholars, and nonacademic experts, these books are authoritative, clearly written, up-to-date, and objective. They provide a good starting point for research by high school and college students, scholars, and general readers as well as by legislators, businesspeople, activists, and others.

Each book, carefully organized and easy to use, contains an overview of the subject, a detailed chronology, biographical sketches, facts and data and/or documents and other primary source material, a forum of authoritative perspective essays, annotated lists of print and nonprint resources, and an index.

Readers of books in the Contemporary World Issues series will find the information they need in order to have a better understanding of the social, political, environmental, and economic issues facing the world today.

Disability

A REFERENCE HANDBOOK

Michael Rembis

ABC-CLIO™

An Imprint of ABC-CLIO, LLC
Santa Barbara, California • Denver, Colorado

Library of Congress Control Number: 2019020788

ISBN: 978-1-4408-6229-8 (print)
      978-1-4408-6230-4 (ebook)

23 22 21 20 19   1 2 3 4 5

This book is also available as an eBook.

ABC-CLIO
An Imprint of ABC-CLIO, LLC

ABC-CLIO, LLC
147 Castilian Drive
Santa Barbara, California 93117
www.abc-clio.com

This book is printed on acid-free paper ∞

Manufactured in the United States of America

Portions of chapter 2 have been adapted from Rembis, Michael A. 2009. "(Re)Defining disability in the 'genetic age': behavioral genetics, 'new' eugenics, and the future of impairment." *Disability & Society* 24; 5: 585–597.

For Carlos

Contents

After decades of activism and advocacy, disability rights have become a global concern in the 21st century. International organizations such as the United Nations (UN) and the World Health Organization (WHO) have redefined the term "disability," recorded the demographic data of disabled people throughout the world, and made official calls for the integration of disabled people into mainstream life. In December 2006, the UN adopted the Convention on the Rights of Persons with Disabilities (CRPD), marking 60 years of human rights measures and more than 50 years of enactments specifically designed to benefit people with a broad range of disabilities. The UN CRPD entered into force in May 2008. In May 2018, the Convention had been ratified by177 countries. As it states on the UN's website:

> The Convention follows decades of work . . . to change attitudes and approaches to persons with disabilities. It takes to a new height the movement from viewing persons with disabilities as "objects" of charity, medical treatment and social protection towards viewing persons with disabilities as "subjects" with rights, who are capable of claiming those rights and making decisions for their lives based on their free and informed consent as well as being active members of society. (UN, 2018)

Through the actions of the UN, and other interested organizations, disabled people came to represent one of the world's

largest minority populations by the beginning of the 21st century. Official reports (WHO, 2011) estimate that between 1
and 1.5 billion people, or 20 percent of the world's population,
are living with a disability. About 85 percent of disability is
acquired. Only 15 percent of the world's population has what
are called "congenital" disabilities—that is, disabilities that developed in utero or upon birth, such as spina bifida, Down
syndrome, cerebral palsy, or muscular dystrophy. Most of the
disability in the world is created through human interaction,
through military violence, malnutrition, childbirth, environmental pollution, injuries, and illnesses. The majority of the
world's disabled population lives outside wealthy Western or
global North areas, such as the United States, Western Europe,
or Canada; 80 percent of disabled people live in what is usually referred to as the global South or the "developing" world.
Because most disabled people live in poverty in places where
access to food, clean water, education, health care, and employment is already precarious, disability and the experiences
of disabled people have become a global concern.

Although the United States has not ratified the UN CRPD,
it is a world leader in disability rights. If we use contemporary
legal definitions, about 19 percent of the U.S. population or
54 million people are living with a disability. The U.S. Congress passed the first federal legislation protecting the civil
rights of people with disabilities in the 1960s. Congress sub-
sequently passed more than 50 laws between the creation of
those early measures, which usually focused on specific concerns such as access to the built environment, access to K–12
education, telecommunications access, or accessible air travel,
and the signing of the Americans with Disabilities Act, the
most comprehensive disability rights legislation in the world,
in July 1990. Following nearly 20 years of legal battles, the U.S.
Congress further fortified legal protections for disabled citizens
with the 2008 Americans with Disabilities Act Amendments
Act (Public Law 110–325, ADAAA, effective January 1, 2009).

In this book, we will journey through America's past in an effort to better understand its present. We will begin with a discussion of disabled people as objects. For nearly two centuries, disabled people increasingly became the objects of state and medical intervention and various charitable efforts to "improve" their lives and "protect" them from harm. Institutionalization, eugenics, and the rise of disability charities will comprise three broad themes that will shape our examination of more recent issues relating to disability and disabled people. This historical background will provide the basis for a discussion of the rise of the modern disability rights movement and its accomplishments, as well as the challenges it faces in the 21st century.

The main focus of the book will be on disabled people as citizen subjects. It will concentrate on the moments when disabled people came together to advocate for their rights and their inclusion in American society. We will begin in the 19th century, when organizations designed to advocate for specific groups of disabled people, such as deaf people or blind people, first made their mark on the country's social and political landscape. We will continue through the first half of the 20th century, when world war, polio, and a growing African American civil rights movement significantly altered not only Americans' views of disability but also disabled people's organizing efforts. Our story will culminate in the second half of the 20th century, when various groups of disabled people came together to forge the modern disability rights movement, which sought to end more than 150 years of the state-sanctioned segregation of disabled people in institutions and "special" schools and hospitals and worked to push for inclusion in the community and equal access to education and employment. The independent living movement, the Mad People's liberation movement, and the self-advocacy movement represent three separate but often-overlapping branches of the modern movement for the full inclusion of disabled people in American society.

Our story ends in the early 21st century, when broad ideas and concerns and specific changes long advocated by disabled people and their allies became an ordinary—although not uncontested—part of our everyday lives. The UN CRPD and the WHO definition of disability set global standards for access, inclusion, development, and empowerment. At home in the United States, changes such as mainstream schooling and accessible public transportation had been woven into the national fabric. The first two decades of the 21st century was a time when real, important, observable transformations were taking place in the United States and abroad. It was also a time when the historically white, middle-class leaders of the modern disability rights movement began to think in more concrete ways about how race, gender, class, sexuality, and religion influenced experiences of disability. It was a time when leadership became more diverse and when white leaders more consciously aligned themselves with other minority groups and the burgeoning global disability rights movement. Finally, it was a time when disability rights became human rights and when efforts for access and inclusion turned into powerful calls for social justice.

Important note on terminology: Throughout this book I use the terms "disabled people" and "people with disabilities" interchangeably. Each term is equally acceptable. The term "disabled people" is more common in the United Kingdom. It is used by people who want to identify disability as an important part of their identity and as something that is both political and positive. Similar to identifying as an African American or a big "D" Deaf person, people who identify as disabled consider themselves part of a sociopolitical minority and wish to claim their citizenship rights as a member of that group in society. The term "people with disabilities" originated in the United States primarily among participants in the self-advocacy movement who wanted to emphasize the "person" and not the disability. People who use the term "disabled people" find the term "people with disabilities" problematic because it implies that disability is something that exists outside of them and it is something that they have or possess, rather than being part of their identity, part of what makes them a person. Critics claim that the term "people with disabilities" removes disability from the social and political realm. Both terms are equally valid and acceptable, and both terms will be used in this text.

References

United Nations. 2018. "Convention on the Rights of Persons with Disabilities (CRPD)." https://www.un.org/development/desa/disabilities/convention-on-the-rights-of-persons-with-disabilities.html (Accessed May 5, 2018).

World Health Organization (WHO). 2011. "World Report on Disability." https://www.ncbi.nlm.nih.gov/books/NBK304079/ (Accessed May 5, 2018).

Disability

Introduction

This chapter will provide the background and history that will frame the rest of the material in this book. Rather than present a comprehensive narrative history of disability in the United States, this chapter will take a more targeted approach and focus on four main areas of concern: institutionalization, eugenics, charity, and the modern disability rights movement. The material in each section and the sections themselves are organized chronologically to show change over time. There are, however, significant themes that run through each section that complicate a simple and progressive linear narrative in which disabled people went from being objects to subjects. The history of disability and disabled people in the United States and the experiences of disabled people in the 21st century are all marked by continual processes of oppression and resistance; of negotiation and compromise; and of liberation, empowerment, and backlash.

While it is safe to say that people with disabilities living in the 21st century are much better off than their historical counterparts, we must always qualify that assertion. Which groups of disabled people are better off, and why? Do disabled people of color have the same experiences or quality of life as their

---

[Black-and-white profile of a young Helen Keller sitting reading a book and smelling a flower] Blind and deaf from a young age, Helen Keller learned to communicate with the help of teacher Anne Sullivan. Keller was a respected writer and social activist. (Library of Congress)

white counterparts? What is life like for women with disabilities? Do women of color with disabilities have different experiences than their white counterparts? How does one's wealth or class position affect one's experience of disability? Do people of various faiths like Christian, Muslim, or Jewish have different experiences with disability? Disability is a social category, not merely or only a medical condition, and as such it requires a more complex and nuanced analysis. This more complex view of disability, often described as the "social model of disability," enables us to explore the ways in which race, gender, religion, sexuality, or class affects experiences of living with a disability.

This book follows the social model of disability and argues that disability is not only or even necessarily a medical problem or concern but rather is a social and political category that is deeply affected by material relations (e.g., the built environment, income, class, access to resources, and the overall economy) and dominant social attitudes. This means that disability is neither static nor ahistorical. It changes from one situation to the next, from one culture to the next, and it is experienced differently at different points throughout history. While this may seem like a fairly straightforward and simple assertion, its effects are profound. When we think of disability as a social category and not a biological condition, we can focus our attention on altering the environment and social attitudes, rather than correcting or fixing individual bodies. If we operate from the premise that disability can and does change, then we can work toward a more socially just and equitable future.

When taken together, the sections in this chapter will show how the material conditions of disability and the social attitudes surrounding disability have changed from the time of the founding of the United States to the early 21st century. Disabled people went from being the objects of medical and state intervention and charitable giving to being citizen subjects capable of demanding their own rights and forging their own historical narratives. This transformation has not been complete, however, and still in the 21st century, most disabled people occupy a place of second-class citizenship and continue to be the objects of state and medical surveillance and intervention. Disabled people have come a long way in securing the rights granted to them under the U.S. Constitution and through various laws passed by the U.S. Congress, but there remains plenty of work to do in achieving full citizenship.

Institutionalization

Institutions of various kinds have long been part of U.S. disability history. The first hospital wards dedicated specifically for people experiencing mental difficulties were created in Philadelphia and Boston in the mid-to-late 18th century. Benjamin Franklin and Benjamin Rush, two signers of the Declaration of Independence, were both important in creating the country's first hospital in Pennsylvania in 1756. Benjamin Rush, who was a well-known physician and one of the leading experts on mental disabilities—he published *Medical Inquiries and Observations upon Diseases of the Mind* in 1812—would remain affiliated with the hospital for his entire career. Other institutions, such as almshouses and jails, also held people with disabilities. One of the earliest almshouses was built in 1736 on the site of what is now City Hall Park in New York City. The almshouse, which grew and expanded its operations over the years, became known as Bellevue Hospital. Bellevue Hospital on New York City's lower east side remains one of the world's most widely recognized psychiatric inpatient facilities in the 21st century.

In the early decades of the 19th century, states began constructing asylums for people considered insane and residential schools for deaf, blind, deaf blind, and "idiot" children. Newly constructed asylums and retreats, which could be funded privately, by the state, or by some combination of both, used moral treatment first implemented in France by Philippe Pinel and in England by Samuel Tuke and somatic or bodily treatments that had been popular since the early 18th century. Between 1817 and 1833, moral treatment asylums opened in Philadelphia,

Boston, Hartford, and New York City. Among the most well-known facilities was the private Charlestown Asylum in Boston, later renamed McLean Hospital, which is still in existence in the 21st century. The first state institutions for insane people were opened in the South in the 1820s, followed by the asylum in Worcester, Massachusetts, in 1833.

Throughout the middle decades of the 19th century, the asylum movement received support from social reformers such as Dorothea Dix; professional organizations such as the Association of Medical Superintendents of American Institutions for the Insane; and prominent physicians such as Philadelphia's Thomas Kirkbride, who created the "Kirkbride Plan" for asylum construction and remained a leader of asylum treatment until his death in 1883. The 1880 census demarcated seven types of insanity: mania, melancholia, monomania, paresis, dementia, dipsomania (alcoholism), and epilepsy. According to the census there were 91,997 insane people in a U.S. population of approximately 50 million people; 1 in every 554 Americans. There were 139 hospitals or asylums treating approximately 74,000 people scattered throughout the United States in 1880. The number of asylums, hospitals, and patients continued to rise until the 1950s, when there were nearly 560,000 institutionalized people in nearly 500 institutions in the United States. Total expenditures on the institutionalized population reached more than $500 million annually, which was still less than $2 per patient per day.

The 19th century was also the time when men like Samuel Gridley Howe and Thomas Hopkins Gallaudet founded specialized schools, many of which were residential schools, to educate deaf, blind, deaf blind, and "idiot" children. Born in 1801 in Boston, Massachusetts, Howe is one of the most well-known 19th-century reformers. He served as the founding director of the New England Institution for the Education of the Blind, which later became known as the Perkins School for the Blind, and the Massachusetts School for Idiotic and Feebleminded Youth. Howe received widespread notoriety during the 19th century for his education of Laura Bridgman, a deaf blind student, whom he taught to communicate through a tactile alphabet. During the 1840s and 1850s, Howe worked with Dix on her efforts to reform asylums and jails in Massachusetts. He was instrumental in introducing her "Memorial to the Legislature of Massachusetts" to both lawmakers and the public (Trent, 2019).

Legend has it that Yale-educated Thomas Hopkins Gallaudet found his calling when on May 25, 1814, he witnessed neighborhood children shunning a nine-year-old girl. Upon inquiry, he found out that the girl, Alice Cogswell, whose father was a wealthy and well-connected physician, was deaf. Gallaudet spent the summer of 1814 teaching little Alice to read and communicate. Her father was so impressed that he funded a trip to Europe so that Gallaudet could learn from European educators who had more experience working with deaf students. When he returned to the United States, Gallaudet, along with Laurent Clerc and Mason Cogswell, founded the Connecticut Asylum for the Education and Instruction of Deaf and Dumb Persons in Hartford on April 15, 1817. The school later became known as the American School for the Deaf.

Gallaudet died in Hartford, Connecticut, on September 10, 1851. He was 63 years old. Six years later, in 1857, the U.S. Congress passed House Resolution 806 chartering the Columbia Institution for the Instruction of the Deaf and Dumb and the Blind in Washington, D.C. In 1864, Congress authorized the institution to award college degrees. In 1865, the institution was renamed the Columbia Institution for the Instruction of the Deaf and Dumb. In 1894, more than four decades after the death of the founder of deaf education in the United States, the college was renamed Gallaudet College. The name was officially changed to Gallaudet University in 1986. Gallaudet University remains one of the only institutions of higher learning in the world exclusively dedicated to educating deaf students through a bilingual American Sign Language (ASL) and English curriculum.

As we will see in both the eugenics and disability rights movement sections later, institutionalization received widespread backing during the first half of the 20th century and faced mounting criticism and challenges during the second half of the 20th century. In the early 20th century, eugenicists sought to use institutionalization as a means of controlling disabled people and limiting or preventing their reproduction. Later in the century, disability rights activists and their allies in the media and the courts challenged institutionalization both as an infringement upon the rights of citizens to live freely in the community and for institution administrators' appallingly negligent and abusive treatment of institution inmates.

The most well-known institutional exposé centered upon the Willowbrook State School on Staten Island in New York City. The school, which was the largest state-run institution for people with mental disabilities in the United States, operated for 40 years from 1947 to 1987. When it was constructed, it was designed to accommodate 4,000 inmates. At its peak population in 1965, more than 6,000 people with (primarily intellectual and developmental) disabilities were incarcerated at Willowbrook. Conditions had become so bad at Willowbrook by 1965 that Sen. Robert Kennedy referred to it as a "snake pit," harkening back to an early 20th-century novel and film that explored the dire conditions and abuses within a fictional mental institution (Disability Justice, n.d.). Kennedy stated that he found "thousands of residents 'living in filth and dirt, their clothing in rags, in rooms less comfortable and cheerful than the cages in which we put animals in a zoo'" (quoted in Disability Justice, n.d.).

In 1972, Geraldo Rivera, who was then an investigative reporter for ABC News, drew national attention to the institution when he entered Willowbrook with cameras. He ultimately produced *Willowbrook: The Last Disgrace*, which exposed the institution's overcrowding, neglect, filth, and generally dangerous conditions. Following the release of Rivera's film, residents' families filed a class action lawsuit in the U.S. District Court for the Eastern District of New York State on March 17, 1972. The lawsuit alleged indefinite confinement of residents; failure to release eligible residents; failure to conduct periodic evaluations to assess progress and refine goals and programming; failure to provide rehabilitation for residents; failure to provide adequate educational programs or services such as speech, occupational, and physical therapy; general overcrowding; lack of privacy; failure to provide protection from theft of personal property, assault, and injury of residents; inadequate clothing, meals, and facilities, including toilets; confining residents to beds, chairs, and solitary confinement; lack of compensation for work performed by residents; inadequate medical facilities; and understaffing and general incompetence of the professional staff. Arguing that the conditions at Willowbrook violated the residents' Fourteenth Amendment rights, the lawsuit sought an immediate injunction to improve conditions at the institution, which the court granted.

The case went to trial and was finally settled on April 30, 1975, when Judge Judd signed the Willowbrook Consent Judgment in *New York State Association for Retarded Children, Inc., et al., v. Hugh L. Carey*, 393 F. Supp. 715 (1975). The ruling, referred to as the Willowbrook Consent Decree, established guidelines and requirements for operating the institution and set the goal of reducing the number of inmates at Willowbrook to no more than 250 by 1981. The institution had about six years to release more than 5,800 residents into the community. The court's ruling in the Willowbrook case added much-needed momentum to an already-growing deinstitutionalization movement. Although the goal of virtually eliminating Willowbrook by 1981 was unrealistic, the ruling set in motion the necessary steps that over the course of the next four decades would result in tens of thousands of people with disabilities in New York State and throughout the rest of the country leaving institutions to live in the community.

Institutions opened their doors and released people back into the community during the 1980s and 1990s and into the

21st century, as disability rights activists and their allies actively secured their rights through federal legislation and key court decisions like the one in the Willowbrook case. The independent living movement, which began on college campuses such as the University of Illinois and the University of California, Berkeley, as well as in major cities such as Boston, Chicago, and San Francisco during the 1960s and early 1970s, gained momentum after the Willowbrook Decree. Likewise, the "people first" or self-advocacy movement also grew and became more powerful during the 1970s and 1980s, and continued to expand in the 21st century. The people first or self-advocacy movement was a movement initiated by people with intellectual and developmental disabilities in which they provided their own leadership and set their own agendas for living in the community. As the ongoing work of the self-advocacy and independent living movement made clear, more people with disabilities were living and thriving in the community by the end of the 20th century than at any other point in U.S. history. Yet there remained a tremendous amount of work for people with all types of disabilities who sought to undo nearly two centuries of institutionalization and to reach full citizenship.

Eugenics

Ideas concerning the mutability of human traits have been part of Western civilization since antiquity, but the science of eugenics had its roots in 19th-century England. Living at the center of a far-flung, powerful global empire and participating firsthand in the rise of modern industrial capitalism, people living in England in the 19th century became increasingly curious about and concerned with what they considered natural differences between various human populations. They asked questions such as: What separated British colonizers from the people they colonized? Why did certain people flourish and prosper while others lived in poverty and filth? What separated capitalist owners, landed aristocrats, and influential government officials from the toiling masses? Influenced by the Enlightenment and the scientific revolution some philosophers, scientists, and social critics looked inward in an attempt to establish rules or laws that would both explain and help to predict human characteristics and behaviors.

Herbert Spencer (1820–1903) is perhaps the most well-known 19th-century intellectual who concerned himself with some of these questions. Spencer, whose reputation rivaled that of Charles Darwin during the 19th century, is best known "for developing and applying evolutionary theory to philosophy, psychology and the study of society—what he called his 'synthetic philosophy'" (Internet Encyclopedia of Philosophy, n.d.). Influenced by the French naturalist, Jean-Baptiste Lamarck (1744–1829), as well as Darwin, Spencer argued that environmental conditions influenced and changed the development of biological organisms, including humans, over time so that there was a "gradual specialization in things . . . towards self-sufficiency and individuation" (Internet Encyclopedia of Philosophy, n.d.). Spencer coined the phrase "survival of the fittest" to describe this evolutionary process. Whereas Darwin emphasized adaptability and ecological balance, Spencer argued that the most "fit" (i.e., strongest) organisms won out in the evolutionary struggle for existence, and that humans, like other biological organisms, gradually, over time became specialized toward a certain role in life. This circular logic made it possible to argue that a worker was a worker because he was a worker, and so on.

Influenced by Spencer and his famous first cousin, Charles Darwin, English aristocrat and scientist Sir Francis Galton developed statistical studies of British families during the second half of the 19th century, which he used to support his argument that heredity governed physical ability, talent, and character, and that socially and economically prominent families were much more likely than ordinary families to produce superior offspring. He argued, moreover, that humans possessed the ability—through a system of selective breeding—to guide the course of human evolution and ultimately improve the race. In 1883, Galton named his new science *eugenics*, which he derived from the Greek word, meaning "good in birth" or "noble in heredity."

Following the publication of Darwin's *On the Origin of Species* in 1859, Galton began his study of human heredity by looking primarily at the English aristocracy, people similar to himself. It has been widely noted, but never conclusively confirmed, that Galton once said, "When in doubt, count." He believed that he could use the newly emerging field of statistics not only to measure the prevalence of "hereditary genius" but also to predict the likelihood that future generations would possess similar mental abilities. Galton and his protégé Karl Pearson (1857–1936) transformed the field of statistics as it relates to human difference and performance. They were instrumental in creating what has become popularly known as the bell curve. Galton's near-obsession with counting, classifying, and categorizing also led to the creation of modern fingerprinting.

Though he had little formal training, Galton's status as an upper-class English man meant that he was able to publish his findings. His first attempt at explaining his thoughts concerning the relationship between human heredity and human ability appeared as a two-part article entitled "Hereditary Talent and Character," published in 1865. In another article entitled "Hereditary Improvement," published in 1873, Galton outlined his method for improving the English population. He declared that his goal was to "improve the race of man by a system which shall be perfectly in accordance with the moral sense of the present time" (quoted in Gillham, 2001). To implement his plan, Galton called for the creation of a state agency that would gather and analyze important information about English families, including photographs and physical measurements. It would then distribute this information to all English citizens interested in using eugenics to alter the perceived quality of the English population. This information would be used to encourage the reproduction of those families perceived to have talent, known as "positive" eugenics, and to discourage the reproduction of the masses of individuals perceived to be of inferior quality, known as "negative" eugenics.

By the beginning of the 20th century, eugenics had become popular among a broad range of Americans. In the decades between the end of the Civil War and the beginning of the 20th century, industrialization, urbanization, and immigration had transformed America. Men such as Charles Davenport and Harry Laughlin of the Station for Experimental Evolution (SEE, 1904–1921) and the Eugenics Record Office (ERO, 1910–1939) at Cold Spring Harbor, New York, sought to use eugenics not only to gather data on what they considered the changing characteristics of the American population, but also to affect reproduction and future generations of Americans. Women reformers working primarily at the local and state levels, and some national figures like Margaret Sanger, also deployed the language of eugenics in their efforts to improve city slums and the lives of working-class people.

Eugenicists received financial backing and became part of the curriculum in American universities. Prominent organizations and individuals such as the Carnegie Institute and the Rockefeller Foundation and Mrs. E. H. Harriman, the widow of a wealthy railroad executive, all supported eugenics. Eugenics became a legitimate topic of research and education in the nation's top universities and a favored topic of discussion among religious leaders. Not all Americans believed in eugenics. Eugenicists had prominent and outspoken opponents, such as the well-known lawyer Clarence Darrow, and every day Americans resisted the intervention of eugenic measures into their lives. Despite this opposition, however, eugenicists and eugenic policies received significant support throughout the first four decades of the 20th century. Eugenic better baby and fitter family contests could be found at state and county fairs, and eugenicists working at both the state and federal levels were instrumental in passing marriage, sterilization, institutionalization, and immigration laws.

In order to make their case for the implementation of eugenic measures, eugenicists needed evidence. In the decades before World War II, eugenicists became increasingly active in gathering eugenic data, organizing professionally, and distributing the knowledge they gained through their studies. They formed groups such as the American Eugenics Society (1926–1972) and the Eugenics Research Association (1912–1939) that along with the SEE and the ERO worked to promote eugenics in the United States. The preferred method among eugenicists was the eugenic family study. Directed by male eugenic leaders such as Davenport, Laughlin, Henry H. Goddard of the Vineland Training School in New Jersey, and Arthur Estabrook of the ERO, and carried out by the mostly female fieldworkers trained at the ERO, eugenic family studies attempted to document and explain the persistent proliferation of ostensibly heritable conditions through detailed genealogical surveys.

In all, there were about 14 family studies published in the United States between 1877 and 1926. Four family studies were published before the founding of the SEE in 1904. The remaining 10 studies were published after the creation of the ERO in 1910. Although it has a complex history, one of the most influential and widely cited family studies is Richard Dugdale's *The Jukes: A Study in Crime, Pauperism, Disease, and Heredity* (1877), which was based on work initially conducted by Elisha Harris, a doctor specializing in public health and infectious diseases. As one scholar has noted, *The Jukes* "focused on reconstructing genealogies of 42 families that could be traced to a common ancestor. A putatively disproportionate number of these family members had been imprisoned, had engaged in behaviour deemed criminal or immoral, or were economically impoverished" (Wilson, 2014). Although Dugdale resisted making straightforward hereditarian arguments to explain persistent poverty, immorality, and criminality, later eugenicists cited his work, which became quite influential in their own family studies.

Of the 10 studies published after the opening of the ERO in 1910, Henry H. Goddard's *The Kallikak Family: A Study in the Heredity of Feeble-Mindedness* (1912) has been the most widely examined by scholars who study eugenics. Written in consultation with his eugenics field worker, Elizabeth Kite, *The Kallikak Family* systematically traced the genealogy of "Deborah Kallikak" (Emma Wolverton, 1889–1978), an inmate in his Vineland Training School for Feebleminded Girls and Boys. By 1939, the book had gone through 12 printings in the United States and many more overseas. It, arguably, made Goddard the most well-known authority on feeblemindedness and eugenics in the United States and perhaps the world. Goddard and the book attracted an equal number of critics, however. Beginning in the 1920s, critics in various fields attacked Goddard's methods and his findings, and by 1940, one critic had pronounced the book and its ideas "dead" (Zenderland, 2004, 165).

As one historian of eugenics asserts, despite all of the criticism (which has also been taken up by scholars), *The Kallikak Family* should be taken seriously, not for its scientific value, but because it served as a powerful parable for people living in the United States during the first 40 years of the 20th century. The study follows two separate seemingly disparate lines of descendants of a single man, Martin Kallikak, Sr., a Revolutionary War veteran who happened to impregnate a hapless barmaid before settling down with an upstanding woman from a "good family" (Zenderland, 2004, 175). The book, which blends morality with medicine and science with religion, brings together the old and the new in ways that spoke to early 20th century Americans. Pedigree charts and explanations of Mendelian laws of inheritance combined with vivid stories of familial degeneration reminded parents "of all that they might bequeath to a child—not only biologically, but also morally and materially" (Zenderland, 2004, 177). Goddard's exploration of the two lines of Deborah Kallikak's family, one illegitimate, "bad," socially and morally degenerate, and the other "good," legitimate, fit, and upstanding, firmly linked in the American public's mind the broad disability category of "feeblemindedness" with both hereditary taint and social decay. By 1915, popular writers and social reformers would issue alarming warnings of the need to control and ideally eliminate the "feebleminded menace" plaguing the United States.

Goddard's study of the Kallikak family and the other family studies were part of a larger, national eugenics movement. On November 7, 1915, *Chicago Daily Tribune* health columnist and eugenicist, Dr. W. A. Evans, informed his readers of a nationwide eugenics program that was being "pushed" by the ERO in Cold Spring Harbor, New York. The program, which was set to receive "heavy financial backing," was based on a proposal that had been outlined in a paper presented by well-known eugenicist Harry Laughlin a year earlier at the first National Conference on Race Betterment held in Battle Creek, Michigan. According to Evans, Laughlin's plan consisted of "cutting off the supply of defectives—by education, restriction, segregation, and sterilization." These four measures would complement one another and over the course of 70 years, from 1915 to 1985, would "purify" the United States by eliminating the lowest 10 percent of the country's racial "stock" (quoted in Rembis, 2011). Evans estimated that 15 million Americans would be sterilized; countless others would be institutionalized; so-called defectives would be barred from entering the country; and all of this would be made possible through an elaborate system of eugenic education that would extol the virtues of being well born. Evans assured his readers that "good lawyers" had informed Laughlin that the eugenics program would not violate the Fourteenth Amendment, which provides equal protection under the law for all Americans. Evans chose to title his column "Rebuilding a Nation" (Rembis, 2011).

By 1915, it had become quite common for reformers, experts, and other advocates interested in "improving" life in America to turn to eugenics. Evans, who regularly wrote on eugenics in his column, "How to Keep Well," first introduced Chicagoans to it in 1912. On March 10, 1912, Evans pleaded with the readers of the *Tribune*: "If you have not seen the *American Magazine* for March, get it and read, 'A New Science and Its Findings,' by Nock" (quoted in Rembis, 2011). Excited to educate the readers of his daily health column, Evans provided a brief definition of eugenics that came straight from Galton himself. According to Evans's reading of Galton, eugenics was the science that dealt with "all influences that improve the inborn qualities of the race." For further clarification, Evans turned to Davenport. "The eugenical standpoint," Davenport declared, "is that of the agriculturist who, while recognizing the value of culture, believes that permanent advance is to be made only by securing the best blood. Man is an organism—an animal—and the laws of improvement of corn and of racehorses hold true of him also. The success of a marriage from the standpoint of eugenics is measured by the number of disease resistant, cultivable offspring that come from it" (quoted in Rembis, 2011). According to eugenicists like Evans, campaigning for pure milk and crusading against infant mortality—both of which he did as Chicago's health commissioner—were vital reform efforts, but they attacked only part of the problem. "We have been so busy with environment," Evans asserted, "that we have forgotten team work. Race betterment is loaded in a two horse wagon, to which is hitched Improved Environment and Eugenics" (quoted in Rembis, 2011). The message in Evans's column was clear. Here at last was a means of making real, lasting change, but only if reformers and the American public embraced the new science and its findings (Rembis, 2011).

Although they harbored lingering reservations concerning the new science, eugenicists made bold assertions about its power to "improve" society. Evans and other eugenicists contended that insanity, alcoholism, drug addiction, cancer, consumption, neurosis, hereditary deafness, multiple sclerosis, and many other "ailments," "conditions," "diseases," and "handicaps" could all be greatly reduced or even eliminated only if society worked toward improving the quality of the gene pool as well as the environment. According to eugenicists, breeding up the human herd would result in improved morals as well; adultery, prostitution, and "illegitimate" births would all be reduced largely because feebleminded "sex delinquents" would be confined to institutions during their reproductive years or permanently sterilized (Rembis, 2011).

American eugenicists played a critical role in the passage of key legislation at both the state and federal levels. They focused their legislative efforts on four main areas: institutionalization or involuntary commitment, marriage restriction, immigration, and sterilization. Numerous states passed laws during the eugenics era that made it possible to involuntarily commit individuals considered feebleminded or mentally defective indefinitely in sex-segregated state institutions. States also enacted laws that made it difficult or, in some cases, illegal for certain people to get married. Perhaps the most well-known marriage restriction legislation was passed in Virginia in 1924. On March 20, 1924, the Virginia state legislature enacted the Racial Integrity Act, which "prohibited interracial marriage and defined as white a person 'who has no trace whatsoever of any blood other than Caucasian'" (Wolfe, 2015). The law, which had deep roots in Virginia's history as a slaveholding state, and was also a direct result of the desire among eugenicists to maintain racial "purity," remained in effect until 1967, when the U.S. Supreme Court in *Loving v. Virginia* found its prohibition of interracial marriage in violation of the Fourteenth Amendment to the U.S. Constitution.

At the federal level, eugenicists, especially Laughlin, played an important role in passing immigration legislation. In the early 1920s the U.S. House of Representatives Committee on Immigration and Naturalization chaired by Congressman Albert Johnson appointed Laughlin as its "Expert Eugenics Agent." Congress had, for decades, since the passage of the 1882 Chinese Exclusion Act, been interested in restricting immigration to the United States. Over the years they passed legislation that prohibited certain groups, such as the feebleminded, mentally defective, epileptic, or persons likely to become a public charge, from entering the United States. Following the onset of World War I, Congress worked to create more comprehensive immigration restrictions. In 1924, with extensive input from Laughlin—he appeared before the House committee five times during the 1920s—Congress passed the Johnson–Reed Immigration Restriction Act, which reduced the number of new immigrants entering the country to 2 percent of their total numbers reported by the 1890 census. The Johnson–Reed Act all but eliminated immigration from southern and eastern Europe, from countries like Russia, Poland, Italy, Greece, and the Balkans—places that had large numbers of Catholics and Jews and people who did not speak English and places that had sent increasing numbers of migrants to the United States in the decades between 1880 and 1920.

Sterilization formed the final part of eugenicists' plans to eliminate defectives and improve America's "racial stock." The state legislature of Indiana passed the country's first sterilization law in 1907. By the 1930s, 32 states had sterilization laws. In 1921, the Indiana Supreme Court overturned Indiana's sterilization law. However, in 1927 in *Buck v. Bell*, the U.S. Supreme Court upheld the constitutionality of Virginia's state sterilization law (1924), making it possible for states to conduct compulsory sterilizations, which they did until the 1970s. Between 1907 and 1963, states sterilized approximately 65,000 people.

Sterilizations were performed overwhelmingly on people defined as developmentally or intellectually disabled, or mentally ill and living in state institutions, asylums, hospitals, or prisons. California, North Carolina, and Virginia performed the most sterilizations. A 1972 Senate investigation revealed that an additional approximately 2,000 black women had been sterilized, without their consent or knowledge in some cases, in hospitals throughout the South. In 1978, the U.S. Department of Health, Education and Welfare issued Federal Sterilization Regulations in an effort to monitor and ultimately reduce or eliminate the number of forced or compulsory sterilizations. Although it is relatively rare, compulsory sterilization continues in the 21st century, and is primarily performed on people defined as developmentally or intellectually disabled.

Eugenics was not limited to England and the United States. Physicians, scientists, and government officials throughout the world embraced some form of eugenics. The most notorious eugenic measures were implemented in Nazi Germany in the 1930s and 1940s. The Nazis performed 400,000 sterilizations, primarily on people considered feebleminded or living with other mental disabilities. In the late 1930s, the Nazis implemented their T4 or "euthanasia" program through which they murdered thousands of disabled people, including children. Throughout the 20th century, various forms of eugenics developed in Eastern Europe, East Asia, Central and South America, the Scandinavian countries, and the Middle East (Bashford and Levine, 2012).

Eugenic thought has influenced public discussions and social policy in numerous countries throughout the world since the late 19th century. Eugenics has assumed many forms, including both "positive" eugenics and "negative" eugenics. Its supporters have spanned the political spectrum, from radical socialists to reactionary racists. Although eugenics fell into disrepute after World War II, it never completely disappeared, and it experienced a resurgence in the late 20th and early 21st centuries.

The rise of the Human Genome Project and advances in various types of reproductive technologies created new concerns about the potential for selective breeding. Known popularly among critics as "the new eugenics," the use of genetic counseling and various reproductive technologies became the subject of much concern and debate among disability studies scholars, activists, historians, and bioethicists. The new eugenics will be discussed in Chapter 2.

Charity

The U.S. religious roots and its commitment to individualism and to the division of power between the states and the federal government, as well as within the federal government, meant that for much of its history it would use nongovernmental sources or at best a mix of governmental and nongovernmental means of providing vital safety nets and social services for its citizens. Disabled veterans, who from the Revolutionary War to World War I received disability pensions from the government, and then after World War I received specialized rehabilitation and health-care services through the Veterans Administration, had a separate and distinct relationship with state and federal governments, and will not be considered in this discussion of charity and its relationship to disability. Disabled people who were not veterans had to rely on family and community, faith-based and secular charities, and the government to provide them with health-care and other services, and the prosthetics and other equipment they would need to survive. A federal welfare state began to emerge in the early decades of the 20th century, but many disabled people would continue throughout the 20th century to rely on charities. The U.S. mix of state-sponsored health-care and disability programs and nongovernmental charities is unique in the world. No other country has relied on charities to the extent that the United States has to provide care to its citizens.

The earliest charitable organizations in the United States were faith-based. Christian community members relied on the local parish to provide them with food and other aid in times of need. As other religious communities established themselves in the United States, they too formed their own faith-based charitable or mutual-aid societies. Americans relied on these local faith-based systems of giving and receiving aid throughout the 19th century and into the early decades of the 20th century. By the early 20th century, it was becoming increasingly clear that massive urbanization, immigration, and industrialization were creating demands for services that private faith-based and secular charities were no longer able to meet. By 1920, the U.S. population had reached 100 million people, the majority of whom were either first- or second-generation immigrants. Although many Americans still lived and worked on farms, the country had become decidedly urban and industrial, with approximately 51 percent of all Americans living in cities. Crowded urban conditions and dangerous industrial working conditions, including extractive industries such as mining, contributed to the rampant spread of diseases, disabilities, and premature death. Local privatized welfare schemes, including those organized through churches and synagogues, could no longer handle the demand for their services. The entire charitable system that had developed in the 150 years since the founding of the nation was strained to the breaking point with the stock market crash in October 1929 and the onset of the Great Depression. It was at this point, under the Roosevelt administration, that the federal government began an earnest attempt to create what has come to be called the modern "welfare state." Despite this move toward state-sponsored social services, disabled people still found themselves marginalized and disenfranchised. They, along with other minority groups such as African Americans, continued to rely on charities for survival.

With the exception of the United Way (1887), the largest and most active disability charities were organized around specific conditions. The National Foundation for Infantile Paralysis, later known as the March of Dimes (1938), the National Society for Crippled Children, later renamed Easter Seals (1919), the American Foundation for the Blind (AFB; 1921), United Cerebral Palsy (1949), and the Muscular Dystrophy Association (MDA; 1950), as well as the United Way, are the largest, most well-known, and most active charitable organizations that provide services and material support (financial assistance and equipment, etc.) to people with disabilities and their families. These organizations were formed in part to meet specific needs that state and federal governments were either unwilling or unable to meet. In the decades since 1950, when the MDA was formed, hundreds of other nonprofit organizations have formed across the country to address the needs of people with all types of disabilities. What one historian (Longmore, 2016) has called the "business of charity" has become big business since the founding of the United Way in 1887.

Although they provide vital, sometimes lifesaving, supports and services that are not provided by the government, large charities have been the subject of criticism among disabled people and their allies almost from the beginning of their formation. As noted in the Disability Rights Movement section of this chapter, the National Federation of the Blind (NFB) was formed by blind people for blind people in part as a response to the creation of the AFB in 1921, which was a charitable organization dedicated to "helping" blind people. Over the decades, disabled people and their allies have criticized charitable organizations for portraying disabled people as helpless, pitiful creatures in need of assistance to survive and live normally. Disabled activists have criticized charitable organizations for infantalizing disabled people by continually using children to represent their organizations and in making calls for charitable donations. Finally, disabled activists have criticized charitable organizations for presenting a one-sided "medicalized" view of disability that does not treat disabled people as whole people with complex, rich, fulfilling lives.

In the decades since the rise of the disability rights movement, from the 1980s into the 21st century, disabled people and their allies have become more vocal in their criticisms of large charitable organizations, forcing them, in some cases, to discontinue or fundamentally alter their fund-raising activities, and to work to "rebrand" themselves, or change their public face in ways that more accurately represent the people they serve. One such group, known as Jerry's Orphans, focused its activism on the MDA's annual telethon, which historically had been hosted by the well-known comedian Jerry Lewis. From the early 1990s through the early 21st century, Jerry's Orphans and other disabled people and groups who identified with their cause protested the MDA telethon and Jerry Lewis, as well as other charitable organizations and events. The results of their protests could be seen by the second decade of the 21st century, when Jerry Lewis retired from hosting the MDA telethon (2011), and when the MDA and other disability charity organizations began actively to change their missions and their messages, and work to incorporate the disabled people they served into their organizations in more meaningful ways.

As long as charitable organizations exist, however, and as long as charitable giving remains big business, the United States may never move to a single-payer health-care system that recognizes the needs of disabled people (and every other American citizen) as a fundamental right, and not an entitlement or benefit. For 150 years, disabled people have had a fraught relationship with "big charity." They have frequently and gratefully benefited from the services and equipment that charities provide, even if in many cases the wait was long and the results were inadequate, because for disabled people many times there was no alternative to the "gifts" provided by charities. This dependence caused disabled people to become the "good cripple," forever humble, and grateful for even the smallest amount of assistance, willing to endure shame, pity, and dehumanizing exploitation to receive life-sustaining supports. As disabled people became increasingly politicized and enfranchised, their collective voice of criticism of charities became louder, but unless real alternatives are created, some disabled people will continue to have to rely on the "benevolent giving" of others, perpetuating their second-class citizenship.

Disability Rights Movement

Most people think that the disability rights movement was an outgrowth of the social movements of the 1960s and in many ways it was part of those broader movements. Yet, disability historians have shown that disabled people have been advocating for their rights since the 19th century. Initially they organized around specific types of disabilities and specific issues and concerns. A more broad-based movement began to emerge in the early 20th century, when groups of people with different disabilities came together to demand equal rights and economic opportunity. Throughout the second half of the 19th century and the first half of the 20th-century survivors of psychiatric institutionalization also increasingly advocated to reform psychiatric treatment and protect patients' rights. These relatively small, widely dispersed movements increasingly coalesced beginning in the 1940s and into the postwar period, when disabled World War II veterans, survivors of the polio virus, and parents of developmentally disabled children added their voices to the call for deinstitutionalization—the movement of disabled people out of large state institutions—equal protection under the law, and increased access to education and employment.

Early History

Deaf people and blind people (and some deaf blind people) were among the first to organize in 19th-century America. Deaf Americans came together in Cincinnati, Ohio, in 1880 to form the National Association of the Deaf (NAD). Formed largely in response to the rise of what has become known as "oralism" in the United States, the NAD fought to protect deaf people's rights, especially their right to speak their own language, ASL, and to promote equal employment opportunities for deaf people. Those referred to as "big D" Deaf people, like those who formed the NAD, did not create ties with other disabled people, and in fact fought to distinguish themselves from people with other types of disabilities. Big D Deaf people argued that they were not disabled but were instead members of a linguistic minority and should be treated not as disabled, but rather as a cultural minority group. The NAD did not support federal programs for disabled people and in fact until the 1940s lobbied for a separate Labor Department specifically for deaf workers. After World War II, an increasing number of deaf people aligned themselves with the disability rights movement, but even in the 21st century, there are big D Deaf people who do not consider themselves disabled and who do not identify with the disability rights movement.

Around the turn of the 20th century, blind people also began to advocate for themselves. By the 1930s, a number of local and state blind organizations had been formed. Activists representing organizations from 16 different states gathered in Wilkes-Barre, Pennsylvania, in 1940 to form the NFB. Formed in part in response to the creation of the AFB in 1921, which was a charity organization founded by philanthropists concerned with the plight of blinded World War I veterans, the NFB was an organization founded by blind people for blind people. Unlike the NAD, the NFB did not shun government intervention into the lives of blind people. Rather, it advocated for Social Security stipends for blind citizens, and federal support for equal access to housing, transportation, public accommodations, and employment. Although the NFB had a much broader agenda than did the NAD, it also was exclusionary; it did not align itself with other disability groups and discriminated against women and racial/ethnic minorities within its own ranks. A growing international movement among blind people began in the 1930s and continues in the 21st century. Helen Keller is perhaps the most well-known representative of the blind community to travel abroad to countries like Japan, China, and India, advocating in their behalf.

People with physical disabilities also became active in the early 20th century. They formed groups such as the Polio Crusaders and the League of the Physically Handicapped during the 1930s to raise awareness about disabilities and the lack of employment and other opportunities for disabled people. The Polio Crusaders formed at the Warm Springs Rehabilitation Institute, which Franklin Delano Roosevelt had opened in 1924 in Georgia. Roosevelt, who continued to frequent Warm Springs after he became president of the United States in 1933, instilled in the institute and the people who went there for rehabilitation a strong sense of independence, which the Crusaders hoped to spread throughout the country through magazine and newspaper articles and other means during the 1930s. Like the Crusaders, the League of the Physically Handicapped also rejected negative stereotypes about disabled people. However, its activist tactics were more straightforward and confrontational than those of the Crusaders. It protested directly outside the Works Progress Administration (WPA) building in New York City in 1935. After six months of protesting, the League managed to convince the WPA to hire more workers with disabilities. The Crusaders and the League were both short-lived and in many ways were a reaction to the economic hardships brought on by the Great Depression during the 1930s. Neither group survived into the post–World War II period. Their relatively brief existence, however, does not mean that these groups are historically insignificant. They are early and important evidence of disabled people's strong desire to change the way people thought about disabilities and disabled people, and to advocate for equal rights and equal opportunities, primarily in employment.

World War II to the Americans with Disabilities Act

The changing political economy and relative prosperity of the postwar world fundamentally shaped the growing disability rights movement in the United States. A wartime labor shortage drew unprecedented numbers of workers with disabilities into the labor force during the war, providing them with a solid base from which to advocate for citizenship rights and continued employment opportunities after the war ended. Though short-lived, the American Federation of the Physically Handicapped (AFPH) was instrumental in making disability rights and the employment of disabled people broad-based federal issues that extended beyond a single program or department. The work of the AFPH after the war resulted in the creation of the President's Committee on the Employment of the Handicapped and the National Employ the Physically Handicapped Week, both of which continue to exist in modified forms in the 21st century. Conscientious objectors to World War II who fulfilled their civil service requirements by working as attendants in state institutions serving people with disabilities during the war documented their experiences, which were used in exposés after the war to reveal in stark terms the grim situation inside the nation's large state institutions. The exposés, in part, led to increased federal oversight and funding of state institutions and further legitimation of Clifford Beers' (see Profiles chapter) long-standing efforts to reform mental health care in the United States. In addition to these groups, a growing number of disabled veterans of World War II added their voices to the calls for civil rights, employment opportunities, and a general improvement in the condition of people with disabilities.

Momentum continued to build in the 1950s and 1960s when parents of institutionalized children deemed "mentally retarded" began to advocate for deinstitutionalization and when disabled veterans of World War II and survivors of the polio virus increasingly called for improved physical access to the built environment, as well as access to education and employment. Pushed from below by disabled activists and their allies, the federal government began to act in the 1960s. The Kennedy administration's Mental Retardation Facilities and Community Mental Health Centers Construction Act of 1963 ushered in a new era of deinstitutionalization in the United States, and the Johnson administration's 1968 Architectural Barriers Act laid the foundation for an accessible built environment. Both pieces of legislation, unfortunately for disability rights activists, were underfunded and usually went unenforced. Much more work remained for the disability rights movement. Yet it was clear by the end of the 1960s that both material conditions and attitudes related to disability were undergoing important transformations.

One of the most crucial moments in the history of the American disability rights movement occurred in the 1970s, with the inclusion of Section 504 in the 1973 Rehabilitation Act. Disappointed that "disability" was not included as part of the 1964 Civil Rights Act, Washington insiders, responding to decades of grassroots activism in places like New York, Illinois, and Berkeley, California, included Section 504 in the 1973 Rehabilitation Act. Section 504 stated in part: "No otherwise qualified handicapped individual in the United States shall, solely by reason of his handicap, be excluded from participation in, be denied the benefits of, or be subjected to discrimination under any program or activity receiving Federal financial assistance." Following two vetoes, President Nixon signed the Federal Rehabilitation Act on September 26, 1973. Although it was limited to entities receiving federal financial assistance, Section 504 of the 1973 Rehabilitation Act was a major victory for disability rights activists. Concerned primarily with costs and enforcement, both the Nixon and Ford administrations attempted to delay the implementation of Section 504 by ordering rewrites of regulations relating to the law and also initiating "impact studies," which attempted to measure the anticipated effects of the law if it were enforced. In 1975, disability rights activists and their allies filed a federal lawsuit, forcing the secretary of Health, Education, and Welfare (HEW)—the government agency charged with overseeing Section 504—to act. In July 1976, a Washington, D.C., federal district court ruled that the Section 504 regulations (essentially the rules of enforcement) should be clarified "with no further unreasonable delays." Outgoing president Gerald Ford and sitting HEW secretary David Matthews did nothing. President Carter, who had promised to act on Section 504 during the election campaign, created a task force headed by new secretary of HEW, Joseph Califano, to study the effects of the law. Disability rights activists and their allies, who had grown weary of delays, and who had attempted other forms of protests, including lobbying, letter writing, and personal pleas, stated that they would initiate a national protest if Califano did not sign the Section 504 regulations by April 4, 1977.

Protests began modestly and grew both in size and in intensity. Initially, approximately 300 protesters in Washington, D.C., gathered outside Califano's home and his office demanding that he sign the regulations. Protests spread to other parts of the country. Disabled people in Boston, Seattle, New York, Atlanta, Philadelphia, Chicago, Dallas, and Denver picketed or occupied HEW regional offices. These protests soon dissipated. The longest and most well-organized protest took place at the HEW offices in San Francisco, California. Home to Ed Roberts, Judy Heumann, Kitty Cone, and other disability rights leaders, as well as the student free speech movement and other student movements, the San Francisco Bay area was the ideal location to stage an occupation of HEW offices. The April 4 deadline passed with no signature. The next day, more than 500 people gathered in San Francisco's Civic Center Plaza, where they discussed the importance of Section 504 and the regulations that governed its implementation and enforcement. After the rally, disabled people and their allies—totaling about 150 people—occupied the federal building at 50 United Nations Plaza.

Primarily the result of Judy Heumann and Kitty Cone's grassroots organizing and networking, the occupation of the HEW offices in San Francisco gained widespread support. The Black Panther Party, Glide Memorial Church, the Gay Men's Butterfly Brigade, Delancey Street, Cesar Chavez and the United Farm Workers, the International Association of Machinists, the Salvation Army, San Francisco mayor George Muscone, Congressman Philip Burton, George Miller, Senator Alan Cranston, and Georgia Senator Julian Bond all supported the occupation. Some even provided material support. The Salvation Army provided mattresses, and the Black Panthers provided daily hot meals. Some of the HEW staff lent their support as well, making the occupation a bit more tolerable for some of the disabled people. Outside the HEW offices, disabled people held daily vigils, keeping the protest in the public consciousness and in the news.

HEW secretary Joseph Califano signed the 504 regulations on April 28, 1977. Remaining protesters left the San Francisco offices two days later, April 30, 1977, ending the longest occupation of a federal building in U.S. history—26 days. HEW protests throughout the country and especially the sit-in at the HEW offices in San Francisco marked an important moment in the history of disability rights in America. Just as the movement was gaining momentum, however, the 1980s ushered in a new era of conservativism that would present increased challenges to disability rights protesters and their allies.

Historians consider the legacies of the 1980s mixed at best. There is no doubt that the disability rights movement grew and became more diverse during the 1980s. Groups such as the National Black Deaf Advocates and the DisAbled Women's Network added their voices and concerns to the expanding movement, and direct-action protest organizations such as Americans Disabled for Accessible Public Transit heightened the stakes of disability protest. The U.S. Congress passed at least six crucial pieces of legislation that helped to ensure accessibility in telecommunications, air travel, and voting, among other areas. Yet, the 1980s was also a time when an increasingly conservative federal judiciary nullified the Bill of Rights for Developmentally Disabled People and considerably weakened Section 504 of the 1973 Rehabilitation Act. The conservative Reagan and Bush administrations also sought to minimize or eliminate Social Security benefits and Medicaid coverage that had been expanding for disabled people since the first Social Security disability insurance scheme was introduced during the Eisenhower administration in the 1950s.

Emboldened by both their successes and setbacks, the disability rights activists of the 1980s actively sought to expand their efforts. Disability rights became an international issue in the 1980s. At home, activists and allies worked to pass comprehensive civil rights legislation. Their work both on the streets and in the halls of Congress ultimately resulted in the passage of the world's most comprehensive disability legislation to date, the Americans with Disabilities Act (ADA, 1990). Although its actual impact has been debated among scholars and activists, the event that became known as the Capitol Crawl marked the culmination of decades of activism.

On Monday, March 12, 1990, more than 1,000 disabled protesters and their allies, from 30 states, met at the steps of the U.S. Capitol building in Washington, D.C., to demand the passage of the ADA. The bill had passed the Senate easily in September 1989. Protesters feared that further delay of the passage of the bill, which was under review by several committees within the House of Representatives, would weaken it through amendments or kill it. Disabled people, who had been organizing and protesting for their rights since the 1960s, had grown impatient. "Two centuries is long enough for people with disabilities to wait before the constitutional promise of justice is kept," Justin W. Dart, Jr., chairman of the President's Committee on Employment of People with Disabilities, told the protesters gathered that day.

At the close of the rally, dozens of protesters—some accounts estimate 60 people—left their wheelchairs or laid down their crutches and crawled up the 83 steps leading into the nation's capitol building. Attention quickly focused on Jennifer Keelan, an eight-year-old girl from Denver, Colorado, living with cerebral palsy, who had come to D.C. to show her support for the ADA and to honor the memory of her friend Kenny Perkins, who had passed away in January 1990. Thirty-three-year-old Paulette Patterson, who had traveled to D.C. from Chicago, told reporters: "I want my civil rights. . . . I want to be treated like a human being." Michael A. Winter (1951–2013), a leader in the disability rights movement who participated in the crawl, later wrote: "Some people may have thought that it was undignified for people in wheelchairs to crawl in that manner, but I felt that it was necessary to show the country what kinds of things people with disabilities have to face on a day-to-day basis." "We had to be willing to fight for what we believed in," he wrote. Winter, a graduate of Southern Illinois University (1974), went on to hold a number of key positions at the federal Department of Transportation and served as an advisor to Norman Y. Mineta, the transportation secretary from 2001 to 2006.

Although it was not widely covered in the media at the time, and some scholars debate whether it was even necessary (Davis, 2016), the Capitol Crawl has since gone on to become an iconic event in the history of the U.S. disability rights movement. It was, and is, a powerful symbol of the barriers disabled people face in society, and of their determination to secure the rights guaranteed to all U.S. citizens under the Constitution. "We're not asking for any favors," asserted I. King Jordan, the first deaf president of Gallaudet University (1988) and a leader in the disability rights movement. "We're simply asking for the same rights and equality any other American has."

The House of Representatives passed the ADA in May 1990 and President George H. W. Bush signed the legislation in a ceremony that included leaders of the disability rights movement on July 26, 1990. Under the ADA, approximately 54 million Americans qualified as disabled, 19 percent of the population, making disabled people the largest minority in the United States.

Post–Americans with Disabilities Act

Unfortunately for disabled activists and the disability community more broadly, conservative federal courts interpreted the ADA narrowly in the decades following its enactment. Some critics tried to argue—unsuccessfully—that the ADA was unconstitutional and that it imposed an undue burden to business owners and the larger society who were now required by law to make the world accessible to people with disabilities. When discrimination lawsuits came before the courts in the 1990s and during the first decade of the 21st century, courts often ruled against disabled plaintiffs, arguing essentially that the plaintiff was not disabled "enough" to qualify for protection under the ADA. In 2008, the U.S. Congress passed the ADA Amendments Act (2008, ADAA) in an attempt to restore the broad definition of disability under the original ADA, effectively nullifying nearly two decades of case law that significantly narrowed that definition. In June 1999, the U.S Supreme Court held in *Olmstead v. L.C.* that disabled people have the right to live as independently as possible in the community. Together, the *Olmstead* decision and the 2008 ADAA have helped to bolster disabled people's ongoing efforts to live in the community, go to school, and work. Disabled people and their allies in the United States and abroad continue to fight to ensure their rights, which includes equal access to the community, to housing, to education, to employment, and to health care.

References

Bashford, Alison, and Philippa Levine. 2012. *The Oxford Handbook of the History of Eugenics*. New York: Oxford University Press.

Davis, Lennard J. 2016. *Enabling Acts: The Hidden Story of How the Americans with Disabilities Act Gave the Largest US Minority Its Rights*. Boston, MA: Beacon Press.

Disability Justice. n.d. "The Closing of Willowbrook." https://disabilityjustice.org/the-closing-of-willowbrook/ (Accessed January 12, 2019).

Dugdale, Richard A. 1877. *The Jukes: A Study in Crime, Pauperism, Disease, and Heredity*. Boston, MA: Putnam.

Gillham, Nicholas Wright. 2001. *A Life of Sir Francis Galton: From African Exploration to the Birth of Eugenics*. Oxford: Oxford University Press.

Goddard, Henry H. 1912. *The Kallikak Family: A Study in the Heredity of Feeble-Mindedness*. New York: Macmillan.

Internet Encyclopedia of Philosophy. n.d. "Herbert Spencer (1820–1903)." https://www.iep.utm.edu/spencer/ (Accessed January 9, 2019).

Kevles, Daniel J. 1985. *In the Name of Eugenics: Genetics and the Uses of Human Heredity*. New York: Alfred A. Knopf.

Longmore, Paul K. 2016. *Telethons: Spectacle, Disability, and the Business of Charity*. New York: Oxford University Press.

Noll, Steven. 2018. "Institutions for People with Disabilities in North America." In Michael Rembis, Catherine Kudlick, and Kim E. Nielsen, eds. *The Oxford Handbook of Disability History*. New York: Oxford University Press.

Oshinsky, David. 2017. *Bellevue: Three Centuries of Medicine and Mayhem at America's Most Storied Hospital*. New York: Anchor Books.

Patterson, Lindsay. 2018. "The Disability Rights Movement in the United States." In Michael Rembis, Catherine Kudlick, and Kim E. Nielsen, eds. *The Oxford Handbook of Disability History*. New York: Oxford University Press.

Paul, Diane B. 1995. *Controlling Human Heredity, 1865 to the Present*. Atlantic Highlands, NJ: Humanities Press.

Proctor, Robert. 1988. *Racial Hygiene: Medicine under the Nazis*. Cambridge, MA: Harvard University Press.

Rembis, Michael A. 2011. *Defining Deviance: Sex, Science, and Delinquent Girls, 1890–1960*. Urbana: University of Illinois Press.

Rembis, Michael A. 2018. "Disability and the History of Eugenics." In Michael Rembis, Catherine Kudlick, and Kim E. Nielsen, eds. *The Oxford Handbook of Disability History*, 85–103. New York: Oxford University Press.

Rothman, David Jay, and Sheila M. Rothman. 1984. *The Willowbrook Wars*. New York: Harper & Row.

Smith, David J., and Michael L. Wehmeyer. 2012. "Who Was Deborah Kallikak?" *Intellectual and Developmental Disabilities* 50 (2): 169–178. doi:10.1352/1934–9556–50.2.169.

Stepan, Nancy. 1991. *The Hour of Eugenics: Race, Gender, and Nation in Latin America*. Ithaca, NY: Cornell University Press.

Trent, James W., Jr. 2019. "Samuel Gridley Howe: American Educator." https://www.britannica.com/biography/Samuel-Gridley-Howe (Accessed January 12, 2019).

Wilson, R. 2014, April 29. "Eugenic Family Studies." http://eugenicsarchive.ca/discover/tree/535eebbb7095aa 0000000225 (Accessed January 9, 2019).

Wolfe, B. Racial Integrity Laws (1924–1930). 2015, November 4. In *Encyclopedia Virginia*. http://www.EncyclopediaVirginia.org/Racial_Integrity_Laws_of_the_1920s (Accessed January 10, 2019).

Zenderland, Leila. 2004. "The Parable of *The Kallikak Family*: Explaining the Meaning of Heredity in 1912." In Steven Noll and James W. Trent, Jr., eds. *Mental Retardation in America: A Historical Reader*, 165–185. New York: New York University Press.

Introduction

Many things related to disability and the lives of disabled people can be considered problematic or controversial, and many solutions have been proposed over the decades. In this chapter, I will explore two broad areas of concern for disabled activists and authors working in a number of different fields.

The first is *access*, a critical concept related to disability. Without access, disabled people cannot enjoy all of the rights and privileges of citizenship. As we saw in Chapter 1, disabled people have made significant gains in accessing the built environment. But access extends well beyond the ramps and automatic door openers that most people have become used to in the 21st century. Access includes access to (1) safe, efficient, and affordable health care; (2) safe, reliable, efficient, and affordable public transportation; (3) safe and affordable housing; (4) the highest-quality public education; and finally, (5) employment opportunities. In the first part of this chapter, I will present the five main "access issues" as they have been addressed since about the time of the Great Recession of 2008,

---

[Group of protesters standing and sitting in their wheelchairs outside] Members of disability and transit groups, and advocates for pregnant women, held a vigil outside of the 53rd and 7th Avenue subway station on January 30, 2019. Protestors asserted that the tragedy of Malaysia Goodson would not be in vain and urged Governor Cuomo to settle the lawsuit with a commitment for a plan of full subway accessibility. (Erik McGregor/Pacific Press/LightRocket via Getty Images) which was also the year that the U.S. Congress passed the Americans with Disabilities Act Amendments Act (ADAAA; see Chapter 5).

The second part of this chapter will focus on something that activists and authors have referred to as "the new eugenics." As we saw in Chapter 1, eugenics, which focused on ridding the world of "defectives," became popular in the United States during the first half of the 20th century. Some historians and bioethicists argue that eugenics ended in the mid-20th century with the revelation of Nazi atrocities and various civil rights struggles that challenged state-sanctioned abuses of minorities and people living on the margins of society. Disability rights activists and bioethicists and historians working within disability studies, as well as in other areas, have argued that a new form of eugenics emerged in the wake of the "old eugenics" that continued its larger project of systematically eliminating people considered "defective." Although the new eugenics does not involve the state in the same ways that characterized its older counterpart, and it is generally not considered coercive, it nevertheless has had dire consequences within the disability community, which in turn have had far-reaching and powerful effects in the broader struggles of disabled people and their allies to achieve full citizenship. The "new eugenics" will be the focus of the second part of this chapter.

Access

Health Care

People with disabilities have had a tenuous relationship with organized health care in the United States. As we saw in Chapter 1, for more than 100 years, disabled people in the United States were forced to endure indefinite commitment in state and private hospitals and asylums, and other institutions that ostensibly provided them with the medical care they needed to survive. While institutionalized, many disabled people were forced to endure various medical experiments and other questionable procedures such as transorbital lobotomy and electroshock therapy.

Changes in the administration of health care in the United States and in the ways in which state institutions were funded contributed to what many scholars and activists have called "deinstitutionalization," the movement of disabled people from large custodial institutions to smaller residential settings, nursing homes, and other community-based arrangements. On October 31, 1963, President John F. Kennedy signed the Mental Retardation and Community Mental Health Centers Construction Act, dramatically altering the provision of care for people experiencing mental health problems and for those individuals who at the time were defined as "mentally retarded," beginning the era of deinstitutionalization and community care. This act was followed by the creation of Medicare and Medicaid by the Johnson administration in 1965. In 1972, the Nixon administration expanded Medicare coverage to Social Security Disability Insurance beneficiaries, and created Supplemental Security Income, which provided monthly cash payments to disabled people. Although all of these measures would undergo revisions in the decades following the 1970s, they combined to fundamentally reshape the provision of health care in the United States. Although health care programs vary from one state to the next, a general shift occurred away from state provision of care for people with disabilities to the federal government, greatly expanding the number of people eligible for health care benefits, and providing them with a small measure of independence in deciding where and how they lived and when and in what ways they would access needed health care.

Because of the high rates of unemployment for disabled people, especially those living with various mental illnesses, and developmental or intellectual disabilities, private health insurance is usually completely inaccessible to them. Many people with disabilities depend on the government to meet their health-care needs, which, for some disabled people, can be both labor- and cost-intensive. Although health-care and disability benefits in most states are comprehensive and generally provide the same quality health care as private insurers, certain things like vision coverage and dental plans are difficult to obtain or are not available to people with disabilities who use state-provided health care. State benefits are also "means tested," which means that disabled people must live in abject poverty, often below the poverty line, in order to continue receiving the health care that they depend on to live. Those disabled people who work often do not qualify for benefits (because the make "too much" money) and must cobble together various private health insurance plans and out-of-pocket fee for service providers in order to meet their health-care needs. Revisions to Medicare, Medicaid, and Social Security since the 1990s have made it possible in most states for disabled people who work to "spend down" their annual income in order to meet the income requirements to qualify for government health benefits. Disabled people and their allies were instrumental in changing Social Security rules to make it easier for people with disabilities to work. Many people within the disability community refer to these changes as the "Longmore Amendment" in honor of the late activist and historian Paul K. Longmore, who was one of the most outspoken advocates for changes in Social Security rules. It is not always possible, however, even with these changes, for disabled people to meet the strict income requirements necessary to receive state-funded health care. Even with these "spend-down" measures in place, some disabled people who cannot qualify for state benefits must use after-tax income to pay out of pocket for much-needed health care, like in-home support services, that enable them to live and work independently.

Accessing health care does not end with accessing much-needed health insurance. Disabled people also have to be able physically to access their health-care providers, and they also often must confront and manage structural and cultural barriers to successful health-care provision. Most disabled people do not drive, and so they must find health-care providers close to fixed-route public transportation, or they must use "paratransit" ride services (introduced in the 1980s), which are incredibly expensive (because they are often private providers billing Medicaid) and notoriously inefficient and unreliable. If these forms of transportation are not available or they prove too burdensome, disabled people must rely on family or friends to take them to the doctor, which adds increased stress and strain on relationships, and may also impair family members and friends' ability to work for wages (because they must take time off of work to help disabled friends or family members). Once at the doctor's office, people with various physical and sensory disabilities must deal with inaccessible waiting and examination rooms and staff who for liability reasons are unwilling to assist patients. Once they make it into the exam room, disabled people must then deal with nurses, physician assistants, and medical doctors who may have preconceived notions about patients on state benefits and about disabled people more generally. People with mental health problems and those people defined as developmentally or intellectually disabled tend to encounter more social and cultural bias among health-care providers than do people with mobility and sensory impairments, who also encounter a significant amount of prejudice and discrimination. If disabled people need to see a specialist, or they need lab work or a prescription filled, this consumes more time and potentially requires disorienting negotiation of the health-care bureaucracy and most likely more trips to far-flung locations that may pose additional access issues.

Some solutions to these access issues include increased and more efficient public transportation (discussed later in this chapter), consolidated and centralized health-care services (the one-stop shop), and improved and more widely utilized "cultural competency training" for all health-care providers. While cultural competency training has become an increasingly common part of medical school curricula and the curricula in other areas such as nursing and other health-care professions (in part because of the activism of disabled people and their allies), the

United States seems to be moving away from centralized and consolidated health-care services and a robust public transportation network. Since the 1980s, cultural competency training has been increasingly included as part of the accreditation process for medical schools and other health professions. Put simply, cultural competency training is meant to provide future doctors and other health-care providers with the tools necessary to provide empathetic care not only to disabled people but also to racial/ethnic minorities, recent immigrants, refugees, and other marginal and minority populations. The recognition that medical practice, or health-care provision more generally, does not only consist of identifying various biological or physiological processes or the management of disease symptoms but also includes a humanistic appreciation for patient experiences, thoughts, feelings, desires, and demands is transforming health-care provision in the United States. Much more work needs to be done, however, especially as it relates to people with disabilities and more specifically people living with mental health issues and those people defined as developmentally or intellectually disabled, both of whom are often the most heavily stigmatized groups of disabled people.

Unfortunately for people with disabilities and other poor people, over the past 40 years the United States has been moving away from state-funded public transportation and centralized health care services. The dominant neoliberal political economy, which favors a decentralized or nonexistent government (at least in the social service sector), privatization, and deeply fragmented service and employment sectors, has given rise to virtual (Internet) economies, widespread distribution, processing and service centers, and decentralized (unregulated) and privatized forms of transportation such as Uber and Lyft. While this new political economy is promoted as providing consumers with increased "choice," independence, and control over their lives, the reality is that much of the work that was once done by service providers and other industries has been offloaded onto consumers (in an effort to increase profits). The overall effect of this new economy has been greatly increased disparities in access (and wealth). Uber and Lyft are not accessible to many people with disabilities, and without an economic incentive or a federal mandate compelling (or even incentivizing) the creation of accessible ride services, this will not change in the foreseeable future. Disabled people who do not have access to the Internet, or who find using the Internet difficult because of their disabilities, cannot participate in virtual ride sharing or in the virtual health-care world, which increasingly includes things like scheduling, advising, referrals, and the distribution of medical knowledge and information. In making health-care services available in multiple and widely dispersed locations, health-care providers are making it nearly impossible for some disabled people to utilize those services because they cannot participate in the virtual health-care world and they cannot travel to multiple locations over vast (or relatively close but inaccessible) distances.

Universal single-payer health care, which was initially introduced to the U.S. Congress by President Harry S. Truman in the 1940s, has become an intensely and widely debated topic since the 1990s. Universal single-payer health care would solve many of the access issues that disabled people experience when they attempt to utilize health-care providers. Universal single-payer health care would eliminate the class bias in health-care provision, the notion that people on "government benefits" are somehow qualitatively different from other patients. Single-payer health care would also offer more comprehensive services to all Americans, including vision, dental, prescriptions, and the durable medical equipment or DME that most disabled people depend on for their survival. Finally, single-payer health care could also incorporate a taxpayer-funded living allowance that would enable disabled people and elderly people to pay for in-home support services that would keep them out of nursing homes, hospitals, and other expensive institutional settings, and would enable them to work (or not). In addition, and this is an especially compelling argument for single-payer health care, employers would no longer be responsible for providing health insurance for their employees. The neoliberal economy in which we live in the 21st century, which demands a flexible and mobile workforce, removes the desirability of employers to provide workers with long-term benefits, such as health-care benefits. If Americans did not have to work in order to receive health insurance (because they received insurance through the government), this would free employers from providing insurance and also simultaneously create a more flexible and mobile workforce, because employees would not live in fear of losing their job and their health insurance. Workers (disabled and nondisabled) could move from one job to the next and one location to the next largely unencumbered. Single-payer health care would provide employers with the type of employees they desire ("free and flexible"), and it would provide workers with the health-care benefits they demand.

Questions to consider: Is single-payer health care a viable option in the United States? Would single-payer health care solve the issues related to access of people with disabilities to health-care provision? What other alternative solutions could be used to provide more accessible health care to both disabled and nondisabled Americans?

Public Transportation

In summer 1978, a group of disabled people in Denver who called themselves "The Gang of Nineteen" began protesting inaccessible public transportation in their city. In 1983, the group officially changed its name to Americans Disabled for Accessible Public Transit, or ADAPT. Taking a cue from Martin Luther King, Jr., Rosa Parks, and other African American civil rights leaders of the 1950s and 1960s, disabled people in the 1970s and 1980s increasingly engaged in direct-action protest of inaccessible public transportation. They blocked buses with their wheelchairs and got out of their wheelchairs and attempted to crawl or drag themselves up the steps of public buses in an effort to dramatize the effects of second-class citizenship and an inaccessible built environment.

Groups like ADAPT, as well as other disabled people and their allies, were instrumental in making disability rights a national issue during the 1970s and 1980s, culminating in the passage of the Americans with Disabilities Act (ADA) in 1990, under the administration of George H. W. Bush. The ADA, combined with legislation such as the Air Carrier Access Act of 1986, made most forms of transportation legally accessible to people with disabilities. Making something legally accessible, however, does not always mean that it will be accessible in the everyday lives of disabled Americans.

Scholars of African American history write about *de jure* and *de facto* segregation, as well as structural racism. When we think about accessible public transportation, it is helpful to use these terms. The term "de jure" simply means "by law." The term "de facto" means "by fact." The idea of structural racism is a bit more complex. It is the idea that it is not necessarily the thoughts or actions of individual people, but rather the way that society is structured that produces segregation and discrimination. Things like housing codes, or voting laws, or even the ways in which scientific knowledge gets produced, can be inherently racist. If we are thinking about how these concepts might apply to people with disabilities, we can argue that most of the built environment, including public transportation and air travel, has been made accessible "by law." That does not mean, necessarily, that de facto accessibility exists in the United States. The law may mandate accessibility, but disabled people do not always experience accessibility in "the fact" of their everyday lives. One way of explaining the disconnect between law and lived experience is through the concept of "ableism," which is very much like structural racism. Ableism is the idea that we live in a society built by and for nondisabled people, and therefore our world is inherently, or structurally, or in fact, inaccessible to most disabled people despite the creation of laws like the ADA that are meant to protect the constitutional rights of disabled people.

The most readily used forms of transportation in the United States (besides individual owner-operated vehicles) are buses, trains, airplanes, and taxis or the new ride-sharing services, such as Uber and Lyft. Disabled people also have access to something called "para-transit," which consists of smaller buses that are usually owned and operated by metro or regional transportation authorities or individual private subcontractors and are meant to provide supplemental transportation services for areas that extend beyond fixed-route public transportation (buses or trains) and to people who may not be able to access fixed-route services independently. Since the passage of the ADA in 1990, nearly all buses and trains in the United States have been made accessible with wheelchair lifts or ramps and accessible seating, signage, and restrooms. In addition, and only after multiple legal actions, interstate bus services such as Greyhound and Megabus have also been made accessible. Airports and airplanes too have been made accessible to disabled travelers. There is absolutely no doubt that tremendous gains have been made in the almost 30 years since the enactment of the ADA in 1990.

Yet transportation options, including public transportation, remain out of reach for many disabled people. This is in large part because the public services sector (of the government and the economy) has been dwindling since the 1980s. Instead of creating more routes, hiring new drivers and mechanics, and creating more modernized, accessible bus stops and train stations, metro and regional transportation authorities, who have seen their resources steadily decline, have been cutting back on services. Many cities in the United States have reached the point where they are unable to invest in the equipment and hire and retain the drivers, mechanics, conductors, and other people necessary to keep their services functioning at full capacity. Expansion of services is usually unthinkable, given the dominant desire among many lawmakers to cut government spending on social services. For many nondisabled travelers, dwindling public sector options have been supplemented by new ride-sharing services such as Uber and Lyft. As mentioned in the previous section, these services remain almost completely inaccessible to people with disabilities, especially those people who use mobility devices. In some of the major cities in the country (e.g., New York City, Chicago, San Francisco, even Buffalo, New York) disability rights activists and their allies have been successful in making a certain percentage of taxis wheelchair accessible, but these services are rare, often difficult to schedule, and in some cases can be exorbitantly expensive. Despite the ADA making it illegal to discriminate against disabled people, many taxi drivers and taxi companies do not use the "metered fare" when transporting people who use mobility devices. Instead, they add on a surcharge, or charge a "flat rate" regardless of the distance traveled, making travel by taxi prohibitively expensive for disabled people, many of whom live in poverty. The only realistic options for many disabled people who need to travel are the understaffed and inconvenient fixed-route public buses and trains, and the notoriously unreliable, inefficient, and burdensome "paratransit" systems. Transportation is such an important issue in disabled people's lives, and public transportation has become so compromised in the United States, that it has become a running theme within disability culture across the country. It has become the subject of much outrage and complaint, and the focus of many jokes.

One possible solution to the transportation problems faced by many disabled people is a countrywide commitment to reinvesting in America's infrastructure and an expansion of its public services. Using a small fraction of America's wealth to expand, update, modernize, and make more efficient and accessible its vast network of public buses and trains would benefit all Americans, not just people with disabilities. Much of the country's infrastructure was built during the Great Depression of the 1930s and in the immediate postwar period, when the federal government in cooperation with the states was willing to take on a greater role in providing vital public services. Buses and trains fueled by renewable energy sources, and modern, accessible bus and train stations electrified and heated by renewable energy sources, like the sun, would also go a long way in promoting environmental sustainability. In addition, a federal mandate that requires all taxi services and ride-sharing services to make a certain percentage of their fleet of vehicles wheelchair accessible, and requires cultural competency training for drivers/operators would provide an improved, sustainable alternative to both fixed-route buses and trains and the existing, badly broken para-transit system. Providing better transportation options would make it easier for more Americans to work, consume, access health care, and pay taxes, which would bring added revenue to businesses, and to local, state, and federal governments. It would improve the quality of life of all Americans, both disabled and nondisabled.

Questions to consider: Is investment in and regulation of various forms of public transportation the only solution to disabled people's transportation issues? Would increased investment in research in "driverless technologies" and other innovations better serve the needs of the American people? It was not mentioned, but do you see a role for unions in supporting and advocating for both workers in and users of public transportation? Why? Why not? Should disabled people be forced to pay more for taxis and other individualized ride services?

Housing

Where to live has always been an especially difficult question for people with disabilities to answer. As we saw in Chapter 1, for most of the 19th and 20th centuries, disabled people were forced to live in residential schools, asylums, hospitals, or other institutions. It was not until the 1960s that disabled people began to move out of these places into various settings within the community. While the majority of disabled people live in the community in the 21st century, their housing situation is less than ideal. Accessing adequate and appropriate housing is an ongoing concern for many disabled people.

Generally, there are three barriers to access related to housing. The first is physical access: Can a disabled person enter the dwelling and use the kitchen, bathrooms, and so on? The second concern is financial: Can a disabled person afford to live in a particular location or in a particular dwelling? The third major concern is the social and cultural backlash that many disabled people face when they attempt to live in the community: Why do *they* have to live in *my* neighborhood, on *my* block, in *my* building, and so on? I will briefly address each one of these concerns and then propose some solutions to these problems.

Since the passage of the ADA in 1990, any new construction intended for public use must be accessible to people with a broad range of disabilities. Contractors or developers building private housing do not have to follow the same rules, but the federal government provides incentives to encourage them to make a certain percentage of their units accessible to people with disabilities. Over the past 30 years, the housing situation for people with disabilities has improved dramatically, but it is still inadequate.

People with physical disabilities who require the use of mobility devices such as wheelchairs, scooters, or walkers have the most difficult time finding accessible housing. Despite the ADA, and various government incentives, physically accessible housing remains scarce. The waiting lists for public housing, which must by law provide accessible units, are long, and "market-rate" accessible housing is either nonexistent or out of the price range of most disabled people. Since the 1990s, cities and counties throughout the United States have been adopting new zoning and building codes that incorporate "visitability" standards, which in most cases require a wheelchair accessible entrance "at grade" (ground level), doorways wide enough to accommodate a wheelchair, and a toilet on the ground floor. These new standards, which do not exist in every city and every county in the United States, have made it easier for people with mobility impairments to visit with friends, family, and neighbors, but this level of access does not adequately address the need for accessible housing. In most cases, people with mobility impairments have to make do with whatever housing they can find, which usually means building makeshift ramps or making other accommodations to get into the home, and relying on DIY or do-it-yourself accessibility modifications inside the home, which can cause significant health and safety risks, especially when internal modifications are made to bathrooms, kitchens, and bedrooms.

Perhaps an even larger access concern related to housing is financial. Most disabled people live in poverty. They do not have the financial resources to access market-rate housing, which has steadily increased in price during the 21st century. Because the waiting lists for public housing are so long, many disabled people's only option is to find affordable market-rate rental units, which are becoming increasingly rare and, because of the rental unit's location and potentially neglected infrastructure, may increase complications related to safety, physical accessibility, access to transportation, and other issues related to health and well-being. People with mental health issues and developmental or intellectual disabilities, who experience incredibly high rates of unemployment, have an especially hard time finding adequate housing.

Many people with developmental or intellectual disabilities live in supported residential settings commonly known as "group homes." Group homes usually accommodate four to eight disabled people, depending on the size of the home and its location. In most cases, group homes are owned and managed by not-for-profit human service agencies who supply the house with staff to support the disabled residents. The staff generally do not live in the home, but come and go on a shift-work schedule. People with developmental and intellectual disabilities began moving into the community in the 1970s and 1980s, after media reports revealed the abhorrent conditions inside state institutions and courts demanded their closure. The U.S. Supreme Court affirmed the right of people with developmental and intellectual disabilities to live as independently as possible in the community with its ruling in *Olmstead v. L. C.* (1999).

Despite nearly 50 years of activism and support from human service agencies and other allies, as well as favorable court rulings, people with developmental and intellectual disabilities still face significant challenges when they attempt to live in the community, especially if they need or desire to live in a group home. Local residents worried about property values and influenced by misconceptions about disabled people and the people who work for them as people who will bring unwanted activities and crime into their neighborhood have put up considerable barriers to disabled people's attempts to live in the community. Resistance from potential neighbors and dwindling governmental fiscal support for community living (in the form of reduced funding for Medicaid and other essential services) have resulted in severe shortages in group homes and other supported living environments in many regions throughout the country. Some parents of developmentally and intellectually disabled children and adults have attempted to combat resistance to community living by advocating for a new form of "voluntary" institutionalization in which parents and other investors pool their resources and create "closed campuses" for their disabled children (Marcum, 2016). Self-advocates and their allies have been understandably alarmed at what they perceive as a return to the institutions of the 19th and early 20th centuries. The latter group supports a more integrated approach to community living for people with disabilities.

If we take the "social model" perspective that disability is created by the environment and is not necessarily the direct result of bodily differences among humans, then it makes sense that the solutions to the housing crisis would be structural. The housing crisis, like other domestic crises facing the United States, must be met head-on by local, state, and federal governments. As part of a renewed investment in the nation's infrastructure, local, state, and federal governments should look toward a deeper investment in mixed-use public housing communities open to a broader range of income levels, to avoid the stigma associated with "living in the projects" as it has been historically characterized. These new mixed-use, multi-income communities should host businesses, retail, restaurants, community health centers (including mental health), and be linked to a robust public transportation network. Housing units should be designed using universal design principles, which would make the built environment accessible to the broadest range of users and minimize the need for accommodations. Housing in these new communities should also be designed in a way that makes it possible to "age in place." Universally designed structures that are able to change to meet the changing needs of humans throughout the various stages of their life should be the new rule in housing development. New housing communities should model "green" sustainable energy production and a sustainable local economy. In addition to creating vibrant and dynamic public housing communities, various levels of government should take a renewed interest in subsidizing housing cooperatives and look again at the importance of rent regulations to control the skyrocketing costs of housing in many regions of the United States. At the end of the second decade of the 21st century, annual rents in some parts of the country exceed 50 percent and even 60 percent of some workers' annual income. Solving even some of these structural problems and making housing accessible would significantly benefit all Americans, not just people with disabilities.

Questions to consider: Should local, state, and federal governments participate in planning residential communities? Should developers and housing contractors be compelled either through positive financial incentives or through negative fines to create a more accessible and affordable built environment? Should people with intellectual and developmental disabilities live in isolated, "closed" residential campuses? What if the parents and other relatives of people with intellectual and developmental disabilities deem this the most appropriate and safe setting for their family members?

Public Education

Since the U.S. Congress passed the Education for All Handicapped Children Act in 1975, schools throughout the United States have been compelled to provide inclusive K–12 education. Although there has been resistance to what is commonly referred to as "mainstreaming" and the level of inclusivity varies from one school to the next and in some cases from one classroom to the next, children with disabilities are much more likely in the 21st century to receive an education in a classroom with their nondisabled peers than at any other point in U.S. history.

Because the federal government began collecting data and monitoring compliance with what is now known as the Individuals with Disabilities Education Act (IDEA), in 1976, we have reliable enrollment data for students with disabilities ages 3–21 (students with developmental and intellectual disabilities can remain in the K–12 system until they are 21). Throughout the first two decades of the 21st century students with disabilities have comprised about 13 percent or 14 percent of all public-school enrollment, between 6.4 and 6.7 million students. Among students with disabilities, approximately 34 percent have a specific learning disability, 20 percent have speech or language impairment, 14 percent have "other health impairment," and the remaining 32 percent of students have autism (9 percent), developmental delays (6 percent), intellectual disability (6 percent), emotional disturbances (5 percent), "multiple disabilities" (2 percent), hearing impairment (1 percent), and orthopedic (mobility) impairment (1 percent) (National Center for Education Statistics, 2018).

Government record-keeping enables access to other data as well, like the racial/ethnic background of students who use services under the IDEA. The largest percentage of students served under the IDEA are American Indian/Alaska Native

(17 percent), followed by black students (16 percent), then white (14 percent), people belonging to two or more races (13 percent), Hispanic and Pacific Islander (12 percent), and Asian (7 percent). In general, more boys than girls use IDEA services, but if we break down the data by disability, we can see that there are significant variations by gender. For example, more boys get labeled as autistic, while more girls receive services for specific learning disabilities (National Center for Education Statistics, 2018).

Perhaps more important are rates of inclusion and educational outcomes. About 95 percent of all students with disabilities ages 6–21 were enrolled in "regular schools" in 2015. Among all of the students served by the IDEA, the percentage of students who spent most of the school day (80 percent or more of their time) in general classes increased from 41 percent in fall 2000 to 63 percent in fall 2015. The rate of inclusion in general classes was highest for students with speech or language impairments, 87 percent. Federal data also show that about two thirds of students with learning disabilities (70 percent), visual impairments (67 percent), other health impairments (65 percent), and developmental delays (64 percent) spent most of their day in general classes. Rates of inclusion for students with intellectual disabilities and multiple disabilities were much lower, at 16 percent and 13 percent, respectively. These data show that a majority of students with certain disabilities are included in general classes in regular schools, while others, namely, those with intellectual and developmental disabilities, are left out of general classrooms (National Center for Education Statistics, 2018).

National data show similar patterns when we look at educational outcomes. Approximately 395,000 disabled students between the ages of 14 and 21 "exited" school in the 2014–2015 academic year. More than two thirds (69 percent) graduated with regular high school diplomas, 18 percent dropped out, and 11 percent received an "alternative certificate." About 1 percent "aged out" of the system and less than 1 percent died.

If we break these statistics down by race/ethnicity we can get a sense of the percentage of students who received a regular diploma or alternative certificate: 88 percent of Asian students, 83 percent of white students, 80 percent of Hispanic students, 77 percent of students who identify as "two or more races," 76 percent of black students, 75 percent of Pacific Islander students, and 70 percent of American Indian/Alaskan Native students. The percentage of students who graduated with a regular high school diploma was lowest among black students at 62 percent. Black students received the highest number of alternative certificates, at 14 percent. The highest percentage of high school dropouts was among students labeled with "emotional disturbances" at 35 percent. Students least likely to receive a regular diploma (42 percent) and most likely to receive an alternative certificate (34 percent) were those students with intellectual disabilities (National Center for Education Statistics, 2018). While rates of inclusion and school outcomes seem impressive on the surface, when we look closer at the connections among race/ethnicity, type of disability, and completion and dropout rates, it starts to become clear that racial/ethnic minorities (blacks, Hispanics, American Indian/Alaska Native) are the least likely to complete K–12 education and the least likely to receive a regular high school diploma.

To put this a different way, statistically speaking, an Asian girl with a learning disability is more likely to receive a high school diploma and go on to college than a black boy or Native American boy labeled as autistic, behaviorally or emotionally disturbed, or intellectual or developmentally disabled (ID). That boy is more likely to drop out of high school or receive an alternative certificate, and less likely to continue on to postsecondary education. Youth with ID, autism, or multiple disabilities were the least likely to be expected to graduate from high school with a regular diploma or to attend postsecondary school (36, 48, and 52 percent, respectively). Overall, the post–high school transition goals of students with ID and students with other disabilities were found to differ significantly.

The National Council on Disability (NCD), an independent federal agency making recommendations to the president and Congress on issues affecting Americans with disabilities, published a report entitled "Improving Educational Outcomes for Students with Disabilities," in 2004. In the report, it made three broad recommendations: to improve the dropout rate among students with disabilities (which was at 34 percent in 2004), to increase the number of students receiving a regular high school diploma (which was at 56 percent in 2004), and finally to increase the likelihood that students with disabilities would transition to postsecondary education after graduation. In the 10 years following the report, the dropout rate decreased and the rate of students receiving diplomas increased. It is more difficult to measure whether students with disabilities successfully transitioned to postsecondary education (National Council on Disability, 2004).

The NCD made some specific recommendations for improving the performance of students with disabilities. Chief among them was expanding the number of qualified teachers to work with students with disabilities. The NCD acknowledged that finding and training those teachers is "a difficult reality faced by schools" (2004, 6). In addition to more and better-trained teachers, the NCD called for more "rigorous, evidence-based research on programs that promote positive outcomes for students with disabilities," which it found to be "severely limited" in 2004. Existing studies, they found, focused most on best practices for teaching young students to read. Existing studies also used very limited sample sizes; that is, they focused their research on a small number of students. Most research only focused on one type of disability. Finally, and perhaps most important, no studies focused on dropout prevention or on the transition from secondary to postsecondary education (2004, 7).

Existing research did, however, provide some mention of useful tools to promote the success of students with disabilities in high school. Effective measures included improved counseling services, reading remediation, tutoring, attendance monitoring, and after-school clubs. Also included among effective strategies for success were "sustained and supportive monitoring interventions focused on school completion" (2004, 7), which could introduce a dangerous and unwanted level of surveillance into students' (and parents') lives, something the NCD did not address. Based on the little work done on dropout rates, the Department of Education found that "five components were common to all [successful] programs: persistence, continuity and consistency; monitoring; relationships; affiliation; and problem-solving skills" (2004, 8). Other more recent research has found that expectations matter. Higher expectations for academic and career success relate to better high school completion rates, higher postsecondary school attendance rates, and more positive parent engagement with their high school students (Grigal, Hart, and Migliore, 2011). Newer research has also found that transition planning teams are helpful in improving outcomes for students with disabilities. Transition planning teams should include, in addition to the student, his or her family school personnel, and representatives from agencies that provide post–high school services to students with disabilities including vocational rehabilitation (VR), mental health agencies, developmental disability providers, and independent living centers (Grigal, Hart, and Migliore, 2011).

Preparation is critical to success. Academic standards for high school students often do not reflect college admissions and placement requirements, and students with and without disabilities get conflicting messages from high schools and colleges about what constitutes adequate preparation. High school teachers estimate that 42 percent of their students are not prepared to transition to postsecondary education. Involving higher education personnel in transition planning for disabled students would offer a valuable opportunity to prepare both the student and their family, the college, and potential support staff to know what types of accommodations are available at the college and which might need to be provided through an outside agency or addressed privately by the family (Grigal, Hart, and Migliore, 2011). In addition to higher education personnel, having people with disabilities who are in college or who have recently completed a postsecondary program serve as mentors for younger people with disabilities would be ideal.

Although the NCD and other researchers do not specifically address it, it becomes clear when listing possible solutions to the problems facing students with disabilities that their success depends on human investment in their education, which is time-consuming, labor-intensive, and incredibly expensive, because schools must hire adequate numbers of teachers and support staff to achieve success. In the early 21st century, when public resources for education are dwindling and the Department of Education is increasingly focusing on privatizing education, it does not appear that many of these measures would be put in place without a significant reorientation of priorities at the federal level of government.

Questions to consider: Should the state fund the necessary improvements to public education to increase the likelihood of success among disabled and nondisabled students? How can the United States better value its students, teachers, and support staff at the K–12 level? Should disabled students be in mainstream classrooms? Why? Why not?

Employment Opportunities

According to the 2010 census, 41 percent of adults aged 21 to 64 with any disability reported being employed, compared to 79 percent of nondisabled adults aged 21 to 64. About 10.8 percent of severely disabled Americans experience persistent poverty, while about 4.9 percent of Americans with "nonsevere" disabilities experience persistent poverty and about 3.8 percent of nondisabled Americans experience persistent poverty. Census takers defined "persistent poverty" as consistent poverty over a 24-month period.

Only 41 percent of disabled adults work. That means that nearly 60 percent of disabled adults are unemployed. The rates are even higher if we focus specifically on people with developmental or intellectual disabilities and people living with mental health problems. The rates of unemployment among these disabled populations are consistently between 70 percent and 80 percent unemployed. Of the 41 percent of disabled people who do work, many are underemployed and overqualified for the jobs they hold. It has been well known within the disability community for many years that disabled people face significant barriers in the job market. As early as the 1940s, mostly in response to the rising numbers of disabled veterans from World War II, the federal government began using "employ the handicapped" campaigns to encourage employers to tap into this unused pool of workers. Despite political rhetoric and more focused efforts over the years to employ disabled people, their rates of employment have not changed much in the early 21st century, and by some accounts they are not even as good as indicated in the 2010 census.

In 2015, the federal Bureau of Labor Statistics (BLS) conducted a more comprehensive survey of unemployment rates among people with disabilities and related those rates to educational attainment. When we look at these figures, the employment status of disabled people comes into stark relief. According to the 2015 BLS study, only 27 percent of people with disabilities were employed; 70 percent of people with disabilities were unemployed, and 3 percent were "not in the labor market," which means they were not seeking any type of employment. Among the nondisabled population, 77 percent of people were employed in 2015 (National Center for Education Statistics, 2018). The BLS study found that as the level of education increased, the unemployment gap between nondisabled and disabled narrowed slightly; 45 percent of disabled people with a bachelor's degree were employed in 2015, versus 84 percent of nondisabled people with a bachelor's degree. Especially concerning, however, was the rate of employment for people with a high school diploma (National Center for Education Statistics, 2018). Only 22 percent of people with disabilities who graduated high school were employed, versus 73 percent of nondisabled people with a high school diploma (National Center for Education Statistics, 2018). Considering that many people do not go to college and an even smaller percentage of people obtain a graduate or professional degree, and that most people move into the labor market upon completion of high school, the percentage of unemployed people with disabilities with a high school diploma (78 percent) are startling. It is clear from these data that disabled people are excluded from the labor market. Figuring out why disabled people do not work is a more difficult task.

Many of the unemployment issues facing disabled people in the 21st century are access issues. Accessing quality education and job training programs is certainly an issue, as is accessing transportation to and from work. Beyond that, however, disabled people face specific forms of discrimination in hiring and retention that result in decreased access to employment. Studies have shown that despite efforts to eliminate bias in hiring, employers consistently discriminate in evaluating people's resumes and in the interview process. Employers like to hire people who look and act like them. Disabled people also face discrimination that is specific to disability. Employers report having concerns about the perceived health-related issues of disabled employees. The dominant misconception is that disabled employees will be unable to work because of multiple health-related issues. Employers also express concern that they will become the subject of ADA lawsuits if the workplace is found to be inaccessible or if employees demand accommodations. Finally, employers have noted their concern that disabled people will be costly, specifically in terms of providing them health-care coverage. Some of these concerns would be removed if, as stated earlier, the United States moved to a single-payer, government-supported health-care system, but other factors, such as deep-seated misconceptions about disabled people being too "different" to employ or being unreliable or especially litigious, would continue to persist and affect the attitudes and worldviews of employers. There are steps that can be taken to change attitudes and promote a more equitable environment in the hiring and retention of disabled workers.

Some solutions to the unemployment problems facing disabled people have presented themselves through larger shifts in the American economy. For example, an increasing reliance on technology and the Internet, as well as "telecommuting"—working from home—could potentially greatly increase the likelihood that disabled people will be increasingly employed in the future. However, the types of jobs that allow for a greater use of technology and also greater freedom to work from home are usually jobs that require specialized training or postsecondary education, something that most disabled people lack. Improving educational outcomes for people with disabilities and providing support and incentives for disabled people to continue their postsecondary education are critical factors in leveling the unemployment rates of disabled and nondisabled people.

Changing employer attitudes is perhaps the most important and difficult challenge facing disabled people and their allies. In 2010, the Obama administration took its own steps in changing attitudes toward disabled people by issuing Executive Order 13548, "Increasing Federal Employment of Individuals with Disabilities," which built upon an executive order issued by President Clinton in 2000, which called for the hiring of 100,000 individuals with disabilities by the federal government over five years (The White House, 2010). President Obama's 2010 Executive Order's preamble states that it would "establish the Federal Government as a model employer of individuals with disabilities" (The White House, 2010). It goes on to state that the "Federal Government has an important interest in reducing discrimination against Americans living with a disability, and eliminating the stigma associated with disability, and encouraging Americans with disabilities to seek employment in the Federal workforce" (The White House, 2010). At the time, in 2010, people with disabilities represented only approximately 5 percent of the nearly 2.5 million federal employees and people with specific disabilities targeted for hiring by the executive order represented less than 1 percent of the total federal workforce (The White House, 2010). The executive order set out specific goals and a specific timeline for achieving those goals. Those goals included mandatory training programs for both human resources personnel and hiring managers, as well as the creation of "agency-specific" plans for hiring and the designation of a "senior-level agency official" to be accountable for hiring people with disabilities (The White House, 2010). In an effort to retain disabled workers, the executive order called for the use of "centralized funds to provide reasonable accommodations, increasing access to appropriate accessible technologies, and ensuring the accessibility of physical and virtual workspaces" (The White House, 2010).

By most accounts, President Obama's executive order was a success. By 2016, the federal government had hired an additional 109,000 employees with disabilities (Bender Consulting Services, Inc., 2017). The consulting company that worked with the federal government's Office of Personnel Management (OPM, 2016) to measure the success (or failure) of the order reported in 2017 that "more people with disabilities now work at the nation's largest employer than anytime over the last 35 years!" (Bender Consulting Services, Inc., 2017). The same report went on to state, "You cannot break down barriers that impede employment of people with disabilities until you start hiring! People with disabilities working at your site, side-by-side with non-disabled employees, is what really increases employment" (Bender Consulting Services, Inc., 2017). The OPM issued a more specific report that conveyed the same message. It stated in October 2016 that "federal employees with disabilities represent 14.41 percent of the overall workforce, accounting for 264,844 people. This is more people with disabilities in Federal service, both in real terms and by percentage, than at any time in the last 35 years" (OPM.GOV, 2016). The hiring and retention of disabled workers initiated under Executive Order 13548 show that disabled people can be integrated into the workforce.

While the vast majority of private employers do not have the resources or the power of the federal government, they can follow its example. One of the most significant barriers disabled people face in the labor market is an unwillingness of employers to hire them. The federal government, through President Obama's executive order, proved that "targeted" hires of disabled people can be successful and that disabled people can succeed in the labor market if given the opportunity. Unfortunately, federal hiring initiatives are often politically motivated and can change with each new administration. If the United States is going to solve its unemployment crisis, it must put in place more robust and permanent solutions to the hiring and retention of people with disabilities, as well as other minorities and people living on the margins of society. More liberal politicians and government officials argue that it should be the responsibility of the federal government to hire people who otherwise cannot find a job and provide them with a sufficient wage, as well as retirement and health-care packages. They argue that these employees could be used for everything from rebuilding and modernizing America's infrastructure to educating its children to maintaining its public spaces and creating art and culture. Jobs do not have to be limited to physical labor or clerical work. During the Great Depression of the 1930s, the federal government employed writers and artists. The materials they produced are still being used by scholars and other people interested in studying the nation's history. Similar undertakings could be achieved in the early 21st century, a time when technology and a changing geopolitical environment are altering the way humans live and interact in the world. More conservative politicians and government officials argue that this is "wasteful" spending and that any projects initiated by the federal government should employ private contractors. Americans need to decide whether they want to commit themselves to making a more equitable and socially just world or whether they believe in the "free market" economics of privatized capitalism. Whatever they decide as a nation, there should be measures put in place that ensure equal opportunity in the labor market for all Americans, including disabled Americans.

Questions to consider: Is it the government's responsibility to employ people who otherwise cannot find work in the private sector? Should the federal government fund the creation of art and culture and work in the humanities, such as that conducted by historians?

The New Eugenics

As we saw in Chapter 1, for nearly 100 years, from the 1860s to the 1950s, eugenic ideas rooted in ableist notions of "fit" bodies occupied a central place in local, national, and international efforts to improve the quality of the "race" and, by extension, society. Most people think that eugenics ended by about 1960. They argue that emerging social and political forces made the continuation of state-led, coercive eugenic programs aimed at improving the "racial stock" increasingly untenable in most countries. They cite changing understandings of human heredity and changing conceptualizations of the causes and consequences of suspect behaviors and bodies, as well as an emerging human rights discourse, and growing civil rights and anticolonial movements to explain the end of eugenics in most places. The old eugenics continued in some countries, however. The People's Republic of China (PRC), for example, created marriage laws in 1950 and 1980 that, according to social philosopher Nikolas Rose, "explicitly identified categories of people unfit for reproduction, especially those where both partners had a history of hereditary disease, or where both partners had a history of 'mental disease.'" In 1994, the PRC created the Law on Maternal and Infant Health Care, which contained four articles that many observers considered eugenic (Rose, 2009,

66–68). Yet even in China state-led eugenics programs faced challenges. In most places in the world, eugenics appeared dead by the 1960s; but was it really gone? Most scholars and activists argue that a "new eugenics" arose immediately after the old eugenics began to decline.

A scientist named R. L. Sinsheimer first referred to genetic engineering as a "new eugenics" in 1969. By the 1990s, public conversations about the new eugenics had increased within the context of major advancements in genetics, biotechnology, and the popular campaign to map the human genome. Bioethicists, journalists, sociologists, historians, and activists from all over the world pondered the implications of the new genetic age. In the United States, *Time* magazine published a special issue on January 11, 1999, entitled "The Future of Medicine," that focused on the changes that genetic engineering would bring to human reproduction in the next century. Inside were articles that explored everything from DNA mapping and genetic screening to the use of genetic fingerprinting in law enforcement and the creation of "designer" babies. In his introductory piece, journalist Walter Isaacson declared that the 21st century would be "The Biotech Century" and that it would be an age in which humans would be able to alter their DNA radically, "encoding [their] visions and vanities while concocting new life-forms" (43). *Time*'s authors were not alone in promoting such claims. Throughout the 1990s, *Atlantic Monthly*, *New Republic*, *Life*, *U.S. News and World Report*, and *Newsweek* all published articles emphasizing the importance of biotechnology to the future of human reproduction (Allen, 2001, 61).

Underlying the new eugenics and the bioethical debates it created was an assumption that major advances in genetic technologies had enabled, and would continue to enable, experts to manipulate the human body in ways that had been previously unimaginable. Everything from the sex of a child to eye color, hair color, skin color, muscle strength, memory, intelligence, height, and athletic or musical talent found their way into discussions of what might be possible in the future of biotechnology and genetic engineering. Rose describes the new genetic age as one where "interventions are scaled at the molecular level" and where "biology is not destiny but opportunity—to discover the biological basis of an illness, of infertility . . . is not to resign oneself to fate but to open oneself to hope" (51). Too often, however, the hope for a better future for one's self and one's offspring manifests in cultural pressures to endure prenatal diagnoses and the elimination of fetuses determined to be "at risk" for disabilities such as spina bifida and Down syndrome, as well as other "genetic" diseases and conditions like cystic fibrosis. Disability activists and scholars are (justifiably) alarmed and quite vocal in their explanations of the implications that the new era of human "enhancement" has for individuals (both living and unborn) who do not measure up to dominant notions of bodily perfection and whose lives are considered by the larger nondisabled society to be not worth living (e.g., Ball and Wolbring; Kerr and Shakespeare, 2002; Rapp and Ginsburg, 2001; Reist, 2010; Shakespeare, 1998; Tokar, 2001).

Critics of the new technologies claim that genetic counseling and other reproductive interventions offered to parents, which in most countries are supposed to be "nondirective," are actually aimed at reducing the number of births of children with congenital and genetic disorders: that they are both eugenic and oppressive (Kerr and Shakespeare, 2002; Reist, 2010). Critics point out that they are not suggesting a conspiracy on the part of medical doctors, scientists, and the state to rid the world of people with disabilities. They maintain, however, that, "structural factors and societal pressures guarantee that allowing parents a 'free choice' result in a systematic bias against the birth of genetically disabled children that can only be called eugenic" (King, 2001, 175). Some critics refer to this as "back-door," "laissez-faire," "do-it-yourself," "user-friendly," or "medical" eugenics, and assert that it is a "major form of disability oppression" (Hampton, 2005; Kazuyo, 2001; King, 2001; Paul, 2007; Pritchard, 2005; Reist, 2010; Rock, 1996; Shakespeare, 1998;

Sharp and Earle, 2002). In addition to these voluntary measures, critics cite cases in which the state has intervened in the reproductive lives of its citizens in more direct ways. Critics, for example, label "eugenic" certain social "reform" measures that target poor women on welfare. Historian Edward Larson argued in 1996 that legislation involving compulsory Norplant—a female birth control device surgically implanted in the upper arm no longer available in the United States—provided an effective means of temporarily sterilizing women whom the state and society deemed "unfit" for parenthood (165–169). According to critics, a new eugenics was indeed afoot.

But are these new forms of genetic screening and intervention eugenic, in the strict sense of the word? The answer to that question depends on what one considers the central tenet or "original sense" (Rose, 2009) of eugenics. Was it a fiercely waged biological battle between nation-states, each determined to create its own "master race"? Or was it a loosely organized, often state-facilitated, global effort to modernize, normalize, and maximize human potential through the elimination of "defectives"? While much of the old eugenics no longer exists, its chief concern—the systematic elimination of people defined as disabled—has endured. Most societies possess a central vision of themselves as steadily progressing toward a future free of disease and impairment, an assumption based in part on the perceived ability of experts, the state, and private stakeholders to gain increasing control over nature through the tools of modern science, an idea that member of former president George W. Bush's Council on Bioethics and Harvard professor Michael Sandel (2007) referred to as a "kind of hyperagency, a Promethean aspiration to remake nature, including human nature, to serve our purposes and satisfy our desires" (26–27). Over 130 years have passed since Francis Galton first used the term "eugenics" to describe his scientific system for "improving" the human race and by extension society. During that time, eugenics has assumed many forms and taken on many meanings. A diverse group of historical actors have debated and implemented a wide range of programs, all in the name of eugenics. Much of the eugenic doctrine that led to the creation of those programs has fallen into disrepute, and the programs themselves have been repealed or dismantled. Yet eugenic thinking continues to occupy an important position in popular culture and in scientific and medical discourse throughout the world. The notion that innate human deficiencies exist, that those deficiencies can be detected or measured, and that modern science and medicine can be used to guide the course of human procreation, thereby improving society, continues to influence experts, politicians, and the individuals and institutions that fund them.

Most people think that eugenics ended after World War II, but we can see from the evidence that despite the changing politics of the postwar world, eugenics persisted. In 1948, largely in response to atrocities committed in Nazi Germany, but also in response to the development of eugenic programs in other countries throughout the world, including the United States, the United Nations passed the *Universal Declaration of Human Rights*. Although the *Declaration* did not carry the force of law, it was extremely influential throughout the world. Eventually written in 370 different languages, it is the world's most translated document. Powerful world leaders, including the pope and various state officials, have said that it is possibly the most important document of our time. Among the *Declaration's* 30 articles, it states that all humans are "born free and equal in dignity and rights"; that everyone "has the right to life, liberty and security of person"; and that "[m]en and women of full age, without any limitation due to race, nationality or religion, have the right to marry and to found a family" (UN). Notably absent from the *Declaration* is any mention of persons with disabilities. The UN would take steps later in the 20th century to recognize the rights of persons with disabilities. In the immediate postwar period, however, the idea that disabled people had human rights did not occur to world leaders, mostly because ideas about disability were still heavily influenced by medicine and eugenics, which saw disability as a defect, a deficiency, or a problem to be mitigated through rehabilitation and various technologies such as prosthetics, or eliminated through medical or eugenic intervention.

The dominant view of disability and eugenics in the postwar world can be found not necessarily in state or federal laws, but in scientific and medical laboratories and institutes. In 1945, zoologist Clarence P. Oliver, the first director of the newly created Dight Institute at the University of Minnesota, announced his goal to "carry out genetic and eugenics programs by collecting information about human traits, analyzing and interpreting the data collected, and making the information available to interested persons" (quoted in Stern, 2012, 78). Oliver went on to state that the primary purpose of the Dight Institute, which had begun operations on July 1, 1941, was to implement a "eugenics program intended to decrease the number of defective children" (quoted in Stern, 2012, 78). Charles Fremont Dight, the man who funded the creation of the Dight Institute at the University of Minnesota, was a physician and a founding member of the Minnesota Eugenics Society. Childless when he died, Dight sought to use his estate to fund eugenic research and education.

Oliver was well aware of the implications of engaging in eugenic research and education in the changing political climate of the postwar world. In stating his vision for the future of the institute, Oliver explained that it "should limit its eugenics program to consultation with persons who have immediate genetic and eugenic problems" and that "an active program by the Institute at this time to bring about legislation for the sterilization of groups or members of families, or an intensive program of propaganda of that sort, would cause the Institute to lose the public support and would make it very difficult for us to follow a research program in human genetics and eugenics" (underline in original, quoted in Stern, 2012, 79). Eugenics would persist after World War II only if it focused on individual "genetic and eugenic problems" and the elimination of "defective children." Anything that extended beyond the systematic elimination of individual "defectives" would draw public alarm, censure, and the ultimate demise of eugenics and possibly the Dight Institute. Medical geneticist Sheldon Reed, who moved from the laboratories of Harvard University to the University of Minnesota to take over as director of the Dight Institute and who coined the term "genetic counseling," both in 1947, agreed with Oliver and carried on the eugenics work of the Dight Institute until his retirement in 1975.

Oliver and Reed and the Dight Institute were not the only individuals and organization interested in continuing eugenics in the postwar period. Despite the events of World War II and the UN's *Declaration*, eugenics continued in the United States and elsewhere after World War II. For example, the British Eugenics Society (BES) continued to operate well into the 1980s. In 1962, at the international meeting of the Ciba Foundation in London, then president of the BES and first director-general of the United Nations Education, Scientific and Cultural Organization (UNESCO), Julian Huxley, argued: "The improvement of human genetic quality by eugenic methods would take a great load of suffering and frustration off the shoulders of evolving humanity and would much increase both enjoyment and efficiency. . . . The general level of genetic intelligence could theoretically be raised by eugenic selection; and even a slight rise in its average level would give a marked increase in the number of the outstandingly intelligent and capable people needed to run our increasingly complex societies. . . . I confidently look forward to a time when eugenic improvement will become one of the major aims of mankind" (quoted in MacKellar and Bechtel, 2014, 29). Throughout its existence, the BES advocated for such measures as contraception, insemination with donor sperm, genetic screening, and prenatal diagnosis. In 1983 the BES celebrated its 75th anniversary. Among its chief concerns at that time were the "eugenic and ethical aspects of new reproductive and genetic technologies" (MacKellar and Bechtel, 2014, 30).

At the center of the conversation led by the BES was a sperm bank created in 1980 in the United States (in Escondido, California) by a 73-year-old multimillionaire businessman Robert Graham, which he named the Hermann J. Muller Repository for Germinal Choice—over the objections of Muller's widow. The repository accepted sperm only from Nobel Prize winners. In 1959, the outspoken American Nobel Prize–winning geneticist Hermann J. Muller (born 1890, New York City) had suggested that sperm donors with the highest physical, mental, and psychological characteristics be used to create genetically superior children. In addition, Muller proposed the establishment of "deep-frozen sperm banks" (MacKellar and Bechtel, 2014, 68) that would provide prospective parents with comprehensive documentation of donor characteristics. He further suggested that sperm donations be used only 20 years after donation "in order to facilitate an adequate evaluation of the donor's genetic heritage" (MacKellar and Bechtel, 2014, 68). The sperm of the "best donors" could then be used to produce multiple children for many years, resulting in a general improvement in the quality of the human population.

After corresponding with Muller, Graham established the Repository for Germinal Choice to provide sperm to women— preferably those married to an infertile husband—who wished to have a child with superior intelligence. When it opened, the repository accepted sperm donations only from Nobel laureates in science. "There's less conjecture and less argument about the standing of scientists than there is in other fields," *People* magazine reported Graham saying in March 1980 (Chen, 1980, n.p.). At the time of its opening, the popular press reported that "to some critics [of Graham's Repository] the project smacks of Nazi Germany's romance with the notion of a 'master race' " and that the idea that intelligence was heritable—that it was passed from one generation to the next—was "highly controversial at best; most experts dispute the theory vigorously" (Chen, 1980, n.p.). Perhaps because of its close resemblance to the old eugenics and the Nazis, the Repository for Germinal

Choice produced relatively few children. In 1999, when it was closed following Graham's death two years earlier, only 215 children had been born using its sperm.

Despite its obscure and questionable origins and negligible impact, the repository remains important in a discussion of the new eugenics because it highlights the ethical dilemmas that arise with the use of modern reproductive technologies. While fertility clinics in the United States and elsewhere do not expect or actively seek to produce highly intelligent children, the sperm they provide can be selected for characteristics such as education level, appearance, and ethnic origin, and donors are always rigorously screened to prevent the transmission of heritable defects, diseases, or disabilities. Artificial insemination with donor sperm is only one of a growing number of reproductive technologies that people use when they wish to have children in the 21st century. In vitro fertilization, genetic screening, preimplantation genetic diagnosis, and prenatal diagnosis are also being used by individuals and couples seeking to have children. Each of these relatively new technologies raises important ethical questions, among them: What traits (if any) may prospective parents select for their unborn child, and which traits (if any) do they have an obligation to avoid?

Ethical questions related to the new eugenics have arisen in response to various reproductive interventions that have expanded and improved since the 1990s, such as sperm or egg donation, artificial insemination, and in vitro fertilization. With these technologies any screening for potential disabilities or diseases takes place before conception or implantation in the uterus. While the frequency with which these technologies are utilized is increasing, the most typical form of intervention occurs after a woman is already pregnant. Most pregnant women in developed countries will be offered some form of prenatal examination. These prenatal screenings are intended to monitor and record the woman's health, and also to help identify a potentially "defective" fetus. Women identified as being at an increased risk, such as women over age 35 or those women who knowingly carry a heritable disorder, are especially encouraged to undergo prenatal testing. Generally, the tests that are performed are either amniocentesis or chorionic villus sampling. These tests involve taking a sample using a needle inserted into either the amniotic sac or the chorion (outer membrane surrounding the fetus). The tests produce what is referred to as a prenatal diagnosis or PND. Tests can determine whether the fetus has a "chromosomal abnormality" such as Down syndrome or a genetic condition such as cystic fibrosis. If one of these or other anomalies is detected, genetic counseling services (if they are available) will be offered and the pregnant woman will be informed of her option to abort the fetus.

Studies have shown that although variations exist among different ethnic and cultural backgrounds, women overwhelmingly choose to abort "defective" fetuses. Large-scale longitudinal studies conducted over the past 40 years show that the overwhelming majority of women who undergo amniocentesis and receive a positive diagnosis for a chronic condition or disability decide to end their pregnancies. The percentage is highest, with averages ranging from 81 percent to 96 percent, for the termination of fetuses that test positive for trisomy 21 (Down syndrome) during the first and second trimesters. Studies have shown that African American and Latina mothers abort fetuses diagnosed with Down syndrome or other anomalies at a lower rate than whites, suggesting that class, religion, and education may play an important role in the decision-making process. More important, however, is the role that dominant ideas about disability play in decisions to terminate pregnancies. The stigma surrounding disability is so powerful that women and the health professionals who counsel them decide that the desire to bring a disabled child into the world is simply untenable. As MacKellar and Bechtel (2014) argue, "Recent trends both amongst health-care professionals and amongst the general public suggest that embryos and fetuses should meet a threshold of quality of life before they are considered to be worthy of postnatal life" (73).

Despite steadily mounting opposition primarily from disability rights groups and parents of disabled children, the use of screening procedures is increasing. The capacity for screening both prospective parents and fetuses is certain to rise as the number of sequenced human genomes increases and testing efficiency improves. In their study of the new eugenics and bioethics in the United Kingdom, MacKellar and Bechtel (2014) report that "private companies already offer prenatal genetic testing for more than 70 disorders by using microarray technology that has the capacity to test for hundreds of different genes at the same time. Some experts predict that prenatal screening for a number of disorders may become quite ordinary if the cost of testing continues to decrease" (71). In 2007, the American College of Obstetricians and Gynecologists (ACOG) revised its guidelines to recommend that all women—not just those over 35—receive multiple levels and types of genetic screening at different stages of their pregnancy, which would enable the detection of various anomalies, greatly increasing the likelihood of the administration of eugenic abortions of "defective" fetuses (Stern, 2012, 99).

Disabled people, their allies, and their organizations have understandably been alarmed at the increasing emphasis on testing and the rising rates of abortion among women suspected of carrying a "defective" fetus. In the United States, the National Down Syndrome Society (NDSS) and the National Down Syndrome Congress each voiced serious concern over the ACOG's revised recommendation, "perceiving it as an attack on their very existence and an attempt to encourage the termination of Down syndrome pregnancies in all expectant women regardless of age or other criteria" (Stern, 2012, 99). Since the early 2000s, the NDSS has engaged in a vigorous, well-financed campaign to educate health-care professionals, including genetic counselors, and the general public about the realities of living with Down syndrome and about the inherent value of including people with Down syndrome in society. The well-known conservative columnist for *Newsweek* magazine,

George Will, has been another especially well-resourced and outspoken opponent of the new ACOG recommendation, as well as the abortion of fetuses that test positive for trisomy 21 (Down syndrome) more generally. He has stated publicly that such measures would eradicate "'from America almost all of a category of citizens, a category that includes Jon', his son, a 'sweet-tempered' man in his 30s able to live independently and work part-time for the Washington Capitals, his favorite hockey team" (quoted in Stern, 2012, 100).

At the center of conversations about which lives are worth living are prospective mothers, genetic counselors, and people living with disabilities and their families and allies. The term "genetic counseling" was first used by Sheldon Reed at the University of Minnesota's Dight Institute in 1947. While the field has changed quite a bit since those early heady days when mostly white, male, nondisabled, culturally elite research scientists, physicians, and academics could speak openly about the perceived importance of eugenics in Americans' reproductive lives, there remain in the first decades of the 21st century certain structural and cultural biases that have influenced the rise of the new eugenics. Since the 1970s, the field of genetic counseling has become progressively more professionalized and increasingly dominated by white women. The leading historian of genetic counseling (Stern, 2012) found that in 2012 there were more than 3,000 certified genetic counselors working in the United States and that 95 percent were women and 92 percent of those women identified as Caucasian. Doctors, nurses, and other health-care professionals engage informally in genetic counseling. Professional genetic counselors, however, are board-certified and many hold a two-year master's degree. They have taken courses in genetics and psychology, and many have participated in clinical and research placements.

Genetic counseling looks much different in the early 21st century than it did in the 1940s. The face of the typical genetic counselor has changed. Their training has become more sophisticated and rigorous. And genetic counseling has been influenced significantly by the social, cultural, and political changes that began in the 1960s and 1970s. Americans living in the early 21st century live in a much different era with respect to disability than existed during the era of the old eugenics. Fundamental shifts in the way most Americans think about disability rights and reproductive rights have transformed the way genetic counselors are trained and have significantly influenced their work. Yet, as the alarmingly high rate of abortion of fetuses that test positive for Down syndrome indicates, some things have not changed. There remains in the 21st century a built-in or structural bias against disability, especially when it could result in a shorter-than-normal life expectancy, or when it may require potentially intensive medical intervention, and when it is considered a developmental or intellectual disability. Things can change, however.

Work done in the United Kingdom and the United States seems to support the argument that ideas about disability and selective abortion are both subjective and malleable, meaning that they vary depending on context and other factors, and that they are able to change. The Human Genetics Commission in the United Kingdom, for example, "emphasizes that individuals with genetic disorders, as well as their families and medical professionals, have different views about which conditions give rise to what may be considered . . . a poor quality of life" (MacKellar and Bechtel, 2014, 75). The commission found that generally disabled people and the people who live with or near disabled people rate the quality of disabled people's lives higher than do medical professionals. Defining what counts as a "serious" disability, MacKellar and Bechtel argue, "therefore, seems to be highly contextual and dependent upon the perceived potential for assistance" (75). In her study of genetic counseling in United States, Stern (2012) found that although genetic counselors are working to change the way they think about disability, a lot of work must be done to change persistent views of disability as a burden or a deficit that must be corrected or eliminated. Stern notes that genetic counselors need continually to examine "their own potential biases toward prenatal testing and the enduring tendency to present a 'narrow description of Down syndrome' that focuses 'on negative aspects of the condition'" (quoted in Stern, 2012, 101). Genetic counselors committed to changing the field's approach to Down syndrome suggest working to cultivate increased interactions at various levels, including student training, in their own practice, and in their own professional organizations among counselors and representatives from the disability community. They also recommend an ongoing evaluation of the field of genetic counseling and its "underlying values" (Stern, 2012, 101).

One way to achieve a more balanced approach and strengthen connections between the disability community and genetic counselors is to build what Rayna Rapp and Faye Ginsberg (2001) have called a "social fund of knowledge" concerning disability, especially intellectual and developmental disabilities. Rapp and Ginsburg have both personal and professional, academic interests in disability. They have written elegantly and persuasively about the ways in which disabled people and their families have formed communities and different types of support networks and how the Internet, other media, and movies, especially documentaries, have been used not only to build kin and other networks but also to inform, educate, and involve the larger public in the lives and concerns of disabled people and their allies. They call this a "social fund of knowledge" and argue that it is imperative for changing dominant views about the value of disabled lives (Rapp and Ginsburg, 2001). The more we know about disabled people, and the more empowered disabled people feel to build networks and share their experiences and their stories, the more likely we as a society are to see disabled people as complex, whole human beings and part of our world. That such a fund of knowledge is needed is testament to the long history of the removal, both figurative and literal, of disabled people from mainstream society. Yet we must also recognize that the existence of such a fund of knowledge and its continual growth is a constant and forceful reminder of the increasingly empowered position people with disabilities occupy in American life. Using this social fund of knowledge, relying on disabled people and their families and allies to tell their stories, is instrumental in achieving a more balanced approach to genetic counseling.

If the new eugenics continues at its current pace, it could have profound implications for our future existence. MacKellar and Bechtel (2014) argue that "frequent and unrestrained" use of reproductive technologies could conceivably "undermine the bedrock of free society: the equality of all its members" (85). If prospective parents are able to eliminate unwanted characteristics or traits and, possibly, someday choose other characteristics for their yet-unborn child, ideas about what is normal and desirable could change drastically over time, making it increasingly difficult for members of society who do not measure up to dominant standards of beauty, productivity, health, and other qualities to survive. Some people may see this as inherently positive, as a way of maximizing human potential. Others contend that this is a new form of eugenics. MacKellar and Bechtel (2014) assert that the discrimination and stigmatization of certain types of people that could result from the unregulated use of reproductive technologies raises serious ethical concerns that become even more complex when we attempt to define the "seriousness" (85) of a disorder or disability and by extension the imagined quality of life of someone who does not yet exist.

This latter point, quality of life, is especially important when we consider the ethical issues related to the elimination of fetuses that test positive for trisomy 21 or Down syndrome. The prenatal tests used to detect the extra chromosome that results in Down syndrome have no way of predicting the extent to which the fetus will be affected by trisomy 21. People living with Down syndrome display a wide range of cognitive and emotional development, and not all people living with Down syndrome are affected equally by the heart defects, vision problems, and other health concerns related to having the extra chromosome. Critics of the new eugenics argue that no parent can ever know or predict the potential health and other outcomes of their unborn child and therefore a fetus with Down syndrome is not unlike any other fetus. Those who favor selective reproduction argue that prospective parents should do everything they can to minimize any risks to their unborn child's health and future well-being, even if that includes aborting a fetus that tests positive for trisomy 21.

One final thing we must consider when we think about the ethical issues related to modern reproductive technologies and the new eugenics are women's reproductive rights. Most disability rights activists and critics of the new eugenics are faced with a perplexing dilemma: they are also in favor of protecting women's reproductive rights. Although about five million "test tube" babies have been born since the first baby conceived using in vitro fertilization was born in Manchester, England in 1978, and preimplantation genetic diagnosis or PGD has become increasingly advanced, the vast majority of selective reproduction occurs after a woman has become pregnant and received a PND. Currently, and for the foreseeable future, selective abortion will be the most common manifestation of the new eugenics. A difficult question we must ask ourselves is: How do we balance or reconcile a woman's right to choose with a desire to end or at least greatly reduce the systematic elimination of "defective" fetuses? This question has no easy answer. Any attempt to address it here would result in a much longer chapter, but we can at least begin to think about this important question.

Various scholars have provided us with tools to help us think about this difficult question. One thing we can say is that all women should have access to the resources, to the social fund of knowledge, that would empower them to make an informed decision when they are deciding whether to terminate a pregnancy. In addition, MacKellar and Bechtel (2014) and Rapp and Ginsburg (2001) each argue that access to material resources after the birth of a child reduces the likelihood that a woman will terminate a pregnancy. Too often, and in too many societies, women are expected to shoulder the burden of caring for infants and young children alone (even if they have a supportive partner and extended family), which can be overwhelming, especially if the child is born with disabilities. Material resources, such as a living allowance, subsidized or free daycare, comprehensive health care, and food assistance, that make infant and child care less of an individual burden could possibly reduce the elimination of "defective" fetuses. A general valuing of all people, including people with disabilities, in society would also help to minimize the reach of the new eugenics.

Humans have been attempting to control reproduction and affect the quality of their offspring for thousands of years. Ancient Greeks resorted to infanticide if a newborn infant did not meet their expectations for health and vigor. Throughout the Middle Ages and into the modern era, learned men and many midwives advised pregnant women to avoid certain experiences for fear that they would permanently mark the fetus inside their womb. For almost 100 years, from the mid-19th century to the mid-20th century, the "old" eugenics increasingly dominated global conversations about reproduction. Then, from the 1960s to the present a new, ostensibly voluntary eugenics came to replace it. Genetic science and reproductive technologies are a tremendous boon to humankind. They should not be disparaged, dismissed, or actively (or passively) undermined. Yet we must always remain vigilant in our efforts to consider the ethical implications of the work being done in these areas. While there are no easy answers to the ethical questions raised by the use of reproductive technologies, we should at least be able to make informed and empowered decisions when we are contemplating bringing new life into the world.

Questions to consider: Are new reproductive interventions a new form of eugenics? How can we, or should we, balance a woman's right to choose to terminate a pregnancy and the valuing of potentially disabled fetuses? To what extent is the "new eugenics" voluntary?

References

Allen, G. E. October 5, 2001. "Is a New Eugenics Afoot?" *Science* 294: 61.

Ball, Natalie, and Gregor Wolbring. "Portrayals of and Arguments around Different Eugenic Practices: Past and Present." *International Journal of Disability, Community and Rehabilitation* 12 (2) http://www.ijdcr.ca/VOL12_02/articles/ball.shtml (Accessed December 19, 2018).

Bender Consulting Services, INC. 2017. "President Obama's Executive Order a Success." https://www.benderconsult.com/blog/president-obamas-executive-order-success (Accessed January 7, 2019).

Chen, Edwin. March 17, 1980. "Sperm Banker Robert Graham Wants the Brave New World to Be Sired by Nobel Prize Winners." *People*. https://people.com/archive/sperm-banker-robert-graham-wants-the-brave-new-world-to-be-sired-by-nobel-prize-winners-vol-13-no-11/ (Accessed December 19, 2018).

Daar, Judith. 2017. *The New Eugenics: Selective Breeding in an Era of Reproductive Technologies*. New Haven, CT: Yale University Press.

Grigal, Meg, Debra Hart, and Alberto Migliore. 2011. "Comparing the Transition Planning Postsecondary Education, and Employment Outcomes of Students with Intellectual and Other Disabilities." *Career Development for Exceptional Individuals* 34(1): 4–17.

Hampton, S. J. 2005. "Family Eugenics." *Disability and Society* 20(5): 553–561.

Isaacson, W. January 11, 1999. "The Biotech Century." *Time* 153(43): 43.

Kazuyo, M. 2001. "The Eugenic Transition of 1996 in Japan: From Law to Personal Choice." *Disability and Society* 16(5): 765–771.

Kerr, Anne, and Tom Shakespeare. 2002. *Genetic Politics: From Eugenics to Genome*. Cheltenham, UK: New Clarion Press.

King, D. 2001. "Eugenic Tendencies in Modern Genetics." In Brian Tokar, ed. *Redesigning Life?: The Worldwide Challenge to Genetic Engineering*, 171–181. New York: Zed Books.

Knowles, Lori P., and Gregory E. Kaebnick, eds. 2007. *Reprogenetics: Law, Policy, and Ethical Issues.* Baltimore: Johns Hopkins University Press.

Larson, Edward John. 1996. *Sex, Race, and Science: Eugenics in Deep South.* Baltimore: Johns Hopkins University Press.

MacKellar, Calum, and Christopher Bechtel. 2014. *The Ethics of the New Eugenics.* New York: Berghahn Books.

Marcum, Andrew. 2016. "Rethinking the American Dream Home: The Disability Rights Movement and the Cultural Politics of Accessible Housing in the United States." In Michael Rembis, ed. *Disabling Domesticity.* New York: Palgrave Macmillan.

National Center for Education Statistics. 2017. "Disability Rates and Employment Status by Educational Attainment." https://nces.ed.gov/programs/coe/indicator_tad.asp (Accessed January 7, 2019).

National Center for Education Statistics. Updated, 2018. "Children and Youth with Disabilities." https://nces.ed.gov/programs/coe/indicator_cgg.asp (Accessed December 29, 2018).

National Council on Disability. 2004. "Improving Educational Outcomes for Students with Disabilities." Washington, DC.

Olmstead v. L. C. (1999)

OPM.GOV. 2016. "Federal Agencies Exceed Disability Hiring Goal." https://www.opm.gov/news/releases/2016/10/federal-agencies-exceed-disability-hiring-goal/ (Accessed January 7, 2019).

Paul, Diane. 2007. "On Drawing Lessons from the History of Eugenics." In Lori P. Knowles and Gregory E. Kaebnick, eds. *Reprogenetics: Law, Policy, and Ethical Issues*, 3–19. Baltimore: Johns Hopkins University Press.

Pritchard, M. 2005. "Can There Be Such a Thing as a 'Wrongful Birth'?" *Disability and Society* 20(1): 81–93.

Rapp, Rayna, and Faye Ginsburg. Fall, 2001. "Enabling Disability: Rewriting Kinship, Reimagining Citizenship." *Public Culture* 13(3): 533–556.

Reist, Melinda Tankard. 2010. *Defiant Birth: Women Who Resist Medical Eugenics.* North Melbourne, Vic.: Spinifex Press.

Rock, P. J. 1996. "Eugenics and Euthanasia: A Cause for Concern for Disabled People, Particularly Disabled Women." *Disability and Society* 11(1): 121–127.

Rose, Nikolas. 2009. *The Politics of Life Itself: Biomedicine, Power, and Subjectivity in the Twenty-First Century.* Princeton, NJ: Princeton University Press.

Sandel, Michael J. 2007. *The Case against Perfection: Ethics in the Age of Genetic Engineering* Cambridge, MA: Belknap Press.

Shakespeare, Tom. 1998. "Choices and Rights: Eugenics, Genetics, and Disability Equality." *Disability and Society* 13(5): 665–681.

Sharp, K., and S. Earle. 2002. "Feminism, Abortion and Disability: Irreconcilable Differences?" *Disability and Society* 17(2): 137–145.

Sinsheimer, R. L. 1969. "The Prospect of Designed Genetic Change." *Engineering and Science* 13: 8–13.

Stern, Alexandra Minna. 2012. *Telling Genes: The Story of Genetic Counseling in America.* Baltimore: Johns Hopkins University Press.

Tokar, Brian. 2001. *Redesigning Life?: The Worldwide Challenge to Genetic Engineering.* London: Zed Books.

The White House. 2010. "Executive Order 13548—Increasing Federal Employment of Individuals with Disabilities." https://obamawhitehouse.archives.gov/the-press-office/executive-order-increasing-federal-employment-individuals-with-disabilities (Accessed January 7, 2019).

Introduction

This chapter expands on the work presented in the first two chapters by exploring the perspectives of people intimately involved in various issues directly addressed within the disability community, including legal concerns, self-advocacy and disability rights, the neurodiversity movement, reproductive and parental rights, artistic production, disabled veterans, domestic violence, cochlear implants, mental health, and race and incarceration.

The Contested Evolution of the Americans with Disabilities Act
Karen A. Kadish and Elizabeth F. Emens

The Americans with Disabilities Act (ADA) broke new ground for disability rights. After much lobbying and deliberation, Congress passed the ADA with overwhelming bipartisan support: over 90 percent of senators and representatives voted for the final version of the ADA (National Council on Disability, 2010). President George H. W. Bush summarized the high hopes for the ADA when he signed the bill into law. He said, "[The ADA]

[Tammy Duckworth standing at a podium speaking into a microphone with her prosthetic leg visible] U.S. Representative Tammy Duckworth speaks during the final day of the 2016 Democratic National Convention at the Wells Fargo Center in Philadelphia, Pennsylvania, on July 28, 2016. (Nicholas Kamm/AFP/Getty Images) will provide our disabled community with a powerful expansion of protections and then basic civil rights. It will guarantee fair and just access to the fruits of American life which we all must be able to enjoy" (EEOC, 1990). The ADA was, in many ways, a continuation of the civil rights dreams that had propelled activists in the 1960s and 1970s to fight against race- and gender-based discrimination and for disability rights.

The ADA was a major step forward for disability rights. Before the ADA, people with disabilities could be restricted from going to public school, voting, or even marrying (Burgdorf, 2015).The ADA prohibited discrimination in hiring and employment practices, mass transportation, telecommunications, and access to public spaces (ADA, 1990; Burgdorf, 2015). The law defined disability to include not only those who had a disability but also those who were "regarded as" having a disability (ADA, 1990). By counting those regarded as disabled, the law seemed to embrace the social model of disability—the idea that disability is not an individual medical problem, but an interaction between impairment and the surrounding social environment (Emens, 2013).

Once enacted into law, however, the ADA ran into roadblocks in the courts. When people with disabilities brought lawsuits seeking enforcement, the courts were not as willing to enforce the ADA as activists had originally hoped. In a series of cases, the Court chipped away at the protections offered by the ADA. The Supreme Court especially focused on the question of whether a plaintiff was *really* disabled. The specific definition of disability under the ADA was "a physical or mental impairment that substantially limits one or more of the major life activities of [an] individual," having a history of such an impairment, or being regarded as having such an impairment (ADA, 1990). The courts narrowed the definition of disability in three key ways, among others. First, the Supreme Court declared that an individual was no longer disabled for purposes of protection under the ADA after he or she used mitigating treatments or devices that ameliorated his or her disability (*Sutton v.*

United Airlines, 1999). Second, the Court defined the "major life activity" that was substantially limited by the impairment narrowly, for instance, by suggesting that the activity must be of central importance to daily life (*Toyota Motor Manufacturing v. Williams*, 2002). Finally, the Court limited the "regarded as" prong of the ADA to individuals whose employers regarded them as impaired in a wide range of jobs, not only in their particular job (*Murphy v. UPS*, 1999). The Court explicitly stated that judges should apply a "demanding standard" when determining whether an individual qualified as disabled under the ADA (*Toyota Motor Manufacturing v. Williams*, 2002).

The net result of the Court's interpretations of the ADA was that individuals with disabilities were caught in a sort of definitional "catch twenty-two." If people could use assistive technology to do their work, but they were nevertheless discriminated against, the Court found that they were not "disabled" under the ADA. But if they could not do the work, they were not considered qualified for the job. That would mean that the ADA did not protect them from being dismissed, because they could not perform their duties at work and therefore disciplinary actions or even firings were not discrimination. Due to the Court's definition, the ADA offered relief only to people who had a disability that significantly impaired them, even with the use of assistive technology (think of someone who cannot stand or walk but uses a wheelchair), but who were *nonetheless* qualified to do their jobs (with or without a legally required accommodation), and were discriminated against based on their disability.

The Supreme Court's narrow construction of the definition of "disability" led to negative outcomes for disabled plaintiffs. Significant portions of the disabled community were not, in the courts' terms, "disabled," and were therefore excluded from ADA protections. For instance, one court declared a cancer patient, after her death from cancer, not disabled enough to be covered by the ADA's definition of disability (*Hirsch v. National Mall Service*, 1997). In addition, courts rarely reached the question of whether the plaintiff was discriminated against; they decided most cases during the preliminary inquiry into whether the person was disabled or not. This meant that there were few court decisions about what counted as "discrimination," and so plaintiffs did not have a clear idea of whether they could win on a discrimination claim even if they did manage to pass the hurdle of being acknowledged as disabled by the court.

Legislators, activists, and scholars reacted strongly to the Court's narrow interpretation of the ADA (Barry, 2010). Congressman Steny Hoyer, one of the drafters of the ADA, lambasted the Supreme Court for invoking Congress's "intent" in order to limit the ADA (Hoyer, 2002). After much lobbying and scholarly writing, Congress eventually responded with new legislation: the ADA Amendments Act of 2008 (ADAAA). In this law, Congress disavowed the Court's rulings on the ADA, asserting that the statute "reinstat[ed] a broad scope of protection" that the original ADA intended, and particularly instructed the courts to understand "disability" more broadly (ADAAA, 2008). This legislation directly responded to some of the Court's prior rulings, for instance, by establishing that people who used assistive technology or other mitigating devices were squarely within the protections of the ADA.

While the ADAAA is still rather new and its full impact is yet to be seen, there are some notable trends in the courts that have so far heard cases under the ADAAA. One cause for optimism is that courts have heeded Congress's words about broadening the definition of disability (Barry et al., 2013; Befort, 2013). For instance, courts have begun to find a much broader range of conditions, such as stuttering, gastrointestinal problems, and high-risk pregnancies, to be "disabilities" under the ADA (*Medvic v. Compass Sign Co.*, 2011; *Price v. UTI. U.S., Inc.*, 2013; *Wells v. Cincinnati Children's Hospital Medical Center*, 2012). This means that many more people are eligible for protection from discrimination (Barry et al., 2013). Whereas people with treatable conditions or less clear-cut disabilities would have been rejected under the old interpretations of the

ADA, the ADAAA reopened that space and forced the courts to acknowledge the discrimination that happens against people with these forms of disability (Barry et al., 2013; see, e.g., *Wolfe v. Postmaster General*, 2012).

Despite these signs of more expansive protections under the ADAAA, there are also reasons for concern. Some scholars suggest that courts have moved toward limiting the causation element of the ADA requirements (Cavaliere et al., 2012). The ADA applies only if an individual is discriminated against *because* of his or her real or perceived disability. Now that the definition of "disability" has been broadened by the ADAAA, there is concern that the courts will limit ADA protections by increasing the proof that plaintiffs have to provide in order to show the causal link between their disability and the discrimination they faced (Barry et al., 2013; Cavaliere et al., 2012). Another concern is that courts will scrutinize more closely whether an individual was actually qualified for his or her job, which is especially problematic for people with disabilities that courts tend to assume limit a person's qualifications, like mental illness (Befort, 2013; Kaminer, 2016).

What does the future hold? As the history of the ADA and the ADAAA shows, progress often takes the form of a back-and-forth between Congress, the courts, and disability advocates. As one group works to broaden disability rights, another group can limit them in serious ways. However, there has been forward movement, even if the trajectory is not linear. The ADA signaled a major change in the approach to disability rights not only in the United States but around the world (Minnesota Department of Administration, 2014). As of this writing, 160 countries have signed the United Nations Convention on the Rights of Persons with Disabilities (United Nations, 2017). Domestically, the change in legal and cultural norms creates avenues for people with disabilities to request and receive accommodations that allow them to participate in American life (Engel and Munger, 2001). The ADA built a framework for disabled Americans to be protected from discrimination and, in so doing, started a decades-long dialogue between Congress and the courts about what it means to be "disabled" and how society can best prevent discrimination against disabled individuals.

References

ADA Amendments Act of 2008. 122 Stat. 3553, 3554, Pub. Law 110–325 (amending 42 U.S.C. 12101).

ADA International Impact. Minnesota Department of Administration Council on Developmental Disabilities. Dec. 1, 2014, http://mn.gov/mnddc/ada-legacy/ada-legacy-moment24.html.

Americans with Disabilities Act of 1990. 42 U.S.C. §12101 (2012).

Barry, Kevin. September 2010. "Toward Universalism: What the ADA Amendments Act of 2008 Can and Can't Do for Disability Rights." *Berkeley Journal of Employment & Labor Law* 31(2): 203.

Barry, Kevin, Brian East, and Marcy Karin. Fall 2013. "Pleading Disability after the ADAAA." *Hofstra Labor & Employment Law Journal* 31(1): 1.

Befort, Stephen F. Fall 2013. "An Empirical Examination of Case Outcomes under the ADA Amendments Act." *Washington & Lee Law Review* 70(4): 2027.

Burgdorf Jr., Robert L. July 24, 2015. "Why I Wrote the Americans with Disabilities Act." *Washington Post.* https://www.washingtonpost.com/posteverything/wp/2015/07/24/why-the-americans-with-disabilities-act-mattered/?utm_term=.705b62041670.

Cavaliere, Frank J., et al. Spring 2012. "Congress Proposes, the Supreme Court Disposes: Is There Room for Courts to Subvert the Will of Congress after the ADAA Act Broadens the Definition of Disability?" *Southern Law Journal* 22(1): 37–60.

EEOC. July 26, 1990. *Remarks of President George Bush at the Signing of the Americans with Disabilities Act.* https://www.eeoc.gov/eeoc/history/35th/videos/ada_signing_text.html.

Emens, Elizabeth. 2013. "Disabling Attitudes." Reprinted in Lennard Davis, ed., *The Disability Studies Reader*, 4th ed. New York: Routledge.

Engel, David M., and Frank W. Munger. 2001. "Re-Interpreting the Effect of Rights: Career Narratives and the ADA." *Ohio State Law Journal* 62(1): 285.

Hirsch v. National Mall & Serv., Inc. 989 F. Supp. 977 (N.D. Ill. 1997).

Hoyer, Steny H. January 20, 2002. "Not Exactly What We Intended, Justice O'Connor." *Washington Post.* https://www.washingtonpost.com/archive/opinions/2002/01/20/not-exactly-what-we-intended-justice-oconnor/41a55301-0d4d-4bfd-8746-37e8f17999a8/?utm_term=.f3093cb11c9e.

Kaminer, Debbie N. 2016. "Mentally Ill Employees in the Workplace: Does the ADA Amendments Act Provide Adequate Protection." *Health Matrix* 26(1): 205.

Maine Rev. Stat. Tit. 19A §701 (2015).

Medvic v. Compass Sign Co., LLC., 2011 WL 3513499 (E.D. Penn. Aug. 10, 2011).

Murphy v. UPS, 527 U.S. 522, 523 (1999).

National Council on Disability. *Equality of Opportunity: The Making of the Americans with Disabilities Act* (Washington, DC, 2010 ed.).

Pietrzak, Brooke. January 1997. "Marriage Laws and People with Mental Retardation: A Continuing History of Second Class Treatment." *Developments in Mental Health Law* 17(1–2): 1–3, 33–46.

Price v. UTI, U.S., Inc., 2013 WL 798014 (E.D. Mo. Mar. 05, 2013).

Sutton v. United Airlines, 527 U.S. 471 (1999).

Toyota Motor Mfg., Ky. v. Williams, 534 U.S. 184, 197 (2002).

United Nations. *Convention on the Rights of Persons with Disabilities*, Division for Social Policy and Development: Disability. https://www.un.org/development/desa/disabilities/convention-on-the-rights-of-persons-with-disabilities.html (Accessed November 17, 2017).

Wells v. Cincinnati Children's Hospital Medical Center, 860 F. Supp. 2d 469 (S.D. Ohio 2012).

Wolfe v. Postmaster General, 488 Fed. Appx. 465 (11th Cir. 2012).

Karen A. Kadish is a JD/MSW candidate at Columbia University. Her disability advocacy work has focused on disabled students' access to education, particularly for youth living in poverty.

Elizabeth F. Emens, Isidor and Seville Sulzbacher Professor of Law at Columbia, is the author of numerous articles on disability law and theory and coeditor of Disability and Equality Law *(Ashgate Press, 2013) with Michael A. Stein.*

"We Can Speak Out the Way We Want": Self-Advocacy, Americans Disabled for Attendant Programs Today, and the Sociopolitical Legacies of the Disability Rights Movement
Andrew Marcum

The disability rights movement in the United States is often understood as an effort to secure legal rights and access to public spaces, jobs, and education for people with disabilities. It has correspondingly been presented as a movement of minorities seeking to forge a distinct identity and history to collectively challenge inequality. But the disability rights movement is also a social, cultural, and intellectual movement that cuts across all identities and communities to challenge assumptions about what it means to be "disabled," what access and inclusion mean, and who is entitled to access and inclusion. Examining self-advocacy alongside Americans Disabled for Attendant Programs Today (ADAPT) illustrates how movements for political power and legal protections are also cultural movements and suggests how a focus on rights alone can obscure—and leave intact—the ideologies that animate disability oppression.

In September 2017, disability activists staged demonstrations on Capitol Hill protesting legislation that would have capped Medicaid spending, restricted Medicaid funding to states in the form of block grants, and eventually shifted much of the costs of Medicaid to recipients themselves. Scores of people (including many wheelchair users) were dragged from Senate offices and committee hearings by U.S. Capitol police. People with disabilities—many of whom depend on Medicaid for health care, support staff, and services that allow them to live in the community—would have been among those most impacted by the changes. As one activist explained, "If Medicaid is cut so dramatically, it will force people into institutions" (Horsley, 2017). Organized by ADAPT, the protests helped bring an end to the legislation.

ADAPT's actions underscored the ongoing struggle of people with disabilities to access the supports necessary to live in the community and showed how the disability rights movement is about more than making the world accessible to "everyone." Rather, ADAPT calls into question who counts as "everyone" while challenging entrenched American ideologies of independence, productivity, and personal responsibility and exposing the relationship between attitudes about disability as a personal deficit to be "overcome" and the architectural practices and socioeconomic structures that systematically exclude people with disabilities. Disabilities may prevent people from working or from processing or producing traditional forms of knowledge. Lack of environmental access amplifies physical and cognitive differences and who is deemed worthy of inclusion is reflected in the spaces that surround us. ADAPT insists that all people are deserving of freedom, choice, and inclusion regardless of the "severity" of their disability or their capacity to approximate able-bodied norms. ADAPT organizer Michael Auberger describes how customers reacted when activists began blocking entryways to protest the inaccessibility of McDonald's restaurants in 1984. "People would crawl over us and fight to get in the doors, three or four people moving people's wheelchairs and then crawling over." One customer bought a soda and poured it over demonstrators, while another pushed a wheelchair user with her car, flattening the wheelchair's tires. Police warned demonstrators they would not protect the demonstrators after dark (Pelka, 2015, 364).

The contempt and entitlement displayed by customers and police in these interactions reveals how architectural problems of inaccessibility are also "attitudinal" problems in an ableist society that believes disabled people should not exist, should stop being disabled or, at least, should not be seen in public. ADAPT activists in Chicago explained to journalist Mary Johnson the socioeconomic dynamics they challenged by making demands for in-home support funding. Those who cannot afford such supports are forced into institutions. As one activist explains, "You can't pay—you don't have the money to pay an attendant at night, when you're on SSI. All these things they're constantly cutting. I haven't been in a nursing home for 15 years—and I don't plan to go." Another states, "I'm tired of the rules and regulations and them telling me what you have to do. None of them has worked as good for me as being at home. In nursing homes, they put you on sleeping pills to keep from getting aggravated with what will occur" (Johnson, 1994, 137). Here, activists assert their right to control their own lives and bodies regardless of their ability to pay for attendant care. ADAPT's legacy is not just one of access or rights, but a critique of American ways of knowing, thinking about, and addressing disability.

Self-advocacy, like ADAPT, has a long and important history. It originated in the 1970s as state-run institutions began closing and people with disabilities (including those with intellectual and developmental disabilities) sought to live in the community. Perhaps the biggest barrier to community integration for these individuals was the assumption that they could not live on their own, have relationships, or make decisions because they were not capable of expressing or distinguishing feelings, desires, or preferences let alone exercising rights or making choices. Segregated into "special education" and group homes, these people were denied choice long after leaving institutions. Frustrated, they began organizing groups to discuss and confront the perception that they were "retarded," defined and constrained by their cognitive differences. With support and encouragement from social workers, they brainstormed solutions to common problems like conflicts with support staff and began organizing around issues, especially access to transportation and housing options that would allow them to exercise more choice and control over their lives. As one early self-advocate who once lived in a state institution in Oregon explained, "We're all people, we all have rights. We can speak out the way we want, we can do what we want, and live where we want, and get married if we want, because back then, we weren't allowed to do all that" (Pelka, 2015, 333). Another noted the importance of letting people speak "even if they don't use words to communicate" (Pelka, 2015, 338). Self-advocates in present-day Western New York carry forth this legacy. They are not merely demanding access to better transportation or inclusion in decision making. They are demanding respect and recognition while showing how a lack of access reflects enduring negative assumptions about their value and place in the community. In addition to actions around access, self-advocates are helping to develop self-advocacy curricula for public schools, teaching peers about self-confidence and healthy relationships, and providing support and advice to those leaving group homes to live on their own.

In July 2013, self-advocates in Western New York marched nearly three miles from the nearest public transit point to the regional headquarters of the state Office of Persons with Developmental Disabilities located on the campus of the former West

Seneca Developmental Center, an institution for people with disabilities intentionally isolated from the community decades earlier. With signs reading "Transportation=Jobs" and "More State Funding for Transportation," the advocates protested the inaccessibility of state offices for people with disabilities. Local officials had long demonstrated "best practices," supporting meaningful inclusion of people with disabilities in not only advisory committees, but also with peer support at individual service plan meetings, in the development of person-centered planning, the exercise of voting rights, and the creation of self-advocacy groups and activities for people with disabilities. In response to decades of activism by residents of former institutions who formed the core of the self-advocacy movement in New York and elsewhere, officials hired self-advocates to do this work and hosted the regional office of the Self-Advocacy Association of New York State. Yet bus service to the site had been cut by the local transit authority years earlier and was only re-established after self-advocates secured sort-term federal transportation funding that would soon run out.

ADAPT's nonviolent, direct-action tactics (drawn from black civil rights struggles) and the work of self-advocates challenged mainstream disability rights conceptions of who is "worthy" of inclusion in American society. Although many ADAPT members are college-educated, most were, and are, people with "severe" disabilities excluded from more "respectable" advocacy organizations. Like self-advocates, many ADAPT members are survivors of institutions, abuse, and exploitation who have had limited access to education and jobs and are living at, or below, the poverty line (Pelka, 2015, 376). They challenge disability oppression not by matching or surpassing social expectations, but by pointing out the exclusionary power of those expectations and the oppressive structures those expectations ultimately produce. In so doing, they are staking a claim to inclusion in American society, not based on equality of ability with others, but based on their humanity and the inherent dignity and value of their difference.

Understanding ADAPT and self-advocacy as critiquing rights regimes premised on achieving parity with nondisabled people allows us to more fully appreciate their evolving historical legacies and enact what ADAPT leaders called a "liberated community," where all people have worth and the power to affect change regardless of their ability. It also reveals how seemingly disparate issues like transit access and attendant care are linked by social, cultural, and economic ideologies of disability that shape both the built environment and access to resources.

References

Horsley, Scott. September 25, 2017. "Graham-Cassidy Health Care Hearing Starts with Eruption of Protests." National Public Radio. https://www.npr.org/2017/09/25/553024686/ in-hearing-sens-graham-and-cassidy-defend-their-namesake-bill-to-repeal-obamacar (Accessed January 30, 2018).

Johnson, Mary. 1994. "On the Barricades with ADAPT." In Barrett Shaw, ed. *The Ragged Edge: The Disability Experience from the First 15 Years of the Disability Rag*, 137–48. Louisville, KY: The Advocado Press, 1994.

Pelka, Fred. *What We Have Done: An Oral History of the Disability Rights Movement.* Amherst: University of Massachusetts Press, 2015.

Andrew Marcum is adjunct assistant professor of disability studies at the City University of New York and program director for the Center for Self Advocacy in Buffalo, New York.

The Neurodiversity Movement
Ari Ne'eman

Like most parts of the disability rights community, the neurodiversity movement emerged out of disabled people's profound frustration with those speaking on our behalf.

When autism was first identified in the 1940s, the diagnosis was considered rare. Initially, clinicians blamed "refrigerator mothers" for causing it, blaming women for their child's developmental disability through lack of maternal warmth. The "refrigerator mother" theory set in place a wrongheaded understanding of autism as something that happens to a normal child that "turns" them into an autistic one. This notion persisted long after the "refrigerator mother" theory was debunked—setting the stage for treatments focused on returning autistic children to a prior normalcy that had never existed. The results were tragic and abusive. A generation of autistic children were educated to believe that the way they naturally moved, thought, and interacted with the world was inherently wrong. Hand-flapping in a special education classroom would be met with a reprimand to have "quiet hands," and valuable instructional time would be spent not on math or reading but on learning to make "eye contact."

Special education professionals working on autism, especially in the popular behaviorist school, were taught to try to make autistic children "indistinguishable from their peers"—a phrase that had its origins in O. Ivar Lovaas's work attempting to "recover" autistic children. Lovaas set as his goal making an autistic child "indistinguishable" from other children and was willing to use painful methods, ranging from slaps to electric shocks, to achieve his goal.

Lovaas operated two behaviorist education projects at UCLA, one focused on making autistic children normal, the other—entitled the Feminine Boys Project—focused on endeavoring to use similar techniques to cure young boys considered "at risk" for homosexuality. The applied behavioral analysis field Lovaas spawned eventually held many views on the appropriateness of "aversives"—the use of pain as a means of behavior modification—but believed (and believes) across the board that autistic traits should be stamped out in favor of the veneer of typicality.

For decades, professionals believed that if autistic people could be pushed, nudged, or threatened to look and act like everyone else, they would no longer be autistic. Instead, autistic people spent their childhoods learning that the most important thing they could do was pretend to be something they are not.

The 1990s saw the rise of the first wave of autistic adults who had grown up with the word "autism" to describe the way their brains worked. As the Internet helped contribute to the creation of an emerging autistic culture, autistic activists began to organize to try to build their own voice. Jim Sinclair's seminal 1993 essay *Don't Mourn for Us* captured the spirit of the emerging neurodiversity—short for "neurological diversity"—movement:

> Autism isn't something a person has, or a "shell" that a person is trapped inside. There's no normal child hidden behind the autism. Autism is a way of being. It is pervasive; it colors every experience, every sensation, perception, thought, emotion, and encounter, every aspect of existence. It is not possible to separate the autism from the person—and if it were possible, the person you'd have left would not be the same person you started with.
>
> This is important, so take a moment to consider it: Autism is a way of being. It is not possible to separate the person from the autism.
>
> > Therefore, when parents say,
> > I wish my child did not have autism,
> > what they're really saying is,
>
> > I wish the autistic child I have did not exist, and I had a different (non-autistic) child instead.

Sinclair and Autism Network International—the first ever autistic-run organization—helped to develop the first stirrings of activism and independent cultural activity among autistic adults. After initially organizing an event alongside a popular autism parent conference, Sinclair organized Autreat, the first independent autistic-run gathering. This was prompted in part due to the parent community's insistence that spaces for autistic adults at parent-run conferences be limited only to those deemed "high-functioning." Instead, the emerging autistic community wanted to develop a culture and identity in which they could all participate.

When I first got involved in autistic advocacy in 2006, Autreat had been in operation for a decade and had spawned a vibrant autistic culture, helped along by the uniquely autistic-friendly nature of online social spaces. But even as the autistic adult community was carving out a niche for themselves at Autreat and on the Internet, the autism parent community was booming with a single message: cure.

With rising numbers, autism was the subject of unprecedented public attention—policy makers, journalists, movies, and TV shows all fell over each other to opine on a diagnosis that seemed to be on the rise. While autism was under discussion everywhere, few sought the views of autistic people themselves. Autistic adults supported services and supports—many of them benefitted from these personally and continue to do so—but they were concerned by treatment models that emphasized making them look and act normal. They wanted services to help teach them skills, like communication and independent living, not ones that focused on how to imitate the appearance of the non-autistic population, an exercise most of them found exhausting and unhelpful.

After Congress passed the Combating Autism Act, I and several other autistic adults worked to form the Autistic Self Advocacy Network (ASAN), the first national autistic-run advocacy organization focused on political and policy advocacy. Our goal was to help shift the autism conversation away from an emphasis on cure and young children. We wanted to help the public understand that autistic people of all ages existed—and we had thoughts and opinions that often were not being acknowledged by the parent organizations that talked about us, without us.

At ASAN, we focused our advocacy in two very different but complementary directions. First, we directly challenged autism organizations that failed to include autistic people in their decision-making process. ASAN activists and the broader neurodiversity movement helped spawn a nationwide protest movement against Autism Speaks, the nation's best-funded autism organization and the driving force behind federal policy focused on "curing autism" and promoting behaviorist intervention to the exclusion of other methods. We also challenged advertising and public representations of autism that presented autistic people as burdens on society, like the New York University Child Study Center's "Ransom Notes" ad campaign or Autism Speaks' *I Am Autism* and *Autism Every Day* films.

In addition, in ASAN we built a strong portfolio of policy advocacy work. We believed that for autistic adults to shape the conversation on autism, we needed to do more than just share their stories and their opinions. It was essential to cultivate strong content area knowledge in the issues we cared about. As a result, ASAN became a leading voice on issues like Medicaid home and community-based services, supported employment services, healthcare discrimination, parenting rights, and other areas where the autistic voice was unique and distinct from that of groups run by non-autistic people. We helped shape federal policy in these areas to emphasize rights protection, community inclusion, and self-determination—the values we believe should govern the national and international conversations on autism.

There remains much work to be done—but the past decade has brought considerable public progress. Federal policy has begun to shift away from "cure" toward promoting service provision, inclusion, and rights protection for autistic people of all ages. In many ways, the autism world continues along a path set for it by other disability rights movements. Autism policy has lagged behind general disability policy by 10–20 years, but autistic people are working hard to catch up. Autistic people deserve to have their voices at the center of policy, research, and services designed for their benefit. This they have learned from the broader disability rights movement. *Nothing about Us without Us* is not just a slogan—it is a way of life, and one with the potential to transform an autism world still in dire need of change.

Ari Ne'eman cofounded the Autistic Self Advocacy Network and served as its president from 2006 to 2016. He was appointed by President Obama to the National Council on Disability in 2010, the first openly autistic presidential appointee in U.S. history, and served until 2015, managing the Council's Medicaid and Affordable Care Act policy portfolios.

Restricted Reproductive and Parental Rights: Challenging What Makes a Person "Fit" to Parent
Brianna Dickens and Michael Gill

In late summer 2017, media coverage picked up the story of Amy Fabbrini and Eric Zeigler, parents who had their first son Christopher and then soon after their second son Hunter taken away from them because a Child Protective Services (CPS) worker said they were "not intelligent enough" to care for their children (Swindler 2017a). Oregon law affords a judge to consider disability status if neglect or harm is assumed to be connected to an individual's disability. In this case, intellectual disability is assumed to be a condition that leads to parental neglect. Fabbrini gave birth to Christopher at Zeigler's home unexpectedly after attributing the changes in her body and pain to kidney issues, which she had a history of having. After calling 9-1-1 and going to the hospital to ensure the safety of both Fabbrini and the baby, Zeigler took Christopher home. Christopher went home with Zeigler because Fabbrini's father, whom she was living with at the time along with her twin boys from her previous marriage, refused to allow Fabbrini to bring the baby to his home. Within a few days, Zeigler's roommate called CPS reporting safety issues. This initial call was followed by Fabbrini's father a few days later claiming neglect. CPS immediately took Christopher (Burke 2017). Hunter was later removed. Over the next four years, Fabbrini and Zeigler fought to get Christopher and his younger brother Hunter back.

There were no signs of abuse or neglect according to several different CPS case workers and volunteers. One volunteer, Sharrene Hagenbach, who supervised visitation between Christopher and his parents for three months, oversaw what she described as "nothing out of line" in the interactions between the parents and child. Hagenbach was asked not to return as a volunteer by a CPS administrator after she testified on Fabbrini and Zeigler's behalf. Hagenbach then volunteered her time as an advocate and mentor to support the couple in regaining custody of their children. She was quoted explaining that the only reason for taking them was that the parents were, according to a CPS worker, "retarded" and that they lacked the intelligence needed to raise their children. Fabbrini and Zeigler both have done everything recommended by the state, including psychological testing, parenting classes, nutrition classes, and CPR classes, in order to prove that they are capable of raising their boys.

What seems to be the leading factor in the question over custody is the intelligence of Fabbrini and Zeigler. Intelligence of the parents was the only documented reason for taking the children, and after being evaluated by several case workers as having the means (house, transportation, income, etc.) and the ability to care for their sons, the assumptions of (lack of) intelligence remained the only reason the couple did not have custody. After Christopher was taken away, both parents agreed to psychological testing, through which they were deemed "intellectually disabled." After a long, emotional battle, Fabbrini and Zeigler were awarded custody of their sons in January 2018.

A 2012 report from the National Council on Disability, "Rocking the Cradle: Ensuring the Rights of Parents with Disabilities and Their Children," discusses how parents with disabilities face tremendous burdens in maintaining custody of their children. Removal rates from parents with disabilities are as high as 80 percent. In addition, two-thirds of states have fitness statutes that allow disability status to be used as the sole justification for child removal recommendations. While activists and lawyers are challenging these rules as discrimination and as a violation of the ADA, for many individuals, including Fabbrini and Zeigler, there remains a culture of surveillance and removal, where having a disability might mean someone's children can be taken away from him or her.

These questions of appropriateness are not new, as historically in the United States there have been many debates about what makes an ideal parent. During the eugenics era "fit parents" were assumed generally to be native-born, white, and nondisabled, although poor whites often did not measure up to eugenicists' standards. Those people who were constructed as potentially "bad" parents were at risk of being sterilized against their will. In the United States, approximately 65,000 individuals were forcibly sterilized under various state laws. In the 1927 U.S. Supreme Court ruling *Buck v. Bell* that permitted compulsory sterilization, Justice Oliver Wendell Holmes wrote in his opinion, "It is better for all the world, if instead of waiting to execute degenerate offspring for crime, or to let them starve for their imbecility, society can prevent those who are manifestly unfit from continuing their kind".

The ruling legalized efforts of state-sponsored sterilization. By the 1970s, an increasing number of women of color, including sisters Mary Alice (age 14) and Minnie Relf (age 12), revealed their experiences of forced sterilization. The Relf sisters were considered to have intellectual disabilities (*Relf v. Weinberger*, 1974). These types of sterilizations, conducted without consent, were referred to as Mississippi Appendectomies, a phrase first used by well-known civil rights activist Fannie Lou Hamer. The documentary *No Mas Bebes* (*No More Babies*; Espino and Tajima-Pena, 2016) recounts how Mexican immigrant women sued the U.S. government because they were sterilized after giving birth. Between 2006 and 2010, 150 female prisoners in California were forcibly sterilized. Questions of parental "fitness" are deeply connected with white, able-bodied, heterosexual, middle-class norms.

In connecting the experiences of Fabbrini and Zeigler to those of other women whose experiences of childbirth, reproduction, and parenting have been either violently restricted or whose families have been fractured because of state oversight and forcible removal, we seek to connect experiences of oppression to historical and contemporary efforts that restrict reproductive and parental rights. In an interview with *Inside Edition*, Fabbrini avers, "I shouldn't be judged on what my IQ level is. It's just a number. It's not how I parent" (Hastings, 2017). Fabbrini is directly challenging the assumption that intelligence levels ought to be used to qualify someone's parenting ability. One of the reasons the public knows a fair amount about this case is because of Fabbrini and Zeigler's willingness to be public about their experiences, much like the Relf sisters, Dolores Madrigal and her co-plaintiffs, and Elaine Riddick. Each of these women—and countless others—has gone public with his or her experience of violence to challenge white supremacist, ableist, heteronormative, and classist assumptions of parental fitness. Women of color activist scholars, including SisterSong, have been at the forefront of moving the conversation around reproduction and parenting beyond the limited discourse of "rights" to recognize that reproductive oppression is best addressed through intersectional examinations that dismantle interlocking systems of oppression based on ability, age, class, gender, immigration status, and sexuality. Reproductive justice work centers parents, like Fabbrini and Zeigler, to challenge false and oppressive assumptions of ability to parent.

We join with these reproductive justice activists to fight against oppressive governmental and social service systems that break apart families under the guise of "fitness" or "appropriateness." Fabbrini and Zeigler's lawyer commented to the *Oregonian*, "How much heartache could have been avoided if the state had opted to, say, provide a parenting aide to coach them rather than a case worker to criticize them? The cost to the state, the cost to these children and the pain for both the biological and foster families might have been mitigated" (Swindler,

2017b). Reproductive justice expands the focus beyond a single issue in order to call upon communities to build inclusive and supportive reproductive and parenting arrangements, including robust, affordable childcare; safe affordable housing; maintaining food security; and opportunities for comprehensive schooling. Currently, individuals who are disabled, of color, queer, or immigrants find themselves under the watchful gaze of social service systems seeking to punitively break apart families. We refuse to valorize one type of parenting above another, and rather demand policies and resources that support all types of parents, including Fabbrini and Ziegler.

References

Buck v. Bell, 274 U.S. 200 (U.S. 1927).

Burke, Minyvonne. August 1, 2017. "Oregon Couple Claims That They Lost Custody of Their Children because of Low IQ." *New York Daily News.* http://www.nydailynews.com/news/national/ore-couple-claims-lost-custody-kids-iq-article-1.3374065.

Espino, Virginia. (Producer), & Tajima-Pena, Renee. (Director). (2016). *No Mas Bebes* [DVD].

Hastings, Deborah. November 1, 2017. *Parents with Intellectual Disabilities Share Heartbreak of Losing Custody of Their Children* [Video File]. http://www.insideedition.com/parents-intellectual-disabilities-share-heartbreak-losing-custody-their-children-38102

National Council of Disability. September 27, 2012. "Rocking the Cradle: Ensuring the Rights of Parents with Disabilities and Their Children." Washington, D.C., pages 1–22.

National Network to End Domestic Violence. *Custody.* https://www.womenslaw.org/laws/or/custody/all.

Relf v. Weinberger, Civ. A. Nos. 73–1557. https://www.splcenter.org/seeking-justice/case-docket/relf-v-weinberger.

Scanlon, Kate. August 1, 2017. "Oregon Mother Says Her Sons Were Removed from Her Home due to Her IQ," *The Blaze*. http://www.theblaze.com/news/2017/08/01/oregon-mother-says-her-sons-were-removed-from-her-home-due-to-her-iq.

Swindler, Samantha. August 1, 2017a. "IQ Costs Oregon Parents Their Kids, but Is That Fair?" *Oregonian*. http://www.oregonlive.com/pacific-northwest-news/index.ssf/2017/07/parents_with_intellectual_disa.html.

Swindler, Samantha. December 23, 2017b. "Judge Rules Oregon Parents with Low IQs Can Take Youngest Son Home." *Oregonian*. http://www.oregonlive.com/pacific-northwest-news/index.ssf/2017/12/judge_rules_oregon_parents_wit.html.

Brianna Dickens is a doctoral student in special education and disability studies at Syracuse University, the United States. She is an autistic self-advocate whose work centers around research methods, alternative communication, and constructions of and labels surrounding intellectual disability.

Michael Gill is an associate professor of disability studies in the Department of Cultural Foundations of Education at Syracuse University. He is also an affiliated faculty member with Women's and Gender Studies. Gill is the author of the book Already Doing It: Intellectual Disability and Sexual Agency *(University of Minnesota Press, 2015). He also coedited, with Cathy Schlund-Vials,* Disability, Human Rights, and the Limits of Humanitarianism *(Ashgate, 2014).*

Starlight Studio and Art Gallery
Carrie Marcotte

In a setting such as Starlight Studio and Art Gallery, founded in Buffalo, New York, in 2005, artists with disabilities are creating and learning in close proximity to their peers and the teaching artists. Starlight proves that creative self-expression and art is an option for every human. Starlight is a place where people get support to explore the ideas and media that interest them.

A strong sense of community quickly develops at Starlight Studio. The artists experiment and make art right next to a peer; some spontaneously solicit feedback throughout the process of creating. This atmosphere contributes to a sense of intimacy and safety. The artists often express a feeling of pride and loyalty for the program.

A studio program such as Starlight also helps individuals to get exposure for their art if this is something to which they are not opposed. The Studio also gives the artwork context for those visitors who have not enjoyed art by people with disabilities.

Support from the larger community comes in many forms: viewership, patronage, hands-on help, demonstration and facilitation of creative arts, and financial support. The presence of Starlight Studio helps society learn more about people with disabilities. This supported and encouraged creative self-expression leads to people with disabilities having a stronger voice and a stronger sense of self. The Studio, as an established location, attracts an audience to experience that voice.

The idea for Starlight emerged from a brainstorming session with the self-advocates of Learning Disabilities Association of Western New York (LDA) who meet once a month. Marc Hennig of LDA had great knowledge and familiarity with Creative Growth in California, perhaps the best-known art studio for people with disabilities in the country. Marc asked the self-advocates to explore what they wanted more of in Buffalo, and of course, he had the studio concept in mind. This conversation led to the design of the Starlight proposal. Exhibitions on- and off-site, hosting visiting artists, and selling art work were integral to the program design.

Starlight's beautiful 5,000 square foot studio is woven into the Buffalo Arts Community. It is ideally located in the most vibrant arts community in Buffalo, directly across the street from Hallwalls Contemporary Art Center, which is in an old church renovated in 2005 by the recording artist Ani DiFranco. The church, known as Babeville, not only houses Hallwalls, but it also offers a large venue for performances and other events. DiFranco's record company, Righteous Babe Records, also owns the building in which Starlight Studio and Art Gallery is located.

The original Starlight proposal was written for 19 people to attend five days per week of "Day Habilitation" service. However, after opening it became apparent that the artists were better served by having various part-time schedules. The Studio currently supports 42 people who come as little as two days a week for at least four hours each, to as many as five days a week. In addition to attending the Starlight program, many of the artists work in competitive employment or other supported employment situations. Participants live in a variety of settings from their own apartments to group homes.

Grants that have been awarded to Starlight over the years have prompted the program to develop rich collaborations and create deeper connections in the Buffalo community. Starlight has enjoyed three formal collaborations with Squeaky Wheel Media Arts Center. Each has provided an opportunity for self-expression through new media and techniques. Stop-action animation was one of the techniques that were learned. The second meaningful partnership with Squeaky Wheel resulted in short documentaries about being an artist; the third, *Of One Mind*, involved the recording of the Starlight artists in conversation about their art and process with artists from the community. Another grant opportunity has resulted in the Starlight artists working with second and third graders in a Buffalo Public School to explore strength through difference. Other grants allowed for a Starlight artist to design and assist in building a sculpture of a full-size woolly mammoth in Buffalo. Still another grant provided for the artists to tour, photograph, and exhibit photos of Buffalo's architectural treasures. Starlight's *Side by Each* exhibition series features five exhibitions in the calendar year that pairs a Starlight artist (or two) with a community artist. *Co-artifact*, Starlight's signature fund-raising event, formalizes this connection between community artist and Starlight artist; together the two artists create finished pieces of art that go up for auction. In 2018, with oversight by a playwright, a Starlight artist wrote a play that was staged at a local theater.

When the Starlight artists were presented with the question "What's the best thing about attending Starlight?" they wrote their answers quite spontaneously and rapidly. In reviewing and categorizing the answers from 26 of the 42 Starlight artists, the responses coalesced around specific themes of experience, artmaking, social support, positive emotions, stimulating new and free thinking, having opportunities to share talents with others, selling and exhibiting art, enjoying ancillary activities, and liking staff. The details and diverse answers, including quotes for each theme, are listed next:

Artmaking
- Having access to supplies and a multitude of different media
- "Being able to do pretty much any kind of artwork." (Alison Mantione)
- "Exploration of a variety of techniques: painting; drawing; embroidery; quilling; clay; needle point; and, animation." (John Budney)
- Attending art demonstrations
- "We work with professional artists." (Janet Harrison)

Stimulating New and Free Thinking
- "I feel artistic freedom." (Kelly Evans)
- "I can create what I want." (Steven Borgisi)
- "The teaching artists help me work through my ideas." (Debbie Medwin)
- "I think of having a pet bunny when I paint." (Mathew Sharp)

- "The teaching artists really challenge me in a very productive way which enables me to put my best foot forward." (Andy Calderon)
- "This place has provided me an arena that I can explore all creative, artistic and poetic concepts and ideas I have." (Andy Calderon)

Liking Staff
- "The teaching artists give me good advice to help me do other things instead of the same old things." (Margaret Meiller)
- "The staff is friendly and helpful and help me work through my ideas." (Debbie Medwin)
- "They help me adapt things to work with my visual impairment." (Debbie Medwin)
- "I like the staff."

After the number of comments regarding the value of art-making, people spoke mostly of the social supports they experience at Starlight Studio.

Social Supports
- Making friends
- Seeing friends
- Getting out of the house
- Attending parties at Starlight
- "It's my home away from home." (Andy Calderon)
- "It feels good to be around others." (Janet Harrison)

Positive Emotions
- "I feel proud of myself to see my paintings hanging." (Mathew Sharp)
- Margaret Meiller and Andy Calderon spoke of setting new goals for themselves and "trying new challenges."

- Two artists spoke of the value in being able to express oneself through art, and Andy Calderon added, "there's value in self-expression."
- Another referred to it as a "release of feelings" (Debbie Bowers) and another said it "relaxes my mind." (Margaret Meiller)
- Debbie Bowers also noted that she can see her potential growing as she witnesses progress in her art skills. She also added, "I'm showing others my abilities not my disability."
- Debbie Medwin and others noted not feeling judged at Starlight.
- One described feeling proud to set a schedule and successfully stick to it (Sonya Lewis).
- Jocelyn Triggle described gaining confidence to take on bigger projects outside Starlight and to try new media.
- "I love my art!" declares Michele Miller.
- "I've gained confidence," says Shirley French.
- "I feel peace of mind without pressure to produce," said John Budney.
- John Montedoro proclaimed that he has "learned how to calm himself down" at Starlight Studio.

Having Opportunities to Share Talents with Others
- Presenting at conferences either about themselves as artists or about the Starlight program.
- Conducting art making demonstrations to peers and children.

Selling and Exhibiting Art
- "It was amazing when I sold my first piece of art," claimed Shirley French.
- Mathew Sharp was pleased that "Mom and Dad can come and see what I made."
- Others are pleased that postcards are made and the exhibit is listed in the papers and sometimes on television.

- Others note that their art has been on display in different galleries.

Enjoying Ancillary Activities
- Many listed the numerous "extra" activities that they enjoy in addition to making art at Starlight, such as seeing movies; attending the writing group ("expressing my thoughts through poetry"); attending the reading group; meditation; running the Starlight snack shop; cooking demonstrations; field trips to galleries and other community locations; sign language classes, "I was able to teach sign language to my peers," said Shirley French.

"Starlight was the best decision I made!" proclaimed Shirley French.

Carrie Marcotte is the founding director of Starlight Studio and Art Gallery. Carrie has a master of arts degree in art therapy with a concentration in addictions treatment from Buffalo State College. After working as an art therapist in various treatment settings, she then worked as the coordinator of the Matter at Hand *program at the Albright-Knox Art Gallery in Buffalo.*

The Contradictory Status of Disabled Veterans
David A. Gerber

Tammy Duckworth is a U.S. senator from Illinois, and a retired U.S. Army lieutenant colonel. She is the first disabled woman to be elected to Congress. Duckworth was a pilot during the Iraq War in November, 2004, when her helicopter was shot down by a rocket-propelled grenade. She had chosen to be a helicopter pilot, because it was one of the few combat roles then open to women. Duckworth immediately lost her left leg below the knee and her right leg below the hip joint in the explosion, and came close to having her right arm amputated at a field hospital in Baghdad. She was evacuated to the army's principal facility for amputees, Walter Reed Army Medical Center in Washington, D.C., where she was to spend months recovering from her injuries and learning to use her prosthetic legs. While at Walter Reed, Duckworth was widely praised as a hero. She received a Purple Heart, an Air Medal, an Army Commendation Medal, and was promoted to the rank of major. On any given day, so many politicians and celebrities came to visit Duckworth, to encourage and cheer her and other injured men and women in the amputation ward, while taking advantage of the opportunity for a voter-pleasing photo op, that Duckworth humorously called it the "amputee petting zoo."

From the Revolutionary War to the current wars in Iraq and Afghanistan, American veterans have been widely used in the media and in the speeches of political leaders as symbols of patriotic devotion to duty to inspire service to state and society. They are widely lauded as heroes, whether they have made the sort of sacrifices that Duckworth has made or simply served in the military without injury. Permanently and visibly physically disabled veterans are especially powerful symbols. The nation has gone well beyond such symbolic gestures as rhetorical praise and medals in recognizing injured military personnel. Since the Revolutionary War, an evolving program of benefits, which initially consisted of pensions and after the Civil War gradually included free lifetime medical care and assistive devices, such as the $4,000 titanium wheelchair Duckworth uses, and subsidies for housing, education, and transportation has evolved. In the 20th century, these benefits grew into a major social investment that now costs billions of dollars a year.

After World War I, to care for the injured soldiers and sailors of that conflict, Congress created veterans hospitals, which can be found in many American cities and towns, and offer lifetime medical care after soldiers leave acute care facilities like Walter Reed and the armed forces, and are back in their own communities as civilians. In sharp contrast, civilians with disabilities, such as those born with physical disabilities or acquiring them as a consequence of accidents or illnesses, may be assisted with public programs, but they hardly have access to such a range of generous benefits, and they have a much lower social status. In light of the special status of veterans, and especially disabled ones, one commentator has spoken of the existence in the United States of a special "veterans' welfare state."

But the special treatment of veterans is more complicated than this recounting of symbolic gestures of praise and long list of material benefits suggests. Though sincere and well-meaning, symbolic gestures do not cost much. Material benefits—such as state-of-the-art wheelchairs and high-tech health care—do. And because they are provided by the government, they have to come out of tax revenues. Not only do voters not like high taxes, but most Americans are deeply divided on whether government should undertake big projects, even to help worthy people who deserve assistance. Money taken in taxes is said to inhibit private investment, and hence to limit economic growth. Programs like the Veterans Administration (VA) are especially controversial in hard economic times, when there is high unemployment and businesses collapse, and there is less money to be derived from taxation.

In addition, however generous the provisions of programs may be on paper, problems have always existed with the provision of services. The system of VA hospitals and the many programs that assist veterans, especially those with disabilities, grew in complexity overtime, so that while parts of the system may be sound, coordination among them has proved difficult. After an injured veteran leaves the hospital (and is no longer a member of the armed forces) the system has often proved inefficient and inadequate in dealing with their needs. The problem tends to lie with failures to anticipate the volume and nature of the problems that each war successively demands be addressed. We as a society are well practiced in waging war, but much less successful in planning for the needs of those injured doing the fighting.

This has been evident in the aftermath of every American war. An example is the psychological injuries, such as posttraumatic stress disorder, that result from the pressures of combat and constant exposure to danger. These are predictable, but the extent and the forms specific to particular times and places have not been easily anticipated or understood. Other examples are environmental and chemical hazards, such as the use of herbicidal defoliants (Agent Orange) or uranium-tipped bullets, both of which may cause illness and disability in those immediately exposed to them and become part of the genetic inheritance of their unborn children.

Every American war for over a century has been followed by a period of crisis in the delivery of services to veterans, especially those with disabilities. Recent wars have been no different, and there has been no greater evidence of this than the closing in 2011 of the army's once-prestigious Walter Reed Army Hospital, where Tammy Duckworth had a few years before received care that she praised. The problem lay not with acute care for the newly injured, but rather with outpatient services for those recently released from hospital wards, but continuing to need medical and rehabilitative care, and often living in facilities on the grounds of the hospital. The hospital was overwhelmed by the number of wounded it was receiving and was forced to release more and more of the seriously injured to outpatient status. Filthy living quarters and endless difficulties accessing services, described at length in a *Washington Post* article, came to haunt the lives of an ever-growing number of those soldiers returning from Iraq and Afghanistan. Finally, there seemed no choice but to close the facility, which had grown to 5,500 rooms covering about 28 acres since its opening in 1909, when it had only 80 beds. It was now combined with the nearby National Naval Medical Center in Maryland, in the hope of achieving better results with a newer, consolidated facility for the navy, army, and marines to form the new Walter Reed National Military Medical Center.

But the collapse of Walter Reed General Hospital was only the tip of an iceberg of problems with services to veterans. From veterans hospitals all over the country came complaints about the endless wait for services and the loss of the case files of individuals that placed the neediest outside the system when they most needed it, and stories of overworked and under-resourced, but dedicated doctors, social workers, and rehabilitation personnel, struggling to do their work amid administrative chaos. The comment of Marine Sergeant Ryan Groves, an amputee who spent 16 months at Walter Reed, could stand for the way many injured veterans came to regard the system. He told the *Washington Post*, "We've done our duty. We fought the war. We came home wounded. Fine. But whoever the people are back here who are supposed to give us an easy transition should be doing it. We don't know what to do. The people who are supposed to know don't have the answers. It's a nonstop process of stalling" (Priest and Hull, 2007). It was left increasingly to the men and women and their families and friends to raise the alarm about the conditions. Among the most insistent voices has been Tammy Duckworth, as head of the Illinois veteran's bureau from 2006 to 2009, then as assistant secretary of the Department of Veterans Affairs and as a member of the House of Representatives, and now as a senator.

References

Kinder, John M. 2015. *Paying with Their Bodies: American War and the Problem of the Disabled Veteran*. Chicago: University of Chicago Press.

Linker, Beth. 2011. *War's Waste: Rehabilitation in World War I America*. Chicago: University of Chicago Press.

Priest, Dana, and Anne Hull. 2007. "Soldiers Face Neglect, Frustration at Army's Top Medical Facility." http://www.washingtonpost.com/wp-dyn/content/article/2007/02/17/AR2007021701172_pf.html (Accessed July 30, 2017).

Skocpol, Theda. 1992. *Protecting Mothers and Soldiers: The Political Origins of Social Policy in the United States*. Cambridge, MA: Harvard University Press.

David A. Gerber is distinguished professor of history emeritus and senior fellow at the University at Buffalo, and the author of books, collections, and essays in 19th- and 20th-century American history.

Violence against People with Disabilities: Still Missing from the Conversation
Miranda Sue Terry

In 2017, Americans and observers from around the world saw the #metoo movement gain momentum through social media and mainstream media. *TIME* magazine's Person(s) of the Year were "The Silence Breakers," which included #metoo movement founder Tarana Burke (Zacharek, Dockterman, and Edwards, 2017). Burke founded the #metoo movement in 2006 "to help survivors of sexual violence, particularly young women of color from economically marginalized communities, find pathways to healing" and to let them know they were not alone (https://metoomvmt.org, n.d.). The #metoo movement brought the topic of sexual violence to the forefront of discussions. The *TIME* article shares the stories of women and men who had experienced sexual violence. It identifies victims of abuse as "those who are often most vulnerable in society—immigrants, people of color, people with disabilities, low-income workers, and LGBTQ people" (Zacharek et al., 2017). Yet, disabled peoples' stories are missing from the article. We have to ask: How are people with disabilities still missing from the conversation about sexual violence and abuse in general?

Violence against People with Disabilities

There are approximately 56.7 million people with a disability in the United States, which is about 19 percent of the population (U.S. Census Bureau, 2012). The 2012 Survey on Abuse of People with Disabilities, conducted by Spectrum Institute, found that more than 70 percent of people with disabilities experienced abuse (Baladerian, Coleman, and Stream, 2013). This survey identified incidences of abuse among types of disabilities.

People with mental health disabilities had a 74.8 percent rate of abuse, people with speech impairments had a 67.1 percent rate of abuse, people with autism had a 66.5 percent rate of abuse, people with intellectual/developmental disabilities had a 62.5 percent rate, and people with mobility impairments had a 55.2 percent incidence rate of abuse (Baladerian, Coleman, and Stream, 2013). These findings are similar to Hughes and colleagues' findings that "adults with disabilities are at a higher risk of violence than are non-disabled adults, and those with mental illnesses could be particularly vulnerable" (Hughes et al., 2012). The Bureau of Justice found that "the rate of violent victimization against persons with disabilities was at least 2.5 times the unadjusted rate for those without disabilities" (BJS, 2017), except in the 65-or-older age group.

With a 40 percent greater risk of violence than women without disabilities (Brownridge, 2006), women with disabilities are more vulnerable to abuse (Nosek, Howland, and Hughes, 2001). An analysis conducted by Diane L. Smith (2008) using the 2005 Behavioral Risk Factor Surveillance System showed "that women who have a disability are twice as likely to be threatened with violence, 1.89 times as likely to be a victim of attempted violence, 2.05 times as likely to be physically abused, and 2.38 times as likely to experience unwanted sex" (Smith, 2008, 22).

"Unwanted sex" is a form of sexual violence. The Centers for Disease Control and Prevention (CDC) define sexual violence as "a sexual act committed against someone without that person's freely given consent" (CDC, 2017). According to the #metoo movement website, "17,700,000 women have reported sexual assault since 1998" (https://metoomvmt.org, n.d.). According to a nationally representative survey of adults by Black and colleagues, 18.3 percent of women and 1.4 percent men reported experiencing rape at some point in their lives, while 13 percent of women and 6 percent of men reported they experienced sexual coercion at some point in their lives (CDC, 2012). Mitra and colleagues found that 8.8 percent of men with a disability reported lifetime sexual violence compared to 6 percent of men without a disability and 4.1 percent of men with a disability reported completed nonconsensual sex compared to 1.4 percent of men without a disability (Mitra, Mouradian, Fox, and Pratt, 2016). Similar to women with disabilities, men with disabilities are more vulnerable to abuse (Mitra, Mouradian, Fox, and Pratt, 2016). As reported by the National Council on Disability, a study by the Association of American Universities found that "31.6 percent of undergraduate females with disabilities reported nonconsensual sexual contact involving physical force or incapacitation, compared to 18.4 percent of undergraduate females without a disability" (NCD, 2018).

The prevalence rates of sexual abuse among people with disabilities provides quite a telling story when breaking it down by specific disabilities. Forty percent of women with physical disabilities reported being sexually assaulted (Young, Nosek, Howland, Chanpong, and Rintala, 1997)—there is no prevalence rate specific for men with physical disabilities. Among adults with developmental disabilities, as many as 83 percent of women and 32 percent of men experienced sexual assault (Johnson and Sigler, 2000). A study conducted by Goodman and colleagues (2001) found that within the previous year, 20 percent of women with a serious mental illness and 8 percent of men with a serious mental illness had experienced sexual assault (Goodman et al., 2001).

Expanding Definitions to Encompass Disability-Related Abuse

Not surprisingly, disability-related abuse is missing from the definitions provided by the CDC, which impacts prevalence rates as disability-related abuse is not captured. For example, disability-related physical abuse may include a perpetrator limiting a woman's mobility (e.g., removing her wheelchair battery), which can be similar to locking her in a closet. Yet such an incident is not captured in surveys because of existing definitions (Hassouneh-Phillips and Curry, 2002). Disability-related sexual abuse may range from more subtle acts such as demanding a kiss before assistance will be given to a woman with a disability to more severe acts such as rape. None of these are currently counted. Terry (2013) proposed the following abuse definitions encompassing disability-related abuse:

> Emotional abuse is defined as "words or behaviors intended to hurt another person, such as abandonment, accusations, belittling controlling, corruption, damaging, property, dominance, exploitation, harming a partner's self-worth, humiliation, ignoring, intimidation, isolation, name calling, put-downs, severely rejected, stalking, terrorizing, threats, threats of abandonment, threatening a partner, threatening of possessions or loved ones, including pets, verbally attacking, or withholding of care."
>
> Physical abuse is defined as "the intentional use of physical force that has the potential to harm or kill such as deprivation of food or water, hitting, slapping, stabbing, choking, burning, biting, limiting mobility, restraining, throwing objects, or otherwise physically assaulting one's partner, including over or under medicating."
>
> Sexual abuse is defined as "being forced, threatened, or deceived into sexual activities ranging from nonconsensual completed or attempted penetration, unwanted non-penetrative sexual contact, or noncontact acts such as verbal sexual harassment, by any perpetrator." (Terry, 2013)

While the CDC states the importance of having a consistent definition of abuse, disability-related abuse is still missing from CDC definitions (CDC, 2017). As Saxton and colleagues state, "The experiences of women with disabilities should not be treated as a special case but as part of the continuum of women's issues" (Saxton, Curry, Powers, Maley, Eckels, and Gross, 2001, 414). This is particularly important when looking at sexual violence among women with disabilities on college campuses. Regardless of setting, however, the definitions and policies must encompass people with disabilities and their experiences, and all stakeholders must ensure appropriate resources are available to them. Men with disabilities who have suffered abuse or violence should also be in this conversation.

Anyone can be a victim of abuse, but people with disabilities have been found to be more vulnerable to abuse than most people (Hughes et al., 2012). It is likely that poor women of color with disabilities experience disproportionate rates of abuse, but we have no way of confirming that. It is time to include people with disabilities fully in the conversation and expand the definitions of abuse: thus, assisting the understanding of the prevalence and effects of abuse within all vulnerable populations.

References

Baladerian, N. J., T. F. Coleman, and J. Stream 2013. "Abuse of People with Disabilities: Victims and Their Families Speak Out." Spectrum Institute, Disability and Abuse Project, A Report on the 2012 National Survey on Abuse of People with Disabilities.

Brownridge, D. 2006. "Partner Violence against Women with Disabilities: Prevalence, Risk, and Explanations. *Violence against Women* 12(9): 805–822. doi: 10.1177/1077801206292681.

Bureau of Justice Statistics (BJS). 2017. "Crime against Persons with Disabilities, 2009–2015—Statistical Tables." https://www.bjs.gov/index.cfm?ty=pbdetail&iid=5986 (Accessed January 2, 2018).

CDC. 2012. "Sexual Violence: Facts at a Glance." https://www.cdc.gov/ViolencePrevention/pdf/SV-DataSheet-a.pdf (Accessed January 2, 2018).

CDC. 2017. "Sexual Violence: Definitions." https://www.cdc.gov/violenceprevention/sexualviolence/definitions.html (Accessed January 2, 2018).

Goodman, L. A., M. P. Salyers, K. T., Mueser, S. D. Rosenberg, M. Swartz, S. M. Essock, F. C. Osher, M. I. Butterfield, & J. Swanson. 2001. "Recent Victimization in Women and Men with Severe Mental Illness: Prevalence and Correlates." *Journal of Traumatic Stress* 14(4): 615–632.

Hassouneh-Phillips, D., and M. A. Curry. 2002. "Abuse of Women with Disabilities: State of the Science." *Rehabilitation Counseling Bulletin* 45(2): 96–104.

Hughes, K., M. A. Bellis, L. Jones, S. Wood, G. Bates, L. Eckley, E. McCoy, C. Mikton, T. Shakespeare, and A. Officer. April 28, 2012. "Prevalence and Risk of Violence against Adults with Disabilities: A Systematic Review and Meta-Analysis of Observational Studies." *Lancet* 379(9826): 1621–29. doi: 10.1016/S0140-6736(11)61851-5.

Johnson, I. M., and R. T. Sigler. 2000. "Forced Sexual Intercourse among Intimates." *Journal of Family Violence* 15(1): 95–108.

me too. n.d. "You Are Not Alone." https://metoomvmt.org/ (Accessed January 2, 2018).

Mitra, M., V. E. Mouradian, M. H. Fox, and C. Pratt. 2016. "Prevalence and Characteristics of Sexual Violence against Men with Disabilities." *American Journal Preventive Medicine* 50(3): 311–317. doi: 10.1016/j. amepre.2015.07.030.

National Council on Disability. 2018. "Not on Radar: Sexual Assault of College Students with Disabilities." https://ncd. gov/publications/2018/not-radar-sexual-assault-college-students-disabilities (Accessed February 2, 2018).

Nosek, M. A., C. A. Howland, and R. B. Hughes. 2001. "The Investigation of Abuse and Women with Disabilities: Going Beyond Assumptions." *Violence against Women* 7(4): 477–499. doi: 10.1177/10778010122182569.

Saxton, M., M. A. Curry, L. E. Powers, S. Maley, K. Eckels, and J. Gross. 2001. "'Bring My Scooter So I Can Leave

You': A Study of Disabled Women Handling Abuse by
Personal Assistance Providers." *Violence against Women*
7(4): 393–417. doi: 10.1177/10778010122182523.

Smith, D. L. 2008. "Disability, Gender and Intimate Partner
Violence: Relationships from the Behavioral Risk Factor
Surveillance System." *Sexuality and Disability* 26: 15–28.
doi:10.1007/s11195-007-9064-6.

Terry, M. S. 2013. "An Exploratory Study of the Effects of
Abuse on the Health of College Women with Mobility
Impairments." Dissertation: University of Illinois,
Urbana-Champaign.

U.S. Census Bureau. 2012. "Nearly 1 in 5 People Have a
Disability in the U.S." Census Bureau Reports. https://
www.census.gov/newsroom/releases/archives/miscellaneous/
cb12-134.html (Accessed January 2, 2018).

Young, M. E., M. A. Nosek, C. A. Howland, G. Chanpong,
and D. H. Rintala. 1997. "Prevalence of Abuse of Women
with Physical Disabilities." *Archives of Physical Medicine and
Rehabilitation Special Issue* 78(12, Suppl.5): 534–538.

Zacharek, S., E. Dockterman, and H. A. Edwards. 2017.
"TIME Person of the Year 2017: The Silence Breakers."
http://time.com/time-person-of-the-year-2017-silence-
breakers/ (Accessed January 2, 2018).

*Miranda Sue Terry, assistant professor, earned her PhD in com-
munity health, specializing in disability studies at University of
Illinois, Urbana-Champaign. Her research interests are diverse,
spanning disability studies, gender and women's studies, and public health. Her overall research objective is to improve the rights
and lives of people with disabilities.*

Deaf Children and Cochlear Implants
Laura Mauldin

The cochlear implant (CI) is a neuroprosthetic device that is
surgically implanted and used to treat individuals who have

qualifying types of severe to profound sensorineural hearing loss. During surgery, the internal component of the device is placed into the skull near the back of the ear and electrodes are threaded into the cochlea, located in the inner ear. Once healed, the external component consisting of a microphone and a speech processor are magnetically attached to the receiver. This external component sits on the skin and has a small wire that attaches to a "behind-the-ear" unit that looks much like a hearing aid. The CI is very different from a hearing aid, however, which only amplifies sound. The CI translates sound waves to a digital signal that is sent through electrical stimulation in the cochlea and directly to the auditory cortex.

While adults do choose to get a CI, deaf children are receiving CIs at increasing rates in the United States and at earlier ages (on average at 12 months old) for a variety of reasons that include the Food and Drug Administration's lowering of the minimum age requirement and mandated newborn hearing screening in all states (Blume, 2010; Mauldin, 2016). Typically, the primary goal of implantation is the acquisition, development, and use of spoken language (Peterson, Pisoni, and Miyamoto, 2010). For pediatric patients specifically, obtaining a CI is often seen as a step toward attempting spoken language development and in lieu of learning sign language. But many are against such goals, and this is why the controversy has brewed for decades, particularly over the use of CIs in children.

The controversy over CIs emerged because there are competing scripts about what deafness means and how it should be responded to, especially when it comes to language choice. Professionals in implantation and many in the general public may characterize deafness as a medical problem that requires medical intervention to "fix" it. For example, audiologists measure the amount and kind of hearing loss a deaf child has and recommend tools like CIs and accompanying therapies to correct or mitigate the "problem." Because of widely accepted norms that deafness or disability is undesirable, parents are expected to adhere to these expectations.

However, there is another script about the meaning of deafness that comes from deaf people who belong to the Deaf community. In the 1970s, deaf people started distinguishing between the lowercase deaf, which describes one's audiological or hearing status, and the capitalized version of Deaf, which refers to an identity of being culturally Deaf (see Padden and Humphries [1990] for more information). The main reason for this cultural identity is shared language and shared experiences of oppression. The primary adaptation used by deaf people to function in society in the United States is a visual-spatial language called American Sign Language (ASL). Many deaf people claim that deafness makes them a member of a linguistic minority and thriving culture. As a result, the Deaf cultural script argues that sign language should be valued and encouraged in deaf children (Blume, 1997; Mauldin, 2016).

Not only does the Deaf cultural script conflict with the medical script of deafness, but the reason CIs are most controversial in children is because more than 90 percent of deaf children have hearing parents, who tend to be unfamiliar with Deaf ideas about what deafness means. Instead, parents are primarily exposed to medical definitions of deafness, where sign language is typically viewed as unnecessary and at times even as suspect (Mauldin, 2016). Proponents of CIs in children tend to argue that a "good" parent will implant his or her child and provide every opportunity by teaching the child to speak. Those who oppose implantation in children tend to argue that their own childhood was marred by a focus on "fixing" them, that parents do not understand the importance of fostering Deaf pride, and there is too much of a focus on speech to the exclusion of sign language.

In light of these differing viewpoints on the CI, it is also important to understand what we know about the realities of opting to obtain one for one's child and its effectiveness. Some parents characterize videos that show a deaf child "hearing for the first time" when the implant is initially turned on as misrepresenting the realities of implantation for children (Mauldin,

2016). Months (and sometimes years) of preparation and therapies precede CI surgery and activation of the device, and years of long-term follow-up care and auditory training are required afterward. Surgery is one moment in a multiyear process of rehabilitation; the CI is not a one-time fix for deafness. Typically, it is mothers of deaf children who are responsible for long-term therapies because childcare is highly gendered. Yet there are few studies of mothers and their experiences (see Mauldin, 2016). It is also well established in the literature that the outcomes of implantation are highly variable and that there are disparities in outcomes across socioeconomic status and race/ethnicity (e.g., Belzner and Seal, 2009; Chang et al., 2010; Hyde and Power, 2006; Kirkham et al., 2009; Stern et al., 2005). If mothers are responsible for the long-term therapeutic care that is essential for the CI to be effective, which mothers have the resources to do so? Which families have access to adequate services? Disparities in health outcomes are highly linked to social status; thus understanding families' experiences is of utmost importance in understanding when and to what degree the CI "works." Finally, there is a dearth of research on family experiences with implantation for their child. There are also no comprehensive data on outcomes at the national level. Without adequate research on families, comprehensive data, and an understanding of the long-term and complex nature of implantation for children, there remain serious gaps in knowledge. It is important not to assume the CI works for everyone or that it instantly enables a child to "hear."

Today, implantation in children who qualify is occurring more often, despite these controversies. And while many in the Deaf community remain opposed to CIs in children, research has shown changing attitudes in the Deaf community toward CIs. For many, the presence of CIs has become more tolerable, yet the decision by hearing parents to implant and exclude ASL is still something to which they object (Christiansen and Leigh, 2010, 2004). Thus, while controversy remains regarding children receiving CIs, the practice is continuing and its consequences will only be known over time as these children age into adulthood.

References

Belzner, K. A., and B. C. Seal. 2009. "Children with Cochlear Implants: A Review of Demographics and Communication Outcomes." *American Annals of the Deaf* 154(3): 311–333.

Blume, Stuart. 1997. "The Rhetoric and Counter-Rhetoric of a 'Bionic' Technology." *Science, Technology, & Human Values* 22 (1): 31–56.

Blume, Stuart. 2010. *The Artificial Ear: Cochlear Implants and the Culture of Deafness*. New Brunswick, NJ: Rutgers University Press.

Boss, Emily F., John K. Niparko, Darrell J. Gaskin, and Kimberly L. Levinson. 2011. "Socioeconomic Disparities for Hearing-Impaired Children in the United States." *The Laryngoscope* 121(4): 860–66. https://doi.org/10.1002/lary.21460.

Chang, David T, Alvin B. Ko, Gail S. Murray, James E. Arnold, and Cliff A. Megerian. 2010. "Lack of Financial Barriers to Pediatric Cochlear Implantation: Impact of Socioeconomic Status on Access and Outcomes." *Archives of Otolaryngology—Head & Neck Surgery* 136(7): 648–57. https://doi.org/10.1001/archoto.2010.90.

Christiansen, John B., and Irene W. Leigh. 2004. "Children with Cochlear Implants: Changing Parent and Deaf Community Perspectives." *Archives of Otolaryngology—Head & Neck Surgery* 130(5): 673.

Christiansen, John B., and Irene W. Leigh. 2010. "Cochlear Implants and Deaf Community Perceptions." In Raylene Paludneviciene and Irene W. Leigh, ed. *Cochlear Implants: Evolving Perspectives*, 39–55. Washington, DC: Gallaudet University Press.

Hyde, Merv, and Des Power. 2006. "Some Ethical Dimensions of Cochlear Implantation for Deaf Children and Their Families." *Journal of Deaf Studies and Deaf Education* 11(1): 102–111. https://doi.org/10.1093/deafed/enj009.

Kirkham, Erin, Chana Sacks, Fuad Baroody, Juned Siddique, Mary Ellen Nevins, Audie Woolley, and Dana Suskind. 2009. "Health Disparities in Pediatric Cochlear Implantation: An Audiologic Perspective." *Ear and Hearing* 30(5): 515–525. https://doi.org/10.1097/AUD.0b013e3181aec5e0.

Mauldin, Laura. 2016. *Made to Hear: Cochlear Implants and Raising Deaf Children*. Minneapolis: University Of Minnesota Press.

Padden, Carol A., and Tom L. Humphries. 1990. *Deaf in America: Voices from a Culture*. Cambridge, MA: Harvard University Press.

Peterson, Nathaniel R., David B. Pisoni, and Richard T. Miyamoto. 2010. "Cochlear Implants and Spoken Language Processing Abilities: Review and Assessment of the Literature." *Restorative Neurology and Neuroscience* 28(2): 237–250.

Stern, Ryan E., Bevan Yueh, Charlotte Lewis, Susan Norton, and Kathleen C. Y. Sie. 2005. "Recent Epidemiology of Pediatric Cochlear Implantation in the United States: Disparity among Children of Different Ethnicity and Socioeconomic Status." *The Laryngoscope* 115(1): 125–131. https://doi.org/10.1097/01.mlg.0000150698.61624.3c.

Laura Mauldin is assistant professor in human development and family studies and women's, gender, and sexuality studies at the University of Connecticut. Her book Made to Hear *(University of Minnesota Press, 2016) won Honorable Mention, Outstanding Publication Award from the American Sociological Association's*

Section on Disability & Society. She is also a nationally certified sign language interpreter.

Gender, Madness, and Commitment
Jessica Lowell Mason

What happens when a woman becomes a ward of the state? What happens when she is deemed incapable of making decisions for herself, when her rights are ripped away from her and the will of an institution is forced upon her?

1. She may be escorted into a hospital by a man with a gun who does not speak to her, who will not look at her, whose presence is there to fulfill a role within a system and to remind her that she does not have a choice.

2. Her possessions may be taken from her, placed in a paper bag, and placed in a locker until she is permitted to be released from captivity.

3. She may be brought through maximum-security doors, doors that she, herself, has no power to open.

4. She may or may not have a room of her own. She may or may not have a room. She may or may not even have a bed. She may have a plastic chair in room packed with 40 other people who have been locked away, too.

5. She may have to wait 20 or more hours just to be recognized by staff.

6. She may have food thrown at her while she waits.

7. She may be brought into a five-by-five room at 2 AM and given a five-minute evaluation by a psychiatrist who does not speak her language.

8. She may be labeled with a serious psychiatric illness after being evaluated for five minutes, and based on this diagnosis, she may not be able to go home.

9. She may be placed in a room, for weeks or months, under the care of a doctor in an institution, and that doctor will

have complete control over her life for as long as that doctor sees fit.

10. She may be forced to consume medications about which she will not be given information.
11. She may lose her job and her credibility.
12. She may be put back out into the world when her insurance, if she has insurance, no longer supports the institution that is keeping and profiting off of her.

The ripping-away of autonomy and identity is a horrific practice that we associate with the past, or perhaps imperialist regimes and genocidal tyrannies, but the belief systems that drive such practices are not unheard of in contemporary America. Women have had to fight for the right to have control over their bodies for a long time. The treatment of women's bodies as property in the United States and abroad is well documented. The denial of human status to women by men in power is a tradition that we have not yet outgrown.

The United States is one of many countries around the world that operates according to a patriarchal ideology in which maleness is privileged and femaleness is underprivileged. Bodies, particularly female bodies, are still a source of conflict when it comes to human rights. Sexism and misogyny, like racism and other forms of discrimination and prejudice, result in power imbalances that hurt those who are marginalized and possess the least agency. Every woman should have the right to own her body and to decide what happens to it, but women continue to have to fight for societal recognition of this right. Women's bodies are often punished when women demand recognition of their autonomy. When a woman's body riots against male power, she will likely be ignored, discredited, or disciplined.

Women's experiences and degrees of liberation are influenced by race, ethnicity, class, age, sex, gender, sexuality, religion, and ability. The social status of a woman's body is determined by its adherence to social rules, or norms, which are often categorized according to divisionary categories such as white or black, rich or poor, young or old, American or un-American, male or female, straight or gay, abled or disabled, and normal or abnormal. Binary social rules, particularly ones rooted in patriarchal beliefs, often result in the dehumanization and criminalization of bodies that do not submit to their assumed obligation to the patriarchal imperative. Bodies can be considered property if they are noncompliant to the will of an authority. A body can be policed, so to speak, according to its adherence to normativity. Disabled and mad bodies are noncompliant bodies, or bodies that do not adhere to social norms. In that regard, they pose a threat to the status quo and to patriarchal authority, especially under capitalism, in which consumption and profit are driven by the dominance and recognition of normal bodies and the submission and negation of laboring and abnormal bodies.

Within the disability social justice movement, there is a push for bodily recognition, for visibility, and for equality and dignity. Institutions are slowly changing to signal recognition of disability rights by moving toward a model of accommodation. Despite this move forward, cognition and mental and emotional distress remain areas of difference that are not always recognized as being worthy of equal treatment. Often, these differences are uncounted and unrecognized. When they are recognized, they are treated with loathing, fear, shame, and criminalization. "Abnormal" minds remain detained on the periphery of society, virtually invisible, except through depictions as dangers and aberrations.

"Mental illness" or what activists within disability rights and social justice movements call "madness" has been addressed by the fields of psychology and psychiatry for over 100 years. These fields have been criticized for relying too heavily on medicalized understandings of human difference and for being too closely aligned with patriarchal points of view and corporate interests. Some critics of the field of psychiatry in Europe and the United States argue that it began as a mechanism for monitoring social normativity and imparting social control. Individuals affected most directly by psychiatry were those with the least power in society: women, immigrants, economically marginalized or homeless people, disabled people, LGBTQ people, and racial/ethnic minorities. Those who had the most power and influence in terms of psychiatric treatment were those with the most power and sway in society: usually, though not always, well-to-do white men.

During the 19th century, when psychiatry was being founded, a woman was not an entity unto herself; she was a possession of a man, and her value in society was determined solely by her relation to the men in her life, through the institution of marriage. An unmarried woman, during this period and long after it, was particularly vulnerable to being demonized or criminalized for her failure to fulfill male expectations of what a woman should be at a time when wives were, by law, required to submit to the wills of their husbands. An uncontrollable woman was one who was not obeying the rules of marriage and patriarchy.

Psychiatry's earliest practices often focused on resolving the supposed problem of gender deviance in women. To be considered insane was to reject the social rules prescribed by men in authority. For example, women who did not behave according to the gender norms of the late 19th and early 20th centuries could be labeled as having "hysteria" and could be sent by men in authority or disgruntled family members to institutions for the insane, where they would be given no choice but to submit to the will of doctors. While men have certainly been harmed by coercive psychiatric practices, women have suffered specifically because they are women.

The problems of early psychiatric practices are many, which makes the fact that such practices have not been more widely condemned, especially disconcerting. The underlying beliefs that women are second-class citizens and that those with mental illnesses are not fully human continue to inform psychiatric practices. Institutions of the present are too much like institutions of the past.

When a woman, or any person, today is admitted or committed into a psychiatric institution, for all intents and purposes, she gives up her human right to make decisions about her own body. It may be illegal for a doctor today to use the abusive treatments used during the 19th century, but a doctor can assert authority over her body in other ways. State psychiatric institutions receive patients from mostly marginalized and minority communities. Many of the patients in such institutions are picked up off the street or brought there by police. Many are poor, many are homeless, many have substance dependency issues, many are people of color, and many are women. Some choose to go into emergency psychiatric care because they feel they have no other option, but many go in by force. The conditions in state mental hospitals are, on the whole, deplorable and reminiscent of prisons—and in fact, jails and prisons are one of the largest providers of psychiatric services in the United States.

A psychiatrist's authority is virtually unquestioned by society and by the court system. While there exist state-provided legal resources for those incarcerated against their will in psychiatric institutions, such resources are no match for the authority of the doctor. The reality is that a female patient forced into treatment does not have a voice in her treatment. She does not have a choice. Her body is not hers. It belongs to the institution. Legally, once she has been labeled by a doctor as a harm to herself or others, without due course and without representation, she can become an object. She can be locked in a room, she can be strapped down to a bed, and she can be injected with powerful drugs that could potentially alter her cognition and body forever. Instead of being property of the institution of marriage, women can now become property of the institution of psychiatry. The origins of both institutions are enmeshed, and they continue to be enmeshed to this day.

Fortunately, there is a growing recognition of the human rights violations inherent in psychiatric institutionalization. Women are getting mad. Women are owning their madness; they are refusing to be treated like property. The movement to liberate people from psychiatric oppression has taken many names over the years, but generally it is referred to as the con-sumer/survivor/ex-patient or C/S/X movement. It is a feminist movement. It is made up of people (men and women) who be-lieve in the human right of every woman, and person, to decide for herself what labels should be applied to her and what she does with her own body. The C/S/X or mad people's movement and the disability rights movement aim to decrease the stigma attached to mental illness labels, to demand visibility and seek restorative justice for psychiatric survivors and consumers of psychiatric services, to end coercive patriarchal psychiatry and its human rights violations, and to raise awareness about cogni-tive differences. Cognitive rights are, perhaps, the last and least recognized frontier of the fight for social justice.

Jessica Lowell Mason is cofounder of Madwomen in the Attic, a grassroots feminist literacy organization for women who have been harmed by the mental health industry. She is a scholar, educa-tor, editor, performer, writer, and recipient of the 2014 Gloria Anzaldúa Rhetorician Award from the Conference on College Composition and Communication.

Minority Students with Disabilities and the School to Prison Pipeline
Leroy Moore, Jr., and Michael Rembis

There is no doubt that America's schools have become increas-ingly policed in the 21st century. In the wake of high-profile school shootings and other forms of violence, school adminis-trators and lawmakers have attempted to use law enforcement to make schools "safer." This is especially true in schools that serve people of color in urban areas (even though school shoot-ings are almost exclusively carried out by white male students). Of particular interest among people who concern themselves with race and disability are the ways in which heightened dis-ciplinary regimes combined with rigidly assessed, standardized academic achievement metrics have created a structure and a culture that unfairly marginalize, discriminate against, and ultimately punish people of color with disabilities. The tracking of people of color, especially those with disabilities, through K–12 educational systems and into the country's jails and prisons has become known popularly as the "school to prison pipeline."

Since the 1980s, school-age children and teenagers of color have been increasingly labeled mentally or developmentally impaired (initially referred to as mentally retarded), and as possessing "behavior disorders." This is especially true in the K–12 setting, where classroom assignments, grade advancement, educational and developmental goals, and other crucial stages of childhood development are intricately linked with psychological, psychiatric, medical, intellectual, and other forms of evaluation. Too often, teachers and school administrators are willing to call the police to respond to behavioral issues, especially when they involve students of color labeled as disabled. Administrators and teachers should be trained to respond to incidents in the school setting without the use of law enforcement.

The school to prison pipeline cannot be easily changed, but parents, schools, advocacy groups, and government authorities are trying to use strategies to protect disabled students. Parents are asking that the police have no contact with their disabled child. Parents are also insisting that their child not be interviewed by the police, or the school's police liaison without a parent being present. At the school and district levels, measures are being taken to remove police officers from schools and increase the number of specialists and counselors. Teacher and administrator training on how to identify and de-escalate "behaviors" without police intervention is important. Similar training and policy changes should be put in place at the state and national levels.

There are a growing number of schools moving away from the "zero-tolerance" policy and taking a more creative approach to breaking the school to prison pipeline. The Ascend Charter High School, in Brooklyn, New York, for example, requires students to take responsibility for their actions, and there are daily activities to build relationships with faculty. The school works to defuse problems before they grow by having the teachers talk about the consequences of one's actions, rather than making suspension the first line of defense in dealing with discipline problems.

People working to end the school to prison pipeline say that the police should be the last resource for schools. Angry outbursts are often part of growing-up. Teachers and administrators should be trained and prepared to handle these kinds of typical behaviors without calling the police. When it comes to disabled students, typical childhood behavior is often looked at as more dangerous because of the negative stereotypes that are associated with disability. Students of color are also discriminated against in similar ways. When race and disability are combined, the negative attitudes about that person increase. A white student without a disability is much less likely to have the police called on him or her for displaying typical (or even problematic or troubling) teenage behavior. It should be noted that extreme outbursts and school shootings while more common are still quite rare. Nevertheless, all students, especially students of color and those with disabilities, have to live with the aftereffects of violence in America's schools.

Disabled students may need a more specialized problem-solving approach than students from the general population. This approach does not require the use of law enforcement. Part of the solution is training teachers to recognize the start of behavioral changes in students. Teachers have to be trained to recognize the problematic behaviors before they grow into something more serious. This also calls for the student, as best he or she can, along with the parents, to discuss the signs that can trigger anger, agitation, or other forms of acting out. The key to ending violence in U.S. schools and the school to prison pipeline is in better training and more empathetic instruction and supervision, not in arming school personnel, like some lawmakers suggest.

Nonprofit organizations, like Parent Advocacy Coalition for Educational Rights, are good resources for teachers and parents. They provide questions to ask school faculty, staff, and administrators, such as whether a student's individual education plan includes guidelines for creating a safe place for them to calm down. There must be consistent rules, and people need to understand the rules at the local, state, and federal levels. One of the difficulties with policies is that they are formed at the district level. As a result, children often lack protection depending on which school or district implements a policy. It also means that many districts and schools may be enforcing policies at the local level that directly conflict with state and federal laws. Because of this localized approach, there is a lack of consistency nationwide when it comes to supporting and protecting students with disabilities. Identifying the exact policies that students are being subjected to and challenging them in court if necessary is important.

Currently, most of the resistance to zero-tolerance policies is at the local level and is in urban settings in districts with high numbers of students of color. For example, the Los Angeles Unified School District is working to reduce overly harsh discipline and eliminate zero-tolerance policies by referring students to counseling and administrative discipline rather than being sent to juvenile court. In other states, such as Florida, students have been arrested for bringing a plastic butter knife to school and throwing an eraser. Legislation has since been passed prohibiting schools from calling the police for nonviolent misdemeanors. Texas also passed a bill that allows officials to consider "mitigating factors" before they punish students. Texas used to have a very harsh zero-tolerance policy. For instance, violations of the code of conduct could end up in a student being expelled or suspended. States are looking at their laws and changing them, but it is up to the school districts, which create and enforce their zero-tolerance policies, to change their stance on zero-tolerance.

In order for programs to work, they have to be fully funded and supported. Again, these policies are left to the discretion of the districts. Measures that will end the school to prison pipeline need to be consistently enforced at the state and federal levels. The implementation of these protections on a school-by-school basis cannot produce the systemic change needed to remove the pipeline nationwide. In some cases, school officials are ignoring federal law. And parents and students are often unaware of their rights, making it difficult to resist things like zero-tolerance and push for change.

Part of the problem with any civil rights legislation is that there are always opponents and ways to get around the law. Federally mandated inclusive education has been in place since the 1970s. It is one policy that can provide some protections for disabled students, especially disabled students of color, but it cannot end discrimination against disabled people. Part of the problem is that the current laws do not provide all of the protections needed by students and parents. This does not mean that the protections that are provided should be removed, but it does mean that additional protections need to be fought for at the federal level. It also means that any protective policies need to be fully funded and supported in order to function properly. Since mandated inclusive education was passed 40 years ago, the federal government has failed to fully fund schools with special needs requirements. Books are outdated; there is a lack of supplies and teaching materials, as well as well-trained teachers, and the costs are shifted to states and local districts. So "special needs" students receive only the materials and services districts can afford—not necessarily what they need or what federal law dictates they should have.

It is also important to talk about how special education really is not a solution in the first place. Critics argue that special education has always been a place to send students to remove them from the school system, the job market, and society, in general. It is a form of social and economic segregation that has always been tied to incarceration. Fully funding and implementing the "mainstreaming" of disabled children is good. But we also need to listen to people from the disabled community who are looking for solutions that extend beyond "inclusive education"—solutions that seek to build upon that solid base.

Civil rights issues deal with unfair discrimination on the basis of characteristics such as race, class, and disability. Filtering students with disabilities into the prison pipeline and otherwise using school policies to discriminate against them is a violation of basic civil rights. At the federal level, legislation such as the Civil Rights Acts, the IDEA, and the ADA provide protections, but they are not enough to secure equal treatment in schools. While schools and districts are fighting to secure these rights more fully, more needs to be done at the state and federal levels to ensure that rights are secured throughout the United States, not just school by school.

States must look to systematically address the role of racism and discrimination in solving chronic inequities in the school system. Many individuals and groups take a similar position. Jane Dunhamn, the founder of the National Black Disability Coalition (NBDC), and the parent of a successful daughter with cerebral palsy, is an important leader in this area. Today NBDC is working on its National Campaign for Minority Disability Legislation and to get black disability studies into college and university curricula. Dunhamn asserts that addressing these inequities will require "reinventing and disrupting policy and practice." She also says that mainstream disability rights organizations and government agencies must actively work on these issues. The disability community must have a meaningful conversation about race, racism, and discrimination. Dunhamn's policy work has had a major effect on black and poor people with disabilities.

Due to a wide array of disability issues that are unique to poor people and people of color it is important to establish legislation that requires state agencies serving underrepresented disability communities to compile data and report to stakeholders. Despite the apparent lack of progress, we are hopeful that people are trying to find solutions. Ultimately, training more students of color who are disabled to become advocates, teachers, legislators, and policy makers would be the most ideal solution to the school to prison pipeline problem.

Leroy Moore, Jr., is the founder of the Krip-Hop movement, which produces hip-hop mix tapes featuring disabled hip-hop artists from around the world. He is one of the founders of the National Black Disability Coalition and the author of The Black Kripple Delivers Poetry & Lyrics. *Moore is the assistant producer of* Where Is Hope, *a film on police brutality against people with disabilities. He lectures around the world on the issues of race, disability, and social injustice.*

This article has been significantly revised from Kathleen Kiley, "Minority Students with Disabilities Fast-Tracked to Prison: Activist Leroy Moore, Jr. Talks Solutions," Huffington Post, *January 6, 2016. Available online at https://www.huffingtonpost.com/kathleen-kiley/minority-students-with-disabilities_b_8912862.html. Excerpted, revised, and reprinted with permission from Kathleen Kiley.*

4   Profiles

This chapter profiles selected people and organizations integral to the field of disability studies. Due to space limitations, it is just a sampling.

ADAPT

ADAPT is a U.S.-based disability rights organization founded in Denver, Colorado, in 1983. ADAPT is an acronym that originally stood for Americans Disabled for Accessible Public Transit. A group of disabled individuals known as "the Gang of Nineteen" formed ADAPT after several years of protesting the inaccessibility of public buses in Denver. The Gang of Nineteen were part of the Atlantis Community, an independent living community started in 1974 by disabled people and by Reverend Wade Blank, a nondisabled former nursing home recreational director who helped nursing home residents create their own community outside the institution. The Gang of Nineteen staged its first protest of inaccessible public buses on July 5 and 6, 1978. They used their wheelchairs and their bodies to prevent public buses from moving, chanting, "We will ride." Some protesters remained in the street blocking buses all night. That first protest has since been commemorated with an official plaque located at the site of the protest.

[Men in wheelchairs crowded into the free-throw lane on a basketball court, with one man shooting the ball] A basketball game between the United States and Turkey during the 2016 Paralympics Games in Rio de Janeiro. (Andre DurÃo/Dreamstime.com)

Throughout the 1980s, members of ADAPT used civil disobedience and direct-action protests to document and dramatize the inaccessibility of public transportation. They positioned themselves in front of buses so that the buses could not move, and they even got out of their wheelchairs and crawled up bus steps to show the inaccessibility of buses. ADAPT spread throughout the United States during the 1980s and came to include protests of interstate travel on Greyhound buses, as well as local public buses. Also during the 1980s, ADAPT sued the Chicago Transit Authority over the issue of inaccessibility in public transportation. ADAPT has long been considered the "militant wing" of the disability rights movement for its direct-action protests and willingness to engage in civil disobedience.

ADAPT is at least partly responsible for the passage of the Americans with Disabilities Act (ADA), which was signed into law by President George H. W. Bush on July 26, 1990. The ADA guarantees that all public transportation must be accessible to a broad range of disabled people, including wheelchair users, people with visual and hearing impairments, people with developmental disabilities, and people living on the autism spectrum.

With the issue of inaccessible public transportation apparently resolved through the passage of the ADA, ADAPT shifted its focus and changed its name in 1990. The acronym "ADAPT" now stands for Americans Disabled for Attendant Programs Today. Many disabled people depend on supports in the community and in their homes in order to live. Because so many disabled people are unemployed and live in poverty, they depend on government programs such as Medicaid and other support services paid for by the state. As the desire among politicians, legislators, and bureaucrats to eliminate state-funded systems of support has grown since the 1990s, many disabled people have seen their quality of life decrease, and many disabled people live in fear that they may be forced into a nursing home or other institutional setting, or even worse that they might suffer and die alone in the community. Since 1991, ADAPT has used lawsuits, petitions, public protests, and direct action to force lawmakers to recognize the needs and listen to the demands of disabled people who require assistance to live in the community.

Over the years, ADAPT has taken the leading role in protests such as the "Free Our People March" that occurred in Maryland, Delaware, and Washington, D.C., in 2003. It has also supported a federal bill known as MiCASSA, or Medicaid Community Attendant Services and Supports Act, which would give disabled people more power in determining how they use their Medicaid dollars. Each time Washington politicians threaten to cut support services and vital health care that directly affects the lives of disabled people, ADAPT descends on Washington, D.C., to represent the interests of those disabled people who rely on government programs for their survival. This happened in 2011, and again in 2017.

Reverend Wade Blank died in 1993, but ADAPT continues to thrive. It has chapters in 30 states and has two national headquarters, one in Denver and the other in Austin, Texas. ADAPT still engages in direct-action protest and civil disobedience, but it also uses its resources to initiate important lawsuits, and to educate the community and government leaders on disability-related issues. ADAPT has an active presence on social media, including Facebook, Twitter, and YouTube.

American Federation of the Physically Handicapped

A former labor organizer and legislative representative for the American Federation of Labor, Paul Strachan founded the American Federation of the Physically Handicapped (AFPH) in 1942 in Washington, D.C. Chartered as a nonprofit, educational, and beneficent organization, the AFPH "grew out of Strachan's personal experiences of being 'broke and dependent' after an automobile accident and several prolonged illnesses, and his vivid memories of how disabled World War I veterans had been cast aside once the embers of war and victory celebrations had faded" (Jennings, 2016, 2).

Mildred Scott, who joined the AFPH in 1943, became its national secretary and treasurer. Scott later recalled concerning the organization's leader, Paul Strachan, that she "had never met anyone before who was so convinced and determined that there must be a real program for the Nation's millions of handicapped, and, a militant organization to back it up." Scott described the AFPH as full of "faith and hope," and as working "for things that are right and just." She described her own activism within the AFPH as "a program which someday would bring about better conditions for the handicapped and the members of their families" (quoted in Jennings, 2016).

Although its emphasis would change over the years, the AFPH focused primarily on economic issues. It worked to create federal services to promote the employment of disabled people. It advocated for greater access to government employment. It sought general employment assistance for people with disabilities, and it advocated for legislation requiring employers to hire people with disabilities. The AFPH also called for a federal pension program for disabled people that would be linked to rehabilitation and provide direct payments based on the "severity" of one's disability. AFPH activists also "demanded improved access to health care and education, increased building access, better safety and hygiene programs, and federally funded research on various disabilities and potential treatments" (Jennings, 2016, 3).

The AFPH was a national, cross disability activist organization that began in the 1940s. As such it represents something new in the history of disability in the United States. Historian Audra Jennings, the foremost scholar of the AFPH, argues that the existence of the AFPH makes it possible to extend the timeline of the modern disability rights movement several decades into the past. Rather than think about the modern disability rights movement as something that began in the 1960s or the early 1970s, we can see that organizations that incorporated people with different types of disabilities advocated for their economic, social, and civil rights as early as the 1940s. The so-called social model of disability, which most disability studies scholars attribute to British activist organizations working in the early 1970s, was preceded by organizations such as the AFPH and others whose calls for social justice were as equally rooted in the elimination of social, cultural, environmental, and economic barriers faced by disabled people. As Jennings argues, "AFPH leaders claimed that all Americans with disabilities had much in common" (2016, 3).

Because of its broad-based organizing and its powerful focus on economic issues, and most likely because the AFPH's leader, Paul Strachan, came to disability rights through the labor movement, the AFPH had the support of prominent labor unions such as the American Federation of Labor, the Congress of Industrial Organizations, the United Mine Workers of America, and the International Association of Machinists.

Despite the wide birth of its organizing efforts and its broad conceptualization of disability rights, the AFPH had its limits. As its name implies, it sought only to organize people with physical disabilities. It did not consider people with intellectual or developmental disabilities, or mental illness as part of its organization. Because it took this stance, the AFPH made claims for civil rights for disabled people based on the perceived mental abilities of its members, a move that historians of disability have noted was common throughout the 19th and 20th centuries. People with disabilities and other marginalized groups like women or African Americans made claims for citizenship based on their ability to exercise that citizenship responsibly and effectively, which they argued could not be assumed for other marginalized groups.

The AFPH proved effective in its own time. At its insistence, the U.S. House of Representatives initiated a two-year investigation on "aid to people with disabilities" in August 1944 (Jennings, 2016, 11). As Jennings argues, the AFPH "used the hearings to highlight the failings of federal disability policy and the discrimination that disabled people faced on the job market and in education" (2016, 11). Among other accomplishments, the AFPH was instrumental in creating the National Employ the Physically Handicapped Week, which was implemented during the Truman administration, and is now part of a broader disability history month, which is observed every October.

Despite its initial promise and its relatively broad focus, the AFPH was a short-lived organization. It entered into a "twilight" (Jennings, 2016, 189) by the mid-1950s. A number of factors contributed to its downfall, including the "window of opportunity" concerning disability, which had been created by World War II, an increasingly conservative political landscape, "changes within the organized labor movement, and the growing prestige and power of medicine" (Jennings, 2016, 189). As Jennings has argued, the AFPH, which relied primarily on the American Federation of Labor and other labor organizations for its funding, "never found sure financial footing" (Jennings, 2016, 189) and when the social and political climate began to change in the early 1950s, it was no longer able to function.

Internal disagreements over financial issues, a lack of support among former allies, and the changing social and political situation contributed to the resignation of both Mildred Scott and Paul Strachan from the AFPH in 1957. The organization hoped to elect a new president at its annual meeting in 1958, but it could not overcome mounting problems. Its national offices "folded" shortly thereafter (Jennings, 2016, 212). Strachan, who battled cancer in the 1960s, died in September 1972 in George Washington University Hospital.

Clifford Beers (March 30, 1876–July 9, 1943)

Clifford Whittingham Beers was born in New Haven, Connecticut, in 1876, to Ida (née Cooke) and Robert Beers. Biographers characterize the young Beers as an average student who attended public school, but who could achieve at higher levels when challenged by instructors. White, male, and upper-middle-class, Beers was able to attend Yale and graduated from its Sheffield Scientific School in 1897. Throughout his undergraduate career, Beers was plagued by anxiety and melancholy. Following graduation, Beers went to work in New York City, where he continued to experience mental distress.

Beers returned home to New Haven in 1900 to convalesce with his family. Shortly after his arrival in the family home, Beers attempted suicide by leaping from his bedroom window. Although he did not succeed in ending his own life, he did sustain serious injuries, which required admission to a local hospital, where Beers experienced "hallucinations and paranoia" while recovering from his injuries (Parry, 2010). Beers's mental distress continued when he left the hospital and returned home to his family. He "gave up speaking" and became convinced that "he and his family were in grave danger" (Parry, 2010). At that point, Beers's family admitted him to a mental institution.

Beers spent the next three years (1900–1903) in Stamford Hall, the Hartford Retreat, and the Connecticut State Hospital at Middletown. Upon his release, he returned to New York City to work, but he continued to experience mental distress. He returned to Connecticut, spending the last few months of 1904 back in the Hartford Retreat. He left the institution at the beginning of 1905.

Appalled and discouraged by the treatment he received in various mental institutions from 1900 to the beginning of 1905, Beers set out to write a book about his experiences. The result was *A Mind That Found Itself: An Autobiography*, published in 1908. In the book, Beers wrote about the ineffective, neglectful, and abusive treatment that he suffered at the hands of untrained attendants and seemingly uncaring physicians. With strong endorsements from philosopher/psychologist William James and psychiatrist Adolph Meyer, both the book and Beers experienced almost immediate success and widespread influence in the mental health field.

Just two months after the publication of his book, Beers, along with the physician William H. Welch and William James, founded the Connecticut Society for Mental Hygiene, with the goal of improving "standards of care and attitudes toward the mentally ill," preventing "mental illness" and promoting "mental health" (Parry, 2010). Other states soon formed their own societies, and in 1909 Beers created the National Committee for Mental Hygiene, which focused on "legal reforms" and provided "grants for research into the causes of psychiatric disorders," as well as funding for the training of medical students (Parry, 2010). The National Committee also published the quarterly magazines, *Mental Hygiene* and *Understanding the Child*.

Along with his allies, and financial backers, Beers spent the next 30 years working to expand the mental hygiene movement that he created. As a white, male "articulate insider" of elite circles that included Yale graduates and prominent psychologists and psychiatrists, Beers was able to craft a successful reform and recovery movement with lasting legacies. Beers formed the International Committee for Mental Hygiene in 1919 and the American Foundation for Mental Hygiene in 1928. In 1930, Beers organized the first International Congress for Mental Hygiene in Washington, D.C. With 3,042 "officially registered participants" from 53 countries, and with "many more actually in attendance" the 1930 conference was, perhaps, the highlight of Beers' career (NASW, n.d.).

Beers continued his work throughout the 1930s, until in 1939 he became "overwhelmed" and "depressed" (Parry, 2010). In 1939, Beers committed himself to the Butler Hospital in Providence, Rhode Island. He died four years later in 1943. Beers had married Clara Louise Jepson in 1912. They had no children.

In 1950, the International Committee joined with the National Mental Health Foundation and the Psychiatric Foundation to form Mental Health America. Still in operation today, Mental Health America is the country's oldest and largest nonprofit organization "addressing all aspects of mental health and mental illness" (NASW, n.d.). It has 320 affiliates nationwide. In April 2018, the Clifford Beers Clinic—a mental health clinic serving children and families in the greater New Haven area—opened in New Haven, Connecticut.

Justin W. Dart, Jr. (August 29, 1930–June 22, 2002)

Justin Whitlock Dart, Jr. (August 29, 1930–June 22, 2002) was born into a wealthy Chicago family that included not only Dart Industries but also Walgreens (on his mother's side). Dart contracted polio in 1948 at age 18 on the eve of leaving Chicago to attend the University of Houston. The effects of the poliovirus left Dart unable to walk. He became a wheelchair user.

Dart's interest in social justice and activism emerged early in his life. While he was an undergraduate student at the University of Houston, Dart formed an "integration club" to combat the university's segregationist policies. Dart graduated with degrees in history and education in 1954. Following graduation, university officials refused to award Dart his teaching certificate despite his having fulfilled the requirements, because, they argued, he was too disabled to become a teacher. Following this setback, Dart briefly attended the University of Texas Law School, but dropped out to work in his family businesses and engage in activist work, which would last the rest of his life.

Though originally a Democrat, Dart left the Democratic Party to work on disability issues in the Reagan (who was a friend of the Dart family) administration in the early 1980s. In 1981, while still a member of the Texas Governor's Committee for Persons with Disabilities, Dart became a member of the National Council on Disability. He served on the National Council until 1984 and the Texas Governor's Committee until 1985. Dart then served as the U.S. Department of Education Commissioner of Rehabilitation Services from 1984 to 1987. The Reagan administration forced Dart to resign his position in 1987 when he criticized Department of Education management in congressional testimony. Following his stint at the Department of Education, Dart served as the chairman of the

President's Committee on Employment of People with Disabilities from 1989 to 1993.

Dart was an instrumental figure in the passage of the landmark 1990 ADA. His gender and race (white and male), his wealth, and his father's close ties to the Reagan administration made Dart an important person able to work with Washington insiders in drafting and passing the ADA. Although he was openly critical of both the Reagan and Bush administrations, Dart remained close to the Republicans throughout the 1980s and early 1990s. His important role in pushing the ADA through Congress and the White House is evidenced by his position seated next to President George H. W. Bush at the public signing of the ADA on July 26, 1990. This iconic image has become one of the most important historical artifacts related to the disability rights movement.

Dart shifted his official political allegiances back to the Democratic Party in 1994. In 1998, President Bill Clinton awarded Dart the Medal of Freedom, the nation's highest civilian honor. At the ceremony, Clinton said Dart had "literally opened the doors of opportunities to millions of our citizens by securing passage of one of the nation's landmark civil rights laws" (quoted in Stevenson, 2002). Throughout his adult life, Dart was a tireless and outspoken advocate for the rights of people with disabilities. As one reporter commented upon his death, Dart was "a longtime advocate for the rights of disabled people who was a familiar sight around Washington in his cowboy hat, boots and wheelchair" (quoted in Stevenson, 2002). Dart died at the age of 71 at his home in Washington, D.C. He was survived by 5 daughters, 11 grandchildren, and 2 great-grandchildren.

Disability Rights Education and Defense Fund

Founded in 1979 by a coalition of people with disabilities and parents whose children had disabilities and currently located in Berkeley, California, in the Ed Roberts Campus, and in Washington, D.C., the Disability Rights Education and Defense Fund (DREDF) is the oldest nonprofit organization providing legal advocacy, training, education, and public policy and legislative development to and on behalf of disabled people.

An outgrowth of the independent living movement and the broader civil rights and feminist movements of the 1960s and 1970s, DREDF made one of its first goals building strong alliances with the national civil rights leadership. In the 1980s, DREDF battled against a conservative federal government that sought to deregulate and defund important institutions, policies, and programs that directly affected the lives of people with disabilities. DREDF worked to maintain and enforce the important section 504 of the 1973 Rehabilitation Act, which, among other things, provided disabled people access to federally funded programs, and the Education for All Handicapped Children Act, which was renamed the Individuals with Disabilities Education Act in 1990.

DREDF also worked during the 1980s and 1990s to pass, maintain, or enforce important civil rights legislation, such as the 1986 Handicap Children's Protection Act, the Civil Rights Restoration Act of 1987, the Individuals with Disabilities Act Amendments, the Fair Housing Act Amendments, and the landmark 1990 Americans with Disabilities Education Act. DREDF played a crucial role in important court decisions such as the U.S. Supreme Court ruling in *Smith v. Robinson* (1984) and the lower court decision in *Board of Education, Sacramento City School District v. Holland* (1992).

DREDF began the 21st century by hosting an international disability law and policy symposium in Washington, D.C., sponsored by the U.S. Social Security Administration between October 22 and 26, 2000. The conference, which attracted 150 attorneys and legal advocates from 57 countries, was called "From Principles to Practice." Among other accomplishments, the five-day symposium marked the launch of "an international disability rights working group of attorneys, policy and legislative experts, and people with disabilities"; participants shared "ideas about laws and policies, enforcement mechanisms, and strategies for reforms"; they discussed "basic legal principles"; they identified "specific strategies and tactics that will advance legal reforms"; and they encouraged "communication among lawyers and advocates" (DREDF, n.d.).

During the five-day conference, participants from all over the world discussed "models of equality," definitions of disability as they were related to disability rights, the conflict between the charity model and the social policy model of disability, and the "emerging right under international and US law to community integration for people with disabilities living in institutions" (DREDF, n.d.). Participants from India, Germany, and the United States discussed community advocacy strategies. And antidiscrimination laws and policies were the topics of discussion among representatives from South Africa, Hungry, and the United States. There were also working groups on architectural accessibility, international development and civil society, transportation, employment under various social and economic circumstances, the United Nations convention on the rights of people with disabilities, and grassroots organizing and coalition building (DREDF, n.d.).

In 2012, DREDF lawyers secured an historic settlement in their case against Netflix, ensuring that 100 percent of the rapidly growing entertainment company's online streaming content (e.g., TV shows and movies) would be closed-captioned within two years, providing access to deaf and hard-of-hearing people and others who wanted to use closed captions. The case was especially significant because it established that the ADA applied to "online-only" businesses.

Judy Heumann (1947–)

Judith E. "Judy" Heumann was born to German-Jewish immigrant parents in Brooklyn, New York, in 1947. She contracted polio when she was only 18 months old. She has used a wheelchair all her life. Heumann faced discrimination based on her disability early in life. New York City public schools refused to admit her when she was a child, claiming she was a fire hazard. Judy's mother challenged the decision, and Judy was able to begin attending school in grade four. Over the next several years, Heumann attended Camp Jened, a summer camp for disabled children in Hunter, New York. While she was at camp, Judy met other disabled children who would become allies in the fight for disability rights.

Heumann became more involved in the disability rights movement while attending college at Long Island University in Brooklyn. Upon graduating with a teaching degree in 1969, the New York State Board of Education denied Heumann her teaching certificate, because, they argued, she would be unable to evacuate students in the event of a fire. As Heumann recalled in an interview, she passed both the written and the oral portions of the certification exam, but "failed" the medical portion of the exam, because she "couldn't walk" (DIA Interview). Heumann challenged the decision in court, and the judge recommended that the city of New York allow Heumann to teach. Following the decision, Judy began teaching grade school. She taught for three years. She was the first visibly physically disabled person to teach in New York City schools.

In 1970, Heumann and other disabled activists formed Disabled in Action (DIA) of Metropolitan New York. The organization was originally called "Handicapped in Action," but Judy and the other organizers agreed early on that the word "handicapped" was unacceptable. DIA, which still exists, continues to fight for disability rights and access, primarily in New York City. According to the organization's website, its mission is to "fight to eliminate the barriers that prevent [disabled people] from enjoying full equality in American society."

In the early 1970s, Heumann moved to the San Francisco bay area, where she earned a master's degree in public health from the University of California, Berkeley, in 1975. While living in the bay area, Heumann expanded her disability rights activism. She served as a legislative assistant to the chairperson of the U.S. Senate Committee on Labor and Public Welfare and was helpful in writing the Education for All handicapped Children Act (1975). She also served as the deputy director of Berkeley's new Center for Independent Living. Heumann later defined independent living as "allowing people to live their lives the way they want to live their lives where disability is not a handicap for them" (DIA Interview). While at the Center for Independent Living, Judy and other disabled people formed the group that would eventually become the Disability Rights Education & Defense Fund. Heumann and other disability rights activists also led the historic "504 Sit-in" at the San Francisco offices of the U.S. Department of Health, Education, and Welfare in April and May 1977. In 1983, Heumann and other leaders of the bay area disability rights movement formed the World Institute on Disability, which Heumann codirected until 1993.

Following her work in California, Heumann moved to Washington, D.C., where she became assistant secretary of the Office of Special Education and Rehabilitative Services in the Department of Education, a new position created under the Clinton administration. She served as assistant secretary from 1993 through 2001. In 2002, Heumann went to work for the World Bank as its first advisor on Disability and Development. She was also lead consultant to the Global Partnership for Disability and Development, and the director of the Department of Disability Services for the District of Columbia. In 2010, Heumann went to work for the Obama administration as its special advisor for International Disability Rights at the U.S. Department of State.

Heumann has won numerous awards, including an Honorary Doctorate of Humane Letters from Long Island University; an Honorary Doctorate of Public Administration from the University of Illinois, Urbana-Champaign; and an Honorary Doctorate of Public Service from the University of Toledo. On

January 20, 2017, Heumann left her post at the State Department and was replaced by paralympian Ann Cody.

Jerry's Orphans

In 1991, Chicago-based disability activist and former Muscular Dystrophy Association (MDA) poster child Cris Matthews and her brother Mike Ervin, who also had muscular dystrophy, organized a boycott of the MDA's annual Labor Day telethon. The MDA telethon was one of the oldest and most successful disability charity events. Hollywood comedian and movie star Jerry Lewis had been hosting the telethon since 1953.

Matthews and Ervin, and other disability activists throughout the country, who called themselves "Jerry's Orphans," opposed the telethon and Jerry Lewis because they promoted a view of disabled people as passive, pitiable recipients of charity incapable of working, and leading active independent lives. People living with muscular dystrophy, and other disabilities, were known as "Jerry's kids," forever dependent and incapable of growing up. Protesters specifically targeted Lewis for his demeaning, dehumanizing view of disabled people. He called them "cripple," and "half a person," and referred to wheelchairs as "steel imprisonment."

On September 1 and 2, 1991, "uncoordinated protests" loosely associated with 'Jerry's Orphans' picketed the MDA telethon in Chicago, Las Vegas, Denver, Charleston, Los Angeles, Detroit, Boston, and Minneapolis/St. Paul. The protesters wanted to reform the telethon and the MDA. They argued that "two thirds of 'Jerry's kids' are adults, [and they want] to be treated that way" (Longmore, 2016, 196). One protester's sign demanded "Dignity Not Charity." Demonstrators chanted "He sells pity day and night! Equal time for equal rights!" (Longmore, 2016, 196). Many of the protesters were veterans of ADAPT, well known as one of the more "militant" disability activist groups.

In October 1991, "Jerry's Orphans" leader Mike Ervin wrote to MDA executive director Robert Ross. Ervin stated in his letter that the protests would grow until Lewis was removed as the host of the annual event. Ervin also demanded that the telethon change its message to one that portrayed disabled people more positively as people living full lives. Finally, Ervin demanded the MDA put disability rights advocates on its governing board. By this time, protests against the telethon were mounting elsewhere. Evan Kemp, disabled and chair of the U.S. Equal Employment Opportunity Commission under the Bush administration, drew media attention when he spoke out against the telethon.

Protests continued throughout the early1990s. Kemp continued to speak out against the telethon, as well as the stereotyping and discrimination faced by disabled people. In September 1992, CNN's Crier & Company invited "Jerry's Orphans" cofounder Cris Matthews to a public debate about the MDA telethon with a disabled MDA spokeswoman and Nancy Mitchell, an economist with Citizens for a Sound Economy, "a right-wing advocacy group fighting for less government, lower taxes, and less regulation" (Longmore, 2016, 202).

Even though activists wanted merely to reform the telethon and not abolish it, media spokespeople harshly criticized "Jerry's Orphans." Media infantilized activists by referring to them as children or kids. They characterized the activists as a loud, ungrateful minority of disabled people. And they defended the use of pity and charity as legitimate means of support for disabled people. Robert A. Jones of the *Los Angeles Times* commented, "As long as the emotional currency [pity] translates into the real currency of cash, who cares?" (Longmore, 2016, 202). Disabled people and their allies cared.

"Jerry's Orphans" momentum began to wane in 1993, but scattered, loosely organized protests continued each year for the next 15 or more years, until finally Jerry Lewis retired from the MDA telethon and the MDA aired its last event on Labor Day 2011.

Helen Keller (1880–1968)

Helen Keller was born in Tuscumbia, Alabama, on June 27, 1880. She died June 1, 1968, in Easton, Connecticut. She was

87 years old. During her long life, Helen Keller was a well-traveled, outspoken social critic. Born into a relatively well-off southern family with a proud Confederate pedigree, Helen had the advantage of both informal and formal education from a young age. After becoming both blind and deaf, the result of an illness when she was only 19 months old, Helen began using her own version of "home signs." She traveled to Massachusetts in 1888 to attend the Perkins Institute for the Blind. In 1894, Helen and her lifelong friend and teacher, Anne Sullivan, moved to New York, where Helen attended the Wright-Humason School for the Deaf and the Horace Mann School for the Deaf. The pair moved back to Massachusetts in 1896, and Helen enrolled in the Cambridge School for Young Ladies. She then entered Radcliffe College in 1900. In 1904, 24-year-old Helen became the first deaf blind person to graduate and earn a bachelor's degree from Radcliffe.

The common, some might say iconic, image of a young Helen Keller learning to communicate at a backyard water pump with her friend and teacher Anne Sullivan is often the only scene from Keller's life that people can recount. Yet, like most disabled people, Keller led a much more interesting and complex life that extended well beyond this single mythologized moment. Keller, for example, remained an "active and visible participant in the American left" from the time she was at Radcliffe through the 1920s (Nielsen 2001, 268). Keller first became interested in socialism under the tutelage of John Macy, a Harvard lecturer and the husband of Anne Sullivan, during which time she read H. G. Wells's utopian novel *New Worlds for Old*. Keller joined the Socialist Party of America in 1909. Though considered radical, even at the time, socialism was not disparaged in the ways that it would be following the first red scare after World War I, and the rise of McCarthyism and the Cold War after World War II. Eugene V. Debs ran for president as a socialist in the election of 1912, gaining about one million votes. During this time, Keller also supported the radical labor union, Industrial Workers of the World, as well as women's suffrage, birth control, assistance for the unemployed, and the newly formed National Association for the Advancement of Colored People. She spoke out against war profiteers during World War I and urged men to resist the draft.

Keller remained active until her death in 1968, albeit in ways that diverged from her early radicalism. By the mid-1920s, Keller and her friend and lifelong companion Anne Sullivan were increasingly dependent on the American Foundation for the Blind (AFB), which had been created in 1921, for their income. At the time, the conservative businessman who led the AFB did not agree with or approve of Keller's radical politics. Although she would later, during the second communist red scare following World War II, speak out against the House Un-American Activities Committee, Keller narrowed her politics significantly beginning in the mid-1920s. For the remainder of her life, she worked nearly exclusively for the AFB. While this work essentially made Keller a spokesperson for "the blind," it afforded her the opportunity to become a national representative and an international star. As historian Kim Nielsen has argued, Keller "made a comfortable living [working for the AFB], visited over twenty foreign countries, met innumerable international figures, and was considered by the State Department one of the most effective public representatives of the United States" (Nielsen 2001, 278). Though she found what Nielsen calls her "civic fitness" challenged, Helen Keller was an important political actor and voice for a number of different marginalized groups during her lifetime, including people with disabilities.

National Association for Retarded Children

The National Association for Retarded Children (NARC) was founded in 1950 as the National Association of Parents and Friends of Mentally Retarded Children. According to the NARC's original secretary, Woodhull Hay, parents began to organize on behalf of their "retarded" children as early as the 1930s. By 1951, there were 125 organizations and 13,000 "active members" in the NARC (Hay, n.d.)

According to Hay, the NARC formed because state institutions, which had been exposed as overcrowded, dysfunctional, and in most cases dangerous, could not meet the needs of "retarded" children, and the "usual regular public school programs" were "unsuited" for "retarded" children. Parents and friends had become aware of advances in technologies for "mentally retarded" children, and they had begun to question and challenge the validity of the popular notion that nothing could be done for "retarded" children. Parents and friends sought more knowledge and information, and they felt that society had a responsibility to care for "retarded" children. Finally, they felt that "spiritually" they needed to do more than simply care for their own child or friend. They wanted to help others in similar situations.

In the early years of the NARC, each of the member or affiliated organizations had its own programs and priorities. Some organizations focused on improving institutions and institutional life. Other organizations focused their efforts on improving care at home or education in the schools. Clinics, classes, play and therapy groups, sheltered workshops, vocational training, and funding for permanent homes and communities were all things for which local NARC organizations worked.

The NARC, which was formally founded in September 1950 and ratified in early 1951, "embraced" all of these activities and all "retarded children" throughout the United States. It served as a "clearinghouse" for information, a sponsor of research and training, and a liaison with other organizations. It also represented the member and associated organizations in the formation of federal policy and programs.

Throughout its history, the NARC has gone through several name changes, reflecting the broader politics of what is considered intellectual or developmental disability in the early 21st century. Following is the chronology of the name changes: 1953–1973, National Association for Retarded Children (NARC); 1973–1981, National Association for Retarded

Citizens (NARC); 1981–1992, Association for Retarded Citizens of the United States (ARC); 1992–present, The Arc of the United States (The Arc). The NARC dropped the use of the word "children" in the early 1970s in response to the rise of the self-advocacy movement led by developmentally disabled adults. During the 1980s, the NARC, which became part of a global movement of people with intellectual and developmental disabilities, added the words "of the United States" to its name. Finally, in 1992, the NARC dropped the word "retarded" from its name, reflecting the disuse of that word among the general population and its disavowal among self-advocates, who recognized its negative connotations and long-troubled history.

National Association of the Deaf

Deaf and hard-of-hearing Americans came together in summer 1880 in Cincinnati, Ohio, to found the National Association of the Deaf (NAD). The organization's mission is "to preserve, protect, and promote the civil, human and linguistic rights of deaf and hard of hearing individuals in the United States of America" (NAD).

American Sign Language (ASL) was, and is, critical to the mission of the NAD. ASL developed over several decades in the early to mid-19th century. Deaf people had always used what have been called "home signs" to communicate with family and friends, and over the course of time, various regional dialects of manual communication emerged in the United States. In the first decades of the 19th century, Thomas Hopkins Gallaudet and other reformers and educators created residential schools to educate "deaf and dumb" children. Manual communication, or the sign language, became the primary mode of communication and instruction at these schools, which helped to foster a shared sense of community among students. As deaf education expanded throughout the United States, ASL became more systematic, until finally by the 1860s and 1870s it was the primary mode of communication for most deaf people.

Toward the end of the 19th century, proponents of oral communication and lip reading, such as Alexander Graham Bell, actively sought to suppress the use of ASL. The thought among many "oralists," as they were called, was that oral communication would make deaf people appear more "normal," and help them to fit into "mainstream" American society. Deaf people formed the NAD in 1880, partly in response to the rise of "oralism." The organization and its founders wanted to preserve their language, ASL, and their culture, and fight for the civil rights of deaf Americans, so that they might have the same freedoms, opportunities, and responsibilities as other citizens, including the right to speak their own language.

The modern NAD advocates on behalf of nearly 50 million deaf and hard-of-hearing Americans. Since 1969, the NAD has supported youth leadership and training programs. In 1976, the NAD created its Law and Advocacy Center. The NAD provides information and referral services, and through a grant from the U.S. Department of Education, it provides a Described and Captioned Media Program, which distributes open-captioned and described media on a free-loan basis to K–12 schools throughout the United States.

National Black Disability Coalition

Founded in 1990, the National Black Disability Coalition (NBDC) is a 501(c)(3) nonprofit organization that focuses specifically on issues related to black disabled Americans. The organization's membership comprises a mix of disabled people, parents, family members, faith-based organizations, other nonprofits, and academic and policy leaders. The NBDC is especially active in the Society for Disability Studies. The organization formed the same year that President George H. W. Bush signed the Americans with Disabilities Act (ADA) in a ceremony on the White House lawn. The NBDC formed to give black disabled people a space to organize around mutual concerns, and to redress the dearth of information and academic studies specifically concerned with black disabled people. The NBDC is "dedicated to examining and improving: community leadership, family inclusion, entrepreneurship, civil rights, service delivery systems, education and information and Black disabled identity and culture" by addressing both ableism and racism (NBDC, n.d.).

The NBDC is especially concerned with the ways in which race, poverty, and disability intersect in the lived experiences of black disabled Americans. Race, poverty, and disability affect everything from access to quality education, employment, and health care to the ability to participate in leisure and other activities. The NBDC seeks to promote unity among black people with disabilities, their families, and their communities, while at the same time advancing equity, social justice, and opportunity for black disabled Americans.

The NBDC has adopted strategies from the African American civil rights movement, as well as other social justice movements to promote "collective power and inclusion" for black people with disabilities, their families, black faith organizations, and the "greater disability community" (NBDC, n.d.). Longtime disability rights activist Leroy Moore, Jr., is a high-profile member of the NBDC.

National Center for College Students with Disabilities and Disability Rights, Education, Activism, and Mentoring

The National Center for College Students with Disabilities (NCCSD) is funded through a Fund for the Improvement of Postsecondary Education grant from the Office of Postsecondary Education, U.S. Department of Education. The NCCSD is part of the Association on Higher Education and Disability (AHEAD), the largest professional organization for postsecondary disability service providers in the United

States. Disability Rights, Education, Activism, and Mentoring (DREAM), started by then undergraduate Allegra Stout and graduate students Nev Jones and Michelle White in 2011, is a program of the NCCSD.

Founded and led by people with disabilities, the NCCSD serves as a clearinghouse of information for disabled students and their parents, as well as college professors and disability services offices on campuses throughout the nation and around the world. It also conducts its own research, which began with a literature review of over 25,000 articles, with the intent of finding and ultimately assessing and rating interventions and studies of disability in higher education. The organization publishes research highlights and research briefs on its website and through its own newsletter, as well as the newsletter of AHEAD. The NCCSD is the "only federally funded national center in the U.S. for college and graduate students with **any** type of disability, chronic health condition, or mental or emotional illness" (NCCSD, n.d. emphasis in original).

Originally formed under the Taishoff Center for Inclusive Higher Education at Syracuse University, DREAM moved to AHEAD in 2015 and became a program of NCCSD in 2016. In that same year, DREAM became a member of the National Disability Mentors Coalition and began its #DREAMMentorMonday program, "featuring guest mentors from the disability community on the second Monday of each month" (DREAM, n.d.). By 2017, DREAM had 10 active board members, an 8-student advisory board, and 7 affiliates and 3 chapters across the United States. Most DREAM activities take place online, through its website, and Facebook, Twitter, YouTube, Instagram, Pinterest, and LinkedIn accounts.

The creation of NCCSD and DREAM marks an important moment in the history of people with disabilities. They are national organizations founded and led by students with disabilities providing peer mentoring and support to their fellow disabled students, as well as valuable resources for college educators and disability service providers.

National Council on Disability

The National Council on Disability (NCD) was first established within the Department of Education in 1978. In 1984, the NCD was made an independent agency and "charged with reviewing all federal disability programs and policies" (NCD, n.d.). The NCD recommended the enactment of the Americans with Disabilities Act (ADA) in 1986 and introduced the first version of the bill into the U.S. House of Representatives and Senate in 1988. Since the enactment of the ADA in July 1990, the NCD has "continued to play a leading role in analyzing the needs of people with disabilities, crafting policy solutions, and advising the President and Congress" (NCD, n.d.). The NCD is also charged with preparing and submitting an annual report to Congress entitled "National Disability Policy: A Progress Report" that assesses the nation's progress in achieving the policies of the ADA.

The NCD is considered a "micro agency" (NCD, 2018) within the massive U.S. federal government. It has an annual budget of approximately $3 million. The NCD consists of 9 part-time council members and 12 full-time staff people. The NCD council members include five members appointed by the president, including the chair, and four members appointed by Senate and House leadership.

The NCD has many stakeholders. Its reach extends beyond the president and Congress. The NCD acts on behalf of all Americans with disabilities, their families, groups and organizations concerned with disabilities, employers, educators, service providers, designers and manufacturers, and other entities concerned with the inclusion and participation in society of Americans with disabilities. It reaches this large constituency through its quarterly reports and meetings, as well as through its e-mail listserv, which in 2018 had 2,420 subscribers; its Facebook account, which in 2018 was followed by over 30,000 people; and its Twitter account, which in 2018 was followed by more than 11,000 people. The NCD also posts vital information, resources, and accounts of its activities on its own website (https://www.ncd.gov).

In 2018, the NCD released its strategic plan for the next five years (FY 2018–FY 2022). One of its most exciting goals was to "gather information from subject matter experts and members of the disability community to help inform policymakers' work" (NCD, 2018). This particular goal is especially important, because since the early 1990s, disability activists and advocates throughout the world have lived by the slogan "nothing about us, without us." The idea that disabled people would no longer be talked about or talked down to is a core conviction held by many people within the disability community. Instead of being treated like second-class citizens, or worse yet, like they did not exist, disabled people would become central players in informing policies and other related matters that directly affected their well-being and their quality of life, as well as their access to the community, to education, and to employment.

The NCD's strategic goal of gathering information from subject matter experts and members of the disability community to help inform policy makers' work was motivated by the council's desire to balance the "hard hitting data" that must form the foundation of federal policies with the "on-the-ground" realities of disabled Americans. The NCD cited the experiences of people with disabilities during Hurricane Katrina (2005) warnings and response as an example of the importance of including this kind of strategic goal in its five-year plan. Emergency warnings were often inaccessible, but without a complete understanding of the lived experiences of people with disabilities, federal officials would have no way of knowing that their warnings were inaccessible. Disabled people perished as a result of inaccessible warnings and inappropriate or un-effective responses.

In its 2018 strategic plan, the NCD stated that it "endeavors to commission policy research projects that honor the blend of [subject matter experts and the lived experiences of people with disabilities] to offer recommendations that are inclusive at the outset of the input and feedback of the very individuals whom the recommendations are intended to service" (NCD, 2018). This is an important goal that shows the extent to which disabled people themselves and their close allies have been able to form important legislative and policy measures at all levels of government.

In the era of social media and virtual conferencing, the NCD will be able to meet its goals of including disabled people themselves, as well as subject matter experts in the creation of the materials and recommendations that it presents to both Congress and the president. It remains to be seen, however, whether Congress and the president honor the perspectives of their constituents.

National Down Syndrome Society

Barton and Betsy Goodwin, whose daughter Carson Goodwin was born with Down syndrome in 1978, formed the National Down Syndrome Society (NDSS) with their friend Arden Moulton in 1979. Originally headquartered in New York, the NDSS focused its initial efforts in the 1980s on two main areas: scientific research and dissemination, and outreach. The NDSS awarded postdoctoral research grants in science, which became known the Charles J. Epstein Down Syndrome Research Award. Awardees focused on investigating the causes of Down syndrome; the cognitive functioning of people living with Down syndrome; and the possible connections among Down syndrome, Alzheimer's disease, obesity, and leukemia. The NDSS hosted 14 scientific symposia during the 1980s, the first of which was entitled, The Molecular Structure of the 21st Chromosome and Down Syndrome. Although disability rights activists and their allies had been focusing for 20 years on advocating for the social model of disability and independent living, this effort by the NDSS to think about Down syndrome scientifically and biologically was decidedly more medical in orientation.

The NDSS balanced this scientific approach with what it called "awareness campaigns" that were more in line with the social model of disability. In the 1980s, the NDSS launched its Project Mainstream, which was funded by the Honeywell Corporation and focused on taking 12 kindergarten students with Down syndrome and placing them in a "typical" classroom as part of each school day. Inclusive K–12 education had only been legally mandated at the federal level since 1975. The NDSS's Project Mainstream was an early and effective way of promoting more inclusive classrooms.

The NDSS also began its Project Child during the 1980s. The program took inner-city children with Down syndrome between the ages of 6 and 12 and placed them for one weekend every six weeks with a family who lived outside New York City. The goal was to have inner-city children experience the suburbs and the countryside, while also enabling adults and families who might have had no exposure or minimal exposure to disabled children an opportunity to spend a weekend with a child with Down syndrome. The program was eventually recognized by the White House, which awarded it its Points of Light Award during the first Bush administration. The program was so successful that NDSS was able to collaborate with groups in Florida and California and expand nationally, eventually resulting in the creation of the NDSS Affiliate Network.

The NDSS continued what could be characterized as its social model organizing and advocacy work, and its scientific research during the 1990s. During that decade, the NDSS created its *News & Views* magazine, which was written for and by people with Down syndrome. The actor and self-advocate Chris Burke, from the television series *Life Goes On* (ABC, 1989–1993), became an NDSS goodwill ambassador and served as the magazine's editor. The NDSS also launched its Educational Challenges program, which was the first national survey of inclusive education for children with Down syndrome. In addition to these activities, the NDSS lobbied, with other disability rights groups, to pass the Ticket to Work and Work Incentives Improvement Act, which was a federal law designed to help people with disabilities gain employment. On the scientific side, the NDSS combined with two other federal agencies to launch a $3.9 million partnership to further Down syndrome research.

Since 2000, and the advent of increasingly sophisticated and effective genetic screening and reproductive technologies, the NDSS has worked to create a more comprehensive and positive image of living life with Down syndrome. It has launched its Changing Lives: Down Syndrome and the Healthcare Professional campaign, which aims to educate physicians, nurses, genetic counselors, and other health-care professionals on the clinical and developmental needs of people with Down syndrome. It has also created its Everyone Counts: Teaching Acceptance and Inclusion curriculum for grades K–6 to help encourage positive relationships among children with and without disabilities. It has also launched its most recent public awareness campaign, My Great Story, which "honors and celebrates" people with Down syndrome by highlighting their stories in an online storybook. At the level of policy, the NDSS was instrumental in persuading Congress to pass the Prenatally and Postnatally Diagnosed Conditions Awareness Act (Public Law 110–374). The act seeks to ensure that pregnant women "receiving a positive prenatal test result and parents receiving a postnatal diagnosis will receive up-to-date, scientific information about life expectancy, clinical course, intellectual and functional development, and prenatal and postnatal treatment options." The NDSS is currently working at the state level to pass measures that will enable the implementation of this law. In 2008, the NDSS began working with the newly created Congressional Down Syndrome Caucus to "support legislative activities that would improve Down syndrome research, education and treatment and promote public policies that would enhance the quality of life for those with Down syndrome" (NDSS, n.d.).

National Federation of the Blind

The National Federation of the Blind (NFB) was founded in 1940, when 16 people representing blind organizations from seven states (California, Illinois, Minnesota, Missouri, Ohio, Pennsylvania, and Wisconsin) came together in Wilkes-Barre, Pennsylvania, to form a national federation of blind organizations that would work to improve the condition of blind Americans. The NFB was formed in part in response to the earlier formation of the American Foundation for the Blind (AFB, 1921), which was a charity organization founded by philanthropists concerned with the plight of blinded World War I veterans. Unlike the AFB, the NFB was founded by blind people themselves and would maintain a majority of blind people in key leadership positions in the organization throughout its history.

One of the NFB's founders, and its president for the first 20 years of its existence, was a professor named Jacobus tenBroek (1911–1968). According to one of his biographers, "Dr. tenBroek was . . . a constitutional law scholar, a civil rights activist, a leader in the reform of social welfare, and a distinguished national and international humanitarian" (Blake, 2006). Born in Alberta, Canada, tenBroek attended the University of California (UC), Berkeley, where he earned an undergraduate degree in history in 1934. He went on to earn a graduate degree in political science in 1935, a law degree in 1938, and a doctorate of law degree in 1940. After spending time at Harvard Law School and the University of Chicago Law School, tenBroek returned to his alma mater where he became a professor. He earned the rank of full professor in 1953 and remained at UC Berkeley for the rest of his career. More than just a successful professor, tenBroek became a prominent blind civil rights leader, "typically [giving] about twenty-five speeches each year" by the 1960s (Blake, 2006). Though his life was cut short by cancer in 1968, tenBroek's scholarly and activist influence endured well beyond his own lifetime, in part through the organization he helped to create, the NFB.

During the NFB's early years, tenBroek led "federationists," as they called themselves, in their fights to gain Social Security stipends for blind citizens, as well as equal access to housing, transportation, public accommodations, and employment.

During the 1960s, the NFB split into two groups over a disagreement concerning the governing structure of the organization. One group believed the organization should be a loose federation with strong state organizations. The other believed in a strong national organization with affiliated state organizations. The group favoring a weak national structure banded together to form the American Council of the Blind (1961), which still exists in the 21st century. During this infighting, tenBroek resigned his presidency, which he regained in 1966.

In the 51 years since tenBroek's death, the NFB has become a multimillion-dollar organization, whose headquarters and research and education center in Baltimore, Maryland, span an entire city block. The "white cane," of which the NFB began promoting the use in the 1940s, has come to symbolize the organization and its mission.

Elizabeth Packard (1816–1897)

Elizabeth Parsons Ware (December 28, 1816–July 25, 1897) was born in Ware, Massachusetts, to Reverend Samuel Ware and Lucy Parsons Ware.

Samuel Ware was a wealthy, well-respected minister of the Calvinist faith who valued education. He enrolled Elizabeth in Amherst Female Seminary. Elizabeth excelled in her studies. She became a teacher in her school when she was only 16 years old. While at home for the Christmas holiday in 1835, Elizabeth began "having headaches and became delirious" (Burns, 2018). The family physicians treated Elizabeth in the family home, but the treatments seemed to have no effect on her. Concerned for his daughter's well-being, Samuel Ware committed Elizabeth to the Worcester State Hospital, an insane asylum. Although relatively brief, Elizabeth's stay in the hospital forever changed her relationship with her father, as well as her perception of what at the time was generally referred to as "insanity," and its treatment.

Although they had no prior romantic involvement or "customary courtship" (Burns, 2018), 22-year-old Elizabeth married 37-year-old Theophilus Packard, a friend of the family and a Calvinist minister, on May 21, 1839. The marriage had been arranged by Elizabeth's father with the intent of providing Elizabeth with the care and protection of a traditional home and husband, and ideally children. Conservative in their beliefs, Calvinists considered the proper role of women to be that of the obedient and submissive wife and selfless mother.

After moving around, Elizabeth, Theophilus, and their six children settled in Kankakee County, Illinois. Though generally content, their marriage was not without conflict. Both Elizabeth and Theophilus had strong views about religion and parenting, and neither was interested in changing their beliefs. Theophilus held traditional Calvinists beliefs, which rested upon the notion that man was the master of both wife and home and that because of Eve's actions in the Garden of Eden and Original Sin, both women and children were inferior to their male masters. Although raised in the Calvinist home, Elizabeth held more egalitarian ideals. She did not condemn marriage or motherhood, but Elizabeth believed that women "did not bring evil upon the world, children were not born with the original sin . . . predestination was not a truth, and it was possible to commune with spirits" (Burns, 2018). As one biographer put it, Elizabeth and her husband "were in total opposition" (Burns, 2018). Elizabeth believed that "a husband should be a woman's protector and allow her to have the right to her own opinions and beliefs, [and should] . . . support her in those rights" (Burns, 2018).

Their arguments at home had become so heated that Elizabeth began openly disagreeing with her husband's preaching in his own church during his sermons. This "prompted" Theophilus to "remove" Elizabeth from the general congregation and "put her" in Bible class, which was run by her brother-in-law, and was thought of as a place where children went to learn about the Bible (Burns, 2018).

The actions of her husband only served to bolster Elizabeth's convictions. According to a biographer, her removal to Bible class "had the opposite effect on Elizabeth" (Burns, 2018). She saw it as an opportunity to voice her beliefs without interference from her husband. She "made her viewpoints clear, that each person was responsible to God in their own way, and that each had the right to freedom of thought between their self and God" (Burns, 2018).

In 1860, after sending their three youngest children to stay with family and friends, Theophilus had Elizabeth declared insane and had her committed to the Illinois State Insane Asylum in Jacksonville, where she remained for the next three years. Elizabeth, who did not believe she was insane, resisted her commitment and continued to resist treatment while in the institution. She continually voiced her concerns to institution doctors and state officials, all the while surreptitiously recording her thoughts, as well as the experiences of other inmates, and events taking place inside the asylum on scraps of paper. When she was finally released from the institution in 1863, Elizabeth became determined to write a book about her experiences and fight for the rights of both women and inmates of insane asylums.

Initially, however, she would have to break free from her husband who attempted to imprison her in their own home upon her release from the asylum and continued to assert that she was "insane." Finally, after a well-publicized trial, a jury declared in January 1864 that Elizabeth was "sane." During the trial, Theophilus sold the family home and moved to Massachusetts. He refused to allow Elizabeth to see her children. Elizabeth too returned home to Massachusetts to live with her father. After receiving a letter from Elizabeth's father, Theophilus allowed Elizabeth to see her children, but only for brief visits and only if he was present.

For the next 30 years, from 1864 through her death in 1897, Elizabeth Packard would support herself by publishing several books. She toured the country going from state to state selling her books and advocating for the rights of married women and inmates of insane asylums. She was successful in establishing what came to be known as "Packard's Laws" in several states, including Illinois, Massachusetts, and Connecticut. Although she attempted to have similar laws passed at the federal level, she was not successful in Washington, D.C. Packard's Laws focused primarily on preventing the wrongful commitment of people to insane asylums and on the rights of inmates of insane asylums—the right to send and receive mail without having it monitored or censored, for example.

Although not widely remembered—like some other 19th-century reformers—Elizabeth Packard was an important early advocate for the rights of people suspected of being "insane" and for inmates of insane asylums.

Paralympics

Sport has been an important part of the lives of many disabled people for nearly 200 years. Deaf people in the United States have formed leagues and participated in organized sports since the 19th century. The early history of modern sport contains many stories of disabled athletes. Since the end of World War II, and even more recently, since the United Nations General Assembly declared 1983–1992 the Decade of Disabled Persons, disabled sports such as wheelchair basketball, road racing, track and field, tennis, and wheelchair rugby (known also as murderball), as well as many other sports, have become global events attracting thousands of athletes and spectators. The Summer and Winter Paralympics have become huge sporting festivals in recent decades. Advances in sporting technology are making ever more difficult athletic feats attainable, which will no doubt continue to enhance the integration of disabled athletes into nondisabled sport and increase the popularity of disabled sport among the nondisabled. Every year, the number of disabled athletes competing at the highest levels grows. These tremendous gains have affected (however unevenly) the lives of all disabled people in what most observers consider positive ways—increased awareness, access, and legitimacy; increased acceptance and inclusion; and a generally more positive public attitude toward disability and disabled people.

Modern disabled sport was born in the wake of a world war that left many soldiers impaired and searching for a way to "re-enter" civilian life. In both the United States and the United Kingdom, disabled sport began as a means of "rehabilitating" disabled veterans of World War II. In the United States, it began amid the cornfields of Illinois and was led by Timothy J. Nugent. In the late 1940s, Nugent, a veteran (though not disabled), formed a wheelchair basketball team for disabled male former GIs attending the University of Illinois. In 1949, Nugent and the University of Illinois hosted the first Wheelchair Basketball Tournament, which at that time was a small local competition. The following year, Nugent formed the National Wheelchair Basketball Association, which he led until 1973. In England, disabled sport began in much the same way. At the end of World War II, Ludwig Guttmann began using sport as a means of "rehabilitating" and "reintegrating" former servicemen (and a few service women) with spinal injuries. The first disabled sporting event, held at the National Spinal Injuries Unit at Stoke Mandeville Hospital in Buckinghamshire, coincided with the opening ceremony of the Olympic Games in London in 1948, an intentional bit of foreshadowing on Guttmann's part.

For the remainder of the 20th century and into the first decade of the 21st century, elite disabled sports grew from these modest beginnings to what it is today—an international community of more than 100 countries and thousands of athletes competing at the highest levels. The first sporting competition at Stoke Mandeville, which took place on July 28, 1948, was an archery competition involving a mere 16 competitors. Word spread quickly among disabled vets and hospital staff, however, and the following year, 60 competitors from five hospitals participated in the second annual Stoke Mandeville Games.

Throughout the 1950s, the games became increasingly international, with seven countries, including France, Israel, Finland, the Netherlands, Canada, the United States, and Australia, participating by 1957. By the end of the 1950s, participants informally dubbed the Stoke Mandeville Games the "Paralympics," initially because of the large number of spinal-injured (paraplegic) competitors. The name stuck, despite the expansion of the games to include competitors with other types of impairment, in part because the Greek preposition *para* means "beside" or "alongside," and it had always been the intent of the game's organizers to have them occur alongside the Olympics.

Although complications arose, usually around issues of physical access, the future of the Paralympics appeared promising in 1959—the year organizers formed the International Stoke Mandeville Games Committee. The Paralympics took place with the Olympics in Rome in 1960 and in Tokyo in 1964. The fate of the Paralympics relied solely on the goodwill of host cities and local sponsors, however, and following the games in Tokyo in 1964, one Olympic city after another refused to host the Paralympics. It would not be until 1988, 24 years after the Tokyo Olympics, that disabled athletes would compete in an Olympic host city. In 1984, the United States agreed to host the Paralympics, but not in the host Olympic city of Los Angeles. Instead, the games took place in Uniondale, New York, and after the University of Illinois withdrew its bid to host, at Stoke Mandeville in England. Established in 1976, the Winter Paralympic Games fared little better than the Summer Paralympic Games. They did not take place in the host Olympic city, either, and in most years they did not even occur in the same country as the Winter Olympics.

Determined to propel disabled sports into the realm of elite competition, the overwhelmingly male, nondisabled leaders of the Paralympic movement began during the early 1980s to intensify their organizing efforts and rebrand their sporting event. One of their first moves was to build a permanent "Olympic Village" near the Ludwig Guttmann Sports Stadium for the

Disabled at Stoke Mandeville in 1981, which physically separated the sporting facilities from the hospital and, in the words of one history of the Paralympics, physically separated disabled sports from the "notion of 'illness' " itself (Rembis, 2013). Over the course of the next decade, organizers and athletes consolidated their power and refined their sporting identity. In 1982, several sports organizations joined forces and formed the International Coordinating Committee of the World Sports Organizations, giving the disabled sports movement a unified voice for the first time in its history. The final phase of the institutional development of disabled sport occurred in 1989, with the establishment of the International Paralympic Committee (IPC). Throughout the next 10 years, the IPC would work out a formal relationship with the International Olympic Committee (IOC) that included, among other arrangements, a lucrative financial agreement. By 2001, the IPC and the IOC had created a "one city, one bid" policy, which compelled potential host cities to construct a comprehensive plan that would fully accommodate both the Paralympics and the Olympics.

An important part of the organizing of elite disabled athletics that took place during the 1980s and 1990s involved the formal integration of people living with various types of impairment into the Paralympic movement. Beginning in 1972, Paralympic organizers gradually allowed the inclusion of a broader range of disabled people in many of the sports included in the games. Women in the United States, for example, had been barred from participating in the all-male National Wheelchair Basketball Association until 1975. In 1988, at the Seoul Paralympics, leaders ratified the participation of all physically impaired groups, including those with spinal injuries, amputees, the blind, and athletes with cerebral palsy. Interestingly, in preparation for the summer games in Barcelona in 1992, often considered a watershed moment in the Paralympic movement, the organizing committee decided to reduce the number of events to 15, highlighting the most popular wheelchair events, and refused to allow mentally impaired athletes to participate in the games. Spectators, who were allowed free admission to the games, and the significant number of television viewers around the world would not know that mentally impaired athletes had traveled to Spain to participate in the Paralympics. Faced primarily with pressure from within the disabled community, the Paralympic organizers haltingly incorporated mentally impaired athletes into the games in Atlanta in 1996. The Paralympics had been formally integrated by the mid-1990s. In 2004, Athens hosted 3,806 disabled athletes from 136 countries, with a total of 1,160 female competitors—31 percent of the total number of athletes.

Ed Roberts (1939–1995)

Born in Burlingame, California, Edward Verne Roberts (January 23, 1939–March 14, 1995) is considered by many people to be the father of the modern disability rights movement. In 1953, when Roberts was only 14 years old, he contracted the polio virus. Although all four of Zona Roberts's boys fell ill that year, only Ed experienced the painful paralysis that is known to occur in about 1 percent of people who contract the virus. Ed spent the next nine months living in a hospital in the large, cumbersome breathing apparatus known as an iron lung and then spent another nine months living in a polio rehabilitation center. Ed finally returned to his family home when he was 16 years old. He would still have to live in the iron lung, which he referred to as his "tank" (Anderson, n.d.). Easter Seals, a prominent charity, funded Ed's home care.

Ed was determined to continue his education. The Soroptomists, a local women's club, provided a telephone and microphone and speakers so that Ed might continue his schooling from home. Spurred on by his mother, Ed began attending school part time. He completed his high school education when he was 20 years old, but the Burlingame High School administration would not allow him to graduate. They argued that Ed did not complete physical education or driver's education, both of which were required components of the high school curriculum. Ed's mother Zona was not swayed. She initially attempted to have Ed's in-home physical therapy count toward his physical education credits and when that did not succeed, she appealed directly to the school board, which ultimately exempted Ed from the physical education and driver's education credits and allowed him to graduate in 1959.

Ed then decided to go to college. With Zona at his side, Ed earned an associate's degree from the College of San Mateo. In 1962, Ed applied for admission to the University of California, Berkeley. School administrators initially rebuffed Ed, reportedly stating, "We've tried cripples before and it didn't work" (Dawson, 2015).

Despite this apparent setback, Ed was admitted to University of California, Berkeley, in 1962. He was not, however, allowed to live in the student dorms. The administration argued that his 800-pound iron lung, which he still required and which he slept in every night, was too heavy and posed a safety risk. Instead of living in the dorm, Ed was forced to live in an empty wing of Cowell, the campus hospital. This was not the only challenge Ed faced at Berkeley. Initially, the California Department of Rehabilitation refused to fund Ed's education. It deemed him "infeasible" (Anderson, n.d.) for employment. With the help of Zona and his former teachers and administrators from the College of San Mateo, Ed was able to gain media attention in California and force the Department of Rehabilitation to pay for his education at Berkeley.

Ed moved into Cowell and began taking classes. He hired his own attendant care workers and figured out ways to become as independent as possible on campus. He devised a creative way to operate a power wheelchair, for example, something his therapists told him he would never be able to do.

While Ed was at Berkeley, other students with disabilities arrived on campus and moved into Cowell. The disabled students made the old hospital wing feel like a college dormitory, complete with parties, drinking, drugs, and sex.

Dedicated to succeeding in school and forging a life for themselves after school, Ed and his fellow students formed an advocacy and activist group that they called the Rolling Quads, but that was officially known as the Physically Disabled Students Program. The group fought to make the campus and community more accessible and to provide disabled students with the support they needed to succeed at the university. They also created a Center for Independent Living that could provide disabled people with support in the community after they left college.

Ed's life was filled with many firsts. He was the first "severely disabled" student to attend UC, Berkeley, earning a bachelor's degree in 1964 and a master's degree in 1966. He and his friends created the first disabled students program in the country, and possibly the world. After graduation, Ed helped to found and served as the first executive director of the world's first Center for Independent Living from 1972 to 1975. In 1975, California governor Edmund G. Brown, Jr., named Ed to head the State Department of Rehabilitation, where Ed oversaw a staff of more than 2,500 employees and a budget of $140 million, and where he served until 1983. In 1983, Ed and his fellow Bay Area disability rights activists founded the World Institute on Disability, a disability policy think tank, research and consulting organization, and center for public education, training, and advocacy.

During his life, Ed traveled to Russia, Australia, Japan, and France, and across the United States to raise public awareness about disability rights and promote the philosophy of independent living for disabled people. In 1984, Ed received a MacArthur Foundation "Genius" Grant, which he used to pay for the activities of the World Institute on Disability.

Opened in Berkeley, California, in 2011, the Ed Roberts Campus is a nonprofit 501(c)(3) situated in a central public transit hub. This universally designed space is meant to provide a central meeting location for the ongoing efforts of disability rights activists and advocacy organizations, as well as a community site dedicated to the memory of Ed and others who fought with him to secure the rights of disabled people everywhere. The campus was opened with the intent of working toward what Ed called our "preferred future" (Ed Roberts Campus, n.d.)—a world where all people work collaboratively to promote social justice.

Society for Disability Studies (and Disability Studies)

In 1982, the Western Social Science Association (USA) created the Section for the Study of Chronic Illness, Impairment, and Disability, which became its own separate organization in 1984. In October 1986, the board of directors of the new organization renamed it the Society for Disability Studies (SDS). The SDS is a 501(c)(3) nonprofit organization based in the United States. It is the primary professional organization for academics engaged in disability studies research and scholarship. The SDS had experienced significant growth since its founding in the 1980s, growing from about a dozen people to an international organization whose annual conference drew more than 500 participants in 2015.

The SDS is responsible for publishing *Disability Studies Quarterly* (*DSQ*). In 1986, Irving K. Zola, university professor and first president of SDS, changed the name of the organization's main publication, the *Disability and Chronic Disease Newsletter*, to *DSQ*. *DSQ* grew from its humble beginnings as a newsletter in the 1980s to one of the most widely known and well-respected peer-reviewed academic journals in the field of disability studies by the turn of the 21st century. By 2015, *DSQ* was publishing dozens of research articles, essays, reviews, and creative pieces each year, which it made available through an "open-access" online journal produced in cooperation with the Ohio State University libraries. *DSQ* is unique among peer-reviewed academic journals, because it is made available for free online (http://dsq-sds.org).

The SDS has worked diligently to promote the academic field of disability studies. The number of degree programs and other initiatives has flourished at colleges and universities throughout North America, Europe, and the rest of the world. One study found that for the 27-year period between 1981 and 2008, disability studies course offerings in English-speaking North America grew a whopping 922 percent. In the United States, the United Kingdom, Canada, Australia, and New Zealand, there were, in 2008, 36 "full" disability studies programs, which grant the bachelor, masters, or PhD degrees in disability studies. There were an additional 31 "partial" disability studies programs that offered students modules, a minor, a diploma, a concentration, or a certificate. Disability studies degree programs, both part time and full time, experienced a growth rate well over 200 percent from the late 1990s to 2008 (Cushing and Smith, 2009). This phenomenal growth continued after 2008. A survey of disability studies degrees offered in the United Kingdom in 2015 revealed 40 different programs. Also in 2015, the University of Toledo, Ohio, launched the first full undergraduate major in disability studies in the United States. Administratively, most disability studies programs are located primarily in three general areas within colleges or universities: independent disability studies departments (primarily in the United States and Canada); hybridized disability studies programs that are integrated with other fields, including the applied fields (common in the United States, Australia, and New Zealand); and disability studies programs that are integrated into existing liberal arts programs and departments (common in the United Kingdom and the United States: Cushing and Smith, 2009).

Although some schools—mostly those in the United States—employ scholars with PhDs in disability studies, most programs recruit their faculty from a number of older, more well-established disciplines, such as English, history, and sociology. They also draw disability studies scholars from American, cultural, women's and gender, media, design, and science studies, and fields such as architecture, occupational therapy, and education. The two elements that unite this diverse group of scholars are an overriding interest in disability and the lives of disabled people and a strong commitment to using some variation of the social model of disability.

The social (occasionally called the socio-political) model of disability originated among disability rights activists in the United Kingdom in the early 1970s. Its primary purpose was to separate disability from impairment and say that disability was something that was socially created, while impairment was merely a biological fact with no cultural values attached to it. Under the social model, what became disabling for people was not their inability to walk, see, or hear, for example, but rather the inaccessibility of a physical, social, and cultural environment that remained hostile to their presence in it. As the British Union for the Physically Impaired Against Segregation explained, disability is "a form of [socially created] disadvantage which is imposed on top of one's impairment, that is, the disadvantage or restriction of activity caused by a contemporary social organization that takes little or no account of people with physical impairments" (quoted in Tremain, 2005, 187). Put simply, the social model of disability makes a critical distinction between impairment (body) and disability (society) and roots disabled people's limitations in societal barriers that disable them, not in any individual-embodied deficit. Disability studies scholars refer to this form of exclusion as "ableism." They argue that ableism and ableist attitudes are present in all societies that are built by and for nondisabled people (Goodley, 2011, 2014).

U.S. Quad Rugby Association

Since the mid-1980s, wheelchair rugby has developed into a well-organized competitive international sport that is part of the summer Paralympics. The U.S. Quad Rugby Association (USQRA) founded in 1988 helps to promote the sport by serving as its governing body and by representing the sport on the world stage, as well as through its efforts to schedule, plan and host events, and recruit and train new athletes. If they have the proper facilities, equipment, training, and expertise, any group of disabled people and their allies can form a quad rugby team. Often teams are associated with a city or community, or a college or university. The first quad rugby team in the United States was affiliated with the University of North Dakota. In 2018, the University of Arizona quad rugby team, the Wildcats, won the Division I national championship.

Wheelchair rugby, also known as murderball, and known in the United States as quad rugby, is an international wheelchair sport that has been around since the 1960s. Wheelchair rugby is played in wheelchairs, indoors, on a hard court, usually on a converted basketball court. There must be four players on each team on the court. Each player is assigned a point value based on his or her level of function. A team may only have a total of eight points on the court at any one time. To play wheelchair rugby, an athlete must have impaired function in three of his or her limbs.

The sport is played with a volleyball. The object of the sport is to score goals by carrying the volleyball over the goal line of the opposing team. Players can block one another and set pics like they do in other sports. Wheelchair rugby is a full-contact sport. Players are allowed to ram into one another with their wheelchairs in order to set up an offensive play, stop an advancing opponent, or dislodge the ball.

The first wheelchair rugby matches were played in the United Kingdom in the 1960s. Wheelchair athletes in Winnipeg, Manitoba, Canada, began participating in the sport in the mid-1970s. By the 1980s, wheelchair rugby had spread to the United States and Australia.

As of 2018, 30 countries participated in the international sport of wheelchair rugby. At the international level, teams are divided into three major zones: Asia/Oceana, Europe, and the Americas. In 1996, wheelchair rugby became a demonstration sport at the Paralympic Games in Atlanta, Georgia. The United States won gold, Canada silver, and New Zealand bronze.

Wheelchair rugby became an official Paralympic sport at the 2000 Games held in Sydney, Australia, where the United States won the gold medal, Australia the silver, and New Zealand the bronze. The United States won its next gold medal in wheelchair rugby at the 2008 Paralympic Games in Beijing, China.

In summer 2005, MTV films, Paramount Pictures, Participant Productions, and A&E Indiefilms released the low-budget documentary *Murderball.* The film, which provides viewers with an inside look at the U.S. wheelchair rugby team's quest for the gold medal at the 2004 Paralympic Games, became an instant favorite among audiences and critics, winning several prestigious awards. Nominated for an Academy Award, the film made an instant star out of its main character, quad rugby player Mark Zupan. Zupan went on to do a number of media spots and guest appearances, and in 2006 he released his own coauthored memoir, *GIMP: When Life Deals You a Crappy Hand, You Can Fold—Or You Can Play.*

Since the mid-1980s, the USQRA and wheelchair rugby have shown the world that people considered "severely" disabled can compete at the highest levels. Although the USQRA welcomes women athletes, it is dominated by men.

"Blind" Tom Wiggins (1849–1908)

Thomas Greene Wiggins was born into slavery on the Wiley Edward Jones Plantation near Columbus, in Harris County, Georgia, on May 25, 1849. His parents were Charity and Domingo "Mingo" Wiggins, slaves who were owned by Wiley Jones. After discovering that the infant Thomas was blind, Jones refused to feed or clothe him. Wiggins's mother intervened to save her son's life. Several months later, in 1850, Jones sold the Wiggins family to a Columbus lawyer and newspaper editor named James Neal Bethune. Some accounts refer to Bethune as a colonel, others as a general. According to Bethune family records, James Neal Bethune served as a lieutenant in the Lawhons County, Georgia, volunteers.

Because young Thomas was disabled, Bethune allowed his mother, Charity, to bring him into the main house, where she worked. While in the main house, Thomas encountered the Bethune children, who spent their time singing and playing the piano. Very early in his life, Thomas displayed an exceptional ability to mimic sounds, including the piano. By age six, he could play the piano from memory, exactly as he had heard other people play it. He soon started improvising on the piano, composing his own musical variations, which he claimed were inspired by the wind, rain, or the birds. Thomas enjoyed mimicking the sounds of animals, machinery, natural phenomena, and even people's voices.

Bethune quickly recognized Thomas's skill on the piano and immediately set about capitalizing financially on his slave's talent. In October 1857, when Thomas was only eight years old, Bethune rented a concert hall in Columbus and for the first time "Blind Tom" performed before a large audience. In 1858, Bethune "hired out" Tom to promoter Perry Oliver. It has been estimated that the Bethune family earned $750,000 through their exploitation of Thomas's labor, touring and playing the piano before live audiences. Thomas, who was only nine years old when his work began, was separated from his family and was made to tour hundreds of cities in the United States and Europe, sometimes performing four shows per day.

During his performances, Thomas would play many of the classics. He would also engage in gimmicks, like playing with his back to the piano and his hands crossed over one another. He engaged in audience challenges in which he reproduced songs note for note after hearing them only one time. Thomas was able to offer the perfect bass accompaniment to the higher treble notes when someone else played them. Often, Thomas would take over during these duets and play the composition entirely on his own. He also mimicked famous people's voices and the sounds of animals. The highlight of Thomas's early career came when President Buchanan invited him to perform at the White House on the eve of the Civil War. After the Civil

War began, Thomas performed almost exclusively in the South, raising funds for the Confederate Army, which drew criticism from some African Americans.

Thomas composed what may well be his most famous piece, "Battle of Manasses," during the Civil War. The North Carolina *Fayetteville Observer* wrote of one of his performances on May 19, 1862: "The blind negro Tom has been performing here to a crowded house. . . . He performs many pieces of his own conception—one, his 'Battle of Manasses,' may be called picturesque and sublime, a true conception of unaided, blind musical genius."

Anticipating the demise of the Confederate states, General Bethune convinced Thomas's parents, Domingo and Charity, to indenture Tom until he reached the age of 21. Tom would receive food, shelter, musical instruction, and an allowance of $20 a month in exchange for his performances. Thomas's parents would receive $500 a year plus food and shelter. Bethune would retain over 90 percent of the remaining profits—an estimated $18,000 a year—from Thomas's performances.

In 1869, Thomas crossed paths with Mark Twain, who was on his own lecture tour. Twain reportedly attended Thomas's concerts three nights in a row. Twain later wrote in the San Francisco *Alta* that Thomas:

> . . . lorded . . . over the emotions of his audience like an autocrat. He swept them like a storm, with his battle-pieces; he lulled them to rest again with melodies as tender as those we hear in dreams; he gladdened them with others that rippled through the charmed air as happily and cheerily as the riot the linnets make in California woods; and now and then he threw in queer imitations of the tuning of discordant harps and fiddles, and the groaning and wheezing of bag-pipes, that sent the rapt silence into tempests of laughter. And every time the audience applauded when a piece was finished, this happy innocent joined in and clapped his hands, too, and with vigorous emphasis.

Twain concluded his account of "Blind Tom" with the following comment:

> Some archangel, cast out of upper Heaven like another Satan, inhabits this coarse casket; and he comforts himself and makes his prison beautiful with thoughts and dreams and memories of another time. . . . It is not Blind Tom that does these wonderful things and plays this wonderful music—it is the other party.

Twain maintained an ongoing interest in Thomas's performances. In *Following the Equator* (1897), Twain wrote:

> The talk passed from the boomerang to dreams—usually a fruitful subject, afloat or ashore—but this time the output was poor. Then it passed to instances of extraordinary memory—with better results. Blind Tom, the negro pianist, was spoken of, and it was said that he could accurately play any piece of music, howsoever long and difficult, after hearing it once; and that six months later he could accurately play it again, without having touched it in the interval.

On Tom's 21st birthday and end of his indenture, General Bethune filed a petition with the court to declare Thomas insane, so that he might retain legal guardianship over the young man and his wealth. The courts complied.

After the Civil War, General Bethune moved his family to a 420-acre estate called Elway about three miles outside of Warrenton, Virginia. At Elway Thomas had his own room and his own Steinway concert grand piano. For the next 20 years, Thomas spent the summers between concert tours on the Virginia estate.

September brought the return of the concert season and his tour manager, to whom Thomas would protest, "Tell him to go to hell. . . . Tom ain't coming!" Thomas apparently enjoyed his quiet life on the farm and did not want to leave. Despite his protests, Thomas toured year after year for the remainder of the 19th century.

During the 1880s, custody of Thomas became an issue for those people in his life seeking to control him and his wealth. John Bethune, the general's son, who had grown up with Thomas, toured with him and took over the management of his career, ensuring that the wealth Thomas generated would remain within the Bethune family. Things became complicated when John married Eliza Stutzbach, and the marriage disintegrated a short while later, with Eliza claiming that John had deserted her. Before the issue of their divorce and the custody of Thomas could be settled, John Bethune died in a tragic train accident in February 1884. John's will barred Eliza from receiving any inheritance, stating she was a "heartless adventuress who sought to absorb his estate." Upon the reading of the will, a battle for the control of Thomas ensued between Eliza and John's father, General Bethune. Eliza, who had convinced Thomas's elderly mother, Charity, to support her ultimately gained custody of Thomas, who was now nearly 40 years old, on July 30, 1887. Reportedly disappointed and grief stricken at the thought of having to leave Virginia and the general, Thomas threatened to "fight them all." But, because of his race and disability, he had no say in the matter.

Now a source of income for Eliza, she promoted Thomas as "the last slave set free by order of the Supreme Court of the United States." "Blind Tom's" performances continued until 1904. He spent the last days of his life in seclusion, playing the piano and holding imaginary receptions. Thomas died on June 13, 1908, at Eliza's home in Hoboken, New Jersey. He was 59 years old.

Throughout his life, "Blind Tom" toured the United States, Canada, Great Britain, Scotland, continental Europe, and South America. His repertoire included about 7,000 pieces, with approximately 100 of his own composition. Over the years, he added the coronet, French horn, and flute to his list of instruments. When medical examiners asked Thomas in the 1860s how he was able to play the piano so well, he responded, "God taught Tom."

World Institute on Disability

Longtime disability rights activists Judy Heumann, Joan Leon, and Ed Roberts founded the World Institute on Disability (WID) as a private, nonprofit corporation in 1983. In 2018, the WID executive director was Anita Shafer Aaron. Before joining WID, Aaron worked nearly 20 years as executive director/CEO of the LightHouse for the Blind and Visually Impaired, headquartered in San Francisco. Under Aaron's leadership, WID plans to strengthen its ongoing mission.

Since its inception, WID has made issues related to personal attendant services a priority; it conducts an extensive research program, engages in policy analysis, and provides technical assistance and public education. No matter what terminology one uses—home care, attendant services, in-home supportive services, homemaker services, long-term care—the issues for many disabled people are the same: the services are usually not available in a way that is appropriate and affordable to the people who need them. The lack of availability of qualified, well-trained, well-paid in-home support workers is made more salient when the federal government cuts funding to or eliminates programs altogether upon which disabled people rely for services. In most cases, when services are cut, in-home support work falls on the backs of family members, especially female family members. Many people also find themselves forced to make do without the services they need and can experience unnecessary isolation, unemployment, deteriorating health, and institutionalization.

The WID has conducted research on personal attendant services since the organization was founded in 1983. It completed its first 50-state survey in 1987. The report and an executive summary, as well as other documents related to the

1987 survey, can be found in the disability rights and independent living movement archive located in the Bancroft Library at the University of California, Berkeley. In 1988, the WID completed a more in-depth study of personal care attendant services in California, Colorado, Connecticut, Massachusetts, and Missouri. This study was followed up by a three-year comparative study of personal attendant delivery systems, which was funded by the National Institute of Disability and Rehabilitation Research. The study focuses on comparisons of cost and advantages and disadvantages of different service delivery models.

The WID uses its research on attendant care services to inform its constituents through a quarterly newsletter that reports on developments at both the state and federal levels and discusses major policy concerns. Representatives of the WID also present information at conferences around the United States and internationally.

In addition to knowledge production and distribution, the WID engages in the day-to-day work of providing technical support to organizations and individuals dealing with personal attendant care service issues. Some examples of organizations that it has worked with in the past include the National Council on the Handicapped (created in 1978, the name was changed to the National Council on Disability in 1988), the Department of Rehabilitation of the state of Illinois, the University of Pennsylvania, and the University of California, San Francisco.

Over the years, the WID has also been concerned with access to affordable health care. It received a major grant from the National Institute of Disability and Rehabilitation Research to develop four policy bulletins on health insurance and disability issues from a "consumer perspective." The bulletins covered four major topics: (1) comparison of different approaches to health insurance in the United States, (2) "characteristics" of persons with disabilities or chronic illness, (3) limitations of existing financing and delivery systems as they relate to people with disabilities and chronic illnesses, and (4) international comparisons of health-care systems as they affect people living with disabilities and chronic illnesses.

The WID has always been at the forefront of the growing global disability rights movement. Although significant differences exist from one country to the next, there are many commonalities that disabled people share, despite their geographical location. In the past, WID received federal grants and collaborated with Rehabilitation International to promote cooperation and exchange of information between the United States and other countries.

In addition to these important areas, the WID has been active over the years in the independent living movement, in issues related to aging and disability, in issues related to public transportation and supported employment, and also in empowering disabled people from diverse ethnic and religious backgrounds. Initially funded by a MacArthur Genius grant awarded to Ed Roberts in 1984, the WID has gone on to become one of the world leaders in the growing global disability rights movement.

References

Anderson, Angela. n.d. "Ed Roberts: The Father of Independent Living." *FoundSF*. http://www.foundsf.org/index.php?title=Ed_Roberts:_The_Father_of_Independent_Living (Accessed May 7, 2018).

Blake, Lou Ann. May 2006. "Who Was Jacobus tenBroek?" *Braille Monitor*. https://nfb.org/images/nfb/publications/bm/bm06/bm0605/bm060503.htm (Accessed September 5, 2017)

Burns, Phyllis Doyle. 2018. "Elizabeth Ware Packard—Advocate for Rights of Women and the Mentally Ill." https://owlcation.com/humanities/Elizabeth-Ware-Packard-Advocate-for-rights-of-women-and-the-mentally-ill (Accessed May 7, 2018).

Clifford Beers Clinic. "About." http://www.cliffordbeers.org/ about-us/ (Accessed May 6, 2018).

Cushing, Pamela, and Tyler Smith. 2009. "A Multinational Review of English-Language Disability Studies Degrees and Courses." *Disability Studies Quarterly* 29(3): n.p.

Dashu, Max. 2014. "Elizabeth Packard's Fight against Legal Tyranny of Husbands." http://www.sourcememory.net/ veleda/?p=757 (Accessed May 7, 2018).

Dawson, Victoria. 2015. "Ed Roberts' Wheelchair Records a Story of Obstacles Overcome." https://www .smithsonianmag.com/smithsonian-institution/ed-roberts-wheelchair-records-story-obstacles-overcome-180954531/ (Accessed May 7, 2018).

DIA. "A Discussion with Judy Heumann on Independent Living." http://www.disabledinaction.org/heumann .html#introduction (Accessed September 3, 2017).

DREAM. n.d. "DREAM Organizational History." https:// www.dreamcollegedisability.org/history-of-dream.html (Accessed May 15, 2018).

DREDF. 2012. "DREDF Secures Historic Settlement in *National Association of the Deaf, et al. v. Netflix.*" https:// dredf.org/2012/10/10/dredf-secures-historic-settlement-in-national-association-of-the-deaf-et-al-v-netflix/ (Accessed May 10, 2018).

DREDF. n.d. "From Principles to Practice." https://dredf.org/ legal-advocacy/international-disability-rights/principles-practice/ (Accessed May 10, 2018).

Ed Roberts Campus. n.d. "Home." https://www .edrobertscampus.org (Accessed May 7, 2018).

Elliott, J. Michael. 1995. "Edward V. Roberts, 56, Champion of the Disabled." *New York Times.* https://www.nytimes .com/1995/03/16/obituaries/edward-v-roberts-56-champion-of-the-disabled.html (Accessed May 7, 2018).

Goodley, Dan. 2011 *Disability Studies: An Interdisciplinary Introduction*. Los Angeles, CA: SAGE.

Goodley, Dan. 2014. *Dis/Ability Studies: Theorising Disablism and Ableism*. Abingdon, Oxon; New York: Routledge.

Hay, Woodhull. n.d. "Associations of Parents and Friends of Mentally Retarded Children." *The Arc*. http://www.thearc.org/who-we-are/history/hay-account (Accessed September 5, 2017).

Jennings, Audra. 2016. *Out of the Horrors of War: Disability Politics in World War II America*. Philadelphia: University of Pennsylvania Press.

Longmore, Paul K. 2016. *Telethons: Spectacle, Disability, and the Business of Charity*. New York: Oxford University Press.

NAD. *America's Charities*. https://www.charities.org/charities/national-association-deaf-nad (Accessed September 5, 2017).

NASW. n.d. "NASW Social Work Pioneers: Clifford Whittingham Beers (1876–1943)." http://www.naswfoundation.org/pioneers/cliffordwhittingtonbooth.htm (Accessed May 6, 2018).

National Black Disability Coalition. http://www.blackdisability.org (Accessed September 9, 2017).

National Council on Disability (NCD). 2018. "STRATEGIC PLAN." https://www.ncd.gov/Accountability/strategicplan (Accessed May 12, 2018).

National Council on Disability (NCD). n.d. "About Us." https://www.ncd.gov/about (Accessed May 12, 2018).

NCCSD. n.d. "Home." http://www.nccsdonline.org (Accessed May 15, 2018).

NDSS History, NATIONAL DOWN SYNDROME SOCIETY (NDSS). https://www.ndss.org/our-story/ndss-history/ (Accessed December 24, 2018).

Nielsen, Kim. 2001. "Helen Keller and the Politics of Civic Fitness." In Longmore, Paul K., and Lauri Umansky, eds. *The New Disability History: American Perspectives*, 268–290. New York: New York University Press.

Parry, Manon. 2010. "From a Patient's Perspective: Clifford Whittingham Beers' Work to Reform Mental Health Services." *American Journal of Public Health* 100(12): 2356–2357. doi: 10.2105/AJPH.2010.191411.

Rembis, Michael. 2013. "Athlete First: A Note on Passing, Disability, and Sport." In Brune, Jeffrey A., and Daniel J. Wilson, eds. *Disability and Passing: Blurring the Lines of Identity*, 111–141. Philadelphia: Temple University Press.

Schmidt, Barbara. "Archangels Unaware: The Story of Thomas Bethune Also Known as Thomas Wiggins Also Known as "Blind Tom," (1849–1908)." http://www.twainquotes.com/archangels.html (Accessed August 8, 2017).

Science Museum. n.d. "Elizabeth Ware Packard (1816–97)." http://brought tolife.sciencemuseum.org.uk/broughttolife/people/elizabethwarepackard (Accessed May 7, 2018).

Stevenson, Richard W. June 24, 2002. "Justin Dart Jr., 71, Advocate for Rights of Disabled People." *The New York Times*. http://www.nytimes.com/2002/06/24/us/justin-dart-jr-71-advocate-for-rights-of-disabled-people.html (Accessed August 30, 2017).

Tremain, Shelley. 2005. *Foucault and the Government of Disability*. Ann Arbor, MI: University of Michigan Press.

World Institute on Disability (WID). *Independent Living Institute*. https://www.independentliving.org/toolsforpower/tools39.html (Accessed May 10, 2018).

World Institute on Disability (WID). *Philanthropedia*. https://www.myphilanthropedia.org/top-nonprofits/national/people-with-disabilities/2011/world-institute-on-disability-wid (Accessed May 10, 2018).

5 Data and Documents

Introduction

This chapter provides a quick look at important data and documents that relate directly to the lives of people with disabilities in the United States. It shows the number of disabled people within the total population, the breakdown of different disability groups, the median monthly earning of disabled people, employment statistics, the percentage of disabled people living in "persistent poverty," and the distribution of disability according to place and race/ethnicity. The documents contained within this chapter are a mix of legislative measures, court decisions, and important cultural artifacts. They are meant to give a sense of the history of the legal enfranchisement of disabled people and also of the significant amount of work that still remained after 50 years of concerted efforts at including people with disabilities in American society. There is no doubt that disabled people living in the 21st century had better lives than disabled people living 50 or 100 years earlier, but most disabled people continued, even in the 21st century, to live with endemic poverty and isolation, and a general lack of opportunities to better their living conditions. Factors such

[A sunny, warm summer day] A young boy in shorts and a T-shirt, in his wheelchair, participates in the first annual Disability Pride Parade in New York City on July 12, 2015. The parade called attention to the rights of people with disabilities and coincided with the 25th anniversary of the Americans with Disabilities Act. (Stephanie Keith/Getty Images)

as gender, race, and geographic location significantly affected people's experiences with disability. These data and documents will provide an excellent starting place for your own research. Each document has its own brief introduction.

Data

As Table 5.1 indicates, Americans reported many different types of disability. People could report having more than one disability. About 31 million Americans reported mobility impairments, including using a wheelchair. About 25 million Americans reported having difficulty completing important activities of daily living. About 20 million people said they had trouble lifting or grasping. About 8 million people reported difficulty hearing, with about 5.6 million Americans using hearing aids. About 7 million Americans reported that depression or anxiety interfered with activities of daily living. Approximately 8 million Americans have visual impairments, with about 2 million reporting blindness. Nearly 3 million Americans are living with the effects of Alzheimer's, senility, or dementia.

Table 5.1   Types of Disability

Disability	Number of People Reporting Disability (in millions)
Mobility	31
Difficulty with activities of daily living	25
Lifting and grasping	20
Hearing	8
Depression and anxiety	7
Vision	6
Blind	2
Alzheimer's, senility, dementia	3

Source: https://www.census.gov/newsroom/releases/archives/miscellaneous/cb12-134.html

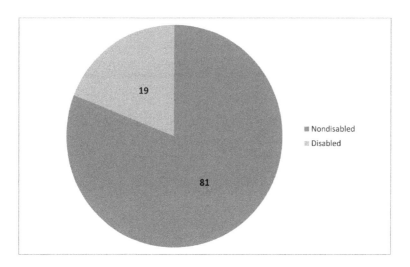

Figure 5.1   Percentage of U.S. Population Identified as Disabled

According to the 2010 census, 56.7 million people or 19 percent of the U.S. population are disabled, making it the largest minority group in the country. More than half of the disabled people reporting stated that their disability was "severe."

Source: https://www.census.gov/newsroom/releases/archives/miscellaneous/cb12-134.html

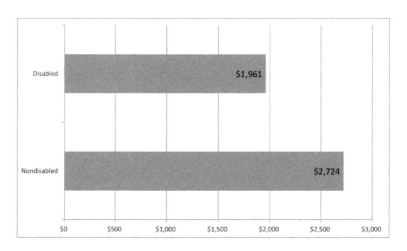

Figure 5.2   Median Monthly Income of Adults with Disabilities

According to the 2010 census, adults age 21 to 64 with disabilities had median monthly earnings of $1,961 compared with $2,724 for nondisabled adults in the same age group.

Source: https://www.census.gov/newsroom/releases/archives/miscellaneous/cb12-134.html

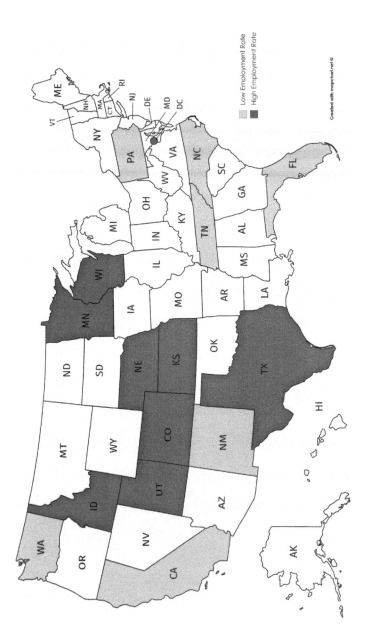

Figure 5.3 Disability Demographics

According to the Brookings Institute and the American Community Survey, 9 percent of adults age 25 to 54 or 11 million Americans reported at least one of six disabilities in 2016. The study also showed that disability is disproportionately concentrated in the Southeast, Midwest, and Appalachian areas, the so-called disability belt, and that people with disabilities have disproportionately low levels of education and income. The study also showed that "at the national level, Native Americans have the highest disability rate [of disability] among working-age adults (16 percent), followed by blacks (11 percent), whites (9 percent), Hispanics (7 percent), and Asians (4 percent)."

Source: https://www.brookings.edu/blog/the-avenue/2018/07/25/only-four-out-of-ten-working-age-adults-with-disabilities-are-employed/

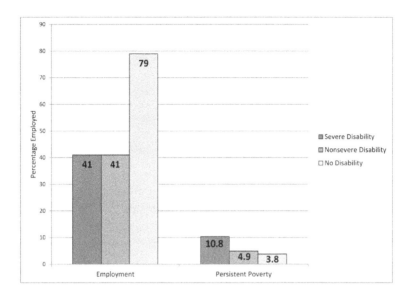

Figure 5.4   Employment of Adults with Disabilities

According to the 2010 census, 41 percent of adults aged 21 to 64 with any disability reported being employed, compared to 79 percent of nondisabled adults in the same age group. About 10.8 percent of severely disabled Americans experienced persistent poverty, while about 4.9 percent of Americans with "nonsevere" disabilities experienced persistent poverty and about 3.8 percent of nondisabled Americans experienced persistent poverty. Census takers defined "persistent poverty" as consistent poverty over a 24-month period.

Source: https://www.census.gov/newsroom/releases/archives/miscellaneous/cb12-134.html

Documents

Section 504 of the Rehabilitation Act (1973)

Disappointed that the 1964 Civil Rights Act did not include disability, disability activists continued to work at the local, state, and federal levels to secure legislation that would protect the rights of disabled citizens. By 1970, four states, Illinois, Wisconsin, New York, and Alaska, passed their own civil rights measures for people with disabilities. Although it was not viewed as the ideal means through which to secure civil rights for people with disabilities at the federal level, the reauthorization of the Federal Rehabilitation Act in 1972 provided an opportunity for disability rights activists and their allies in Congress to secure a federal mandate. During revisions of the bill that would become the 1973 Rehabilitation Act, congressional aides who were sympathetic to disability rights activists demands for equal protection under the law added Section 504, which stated in part: "No otherwise qualified handicapped individual in the United States shall, solely by reason of his handicap, be excluded from participation in, be denied the benefits of, or be subjected to discrimination under any program or activity receiving Federal financial assistance." Following two vetoes, President Nixon signed the Federal Rehabilitation Act on September 26, 1973. Although it was limited to entities receiving federal financial assistance, and it would prove difficult to enforce, Section 504 of the 1973 Rehabilitation Act was a major victory in the battle for civil rights for disabled Americans. Congress amended the Rehabilitation Act in December 2015. Following is an excerpt from the amended text of the act.

Section 794. Nondiscrimination under Federal Grants and Programs; Promulgation of Rules and Regulations

(a) Promulgation of Rules and Regulations

No otherwise qualified individual with a disability in the United States, as defined in section 705 (20) of this title, shall, solely by reason of his or her disability, be excluded from the participation in, be denied the benefits of, or be subjected to discrimination under any program or activity receiving Federal financial assistance or under any program or activity conducted by any Executive agency or by the United States Postal Service. The head of each such agency shall promulgate such regulations as may be necessary to carry out the amendments to this section made by the Rehabilitation, Comprehensive Services, and Development Disabilities Act of 1978. Copies of any proposed regulations shall be submitted to appropriate authorizing committees of the Congress, and such regulation may take effect no earlier than the thirtieth day after the date of which such regulation is so submitted to such committees.

(b) "Program or Activity" Defined

For the purposes of this section, the term "program or activity" means all of the operations of—

(1) (A) a department, agency, special purpose district, or other instrumentality of a State or of a local government; or

(B) the entity of such State or local government that distributes such assistance and each such department or agency (and each other State or local government entity) to which the assistance is extended, in the case of assistance to a State or local government;

(2) (A) a college, university, or other postsecondary institution, or a public system of higher education; or

(B) a local educational agency (as defined in section 8801 of Title 20), system of vocational education, or other school system;

(3) (A) an entire corporation, partnership, or other private organization, or an entire sole proprietorship—

(i) if assistance is extended to such corporation, partnership, private organization, or sole proprietorship as a whole; or

(ii) which is principally engaged in the business of providing education, health care, housing, social services, or parks and recreation; or

(B) the entire plant or other comparable, geographically separate facility to which Federal financial assistance is extended, in the case of any other corporation, partnership, private organization, or sole proprietorship; or

(4) any other entity which is established by two or more of the entities described in paragraph (l), (2) or (3); any part of which is extended Federal financial assistance.

(c) Significant Structural Alterations by Small Providers

Small providers are not required by subsection (a) to make significant structural alterations to their existing facilities for the purpose of assuring program accessibility, if alternative means of providing the services is available. The terms used in this subsection shall be construed with reference to the regulations existing on March 22, 1988.

(d) Standards Used in Determining Violation of Section

The standards used to determine whether this section has been violated in a complaint alleging employment discrimination under this section shall be the standards applied under title I of the Americans with Disabilities Act of 1990 (42 U.S.C. 12111 et seq.) and the provisions of sections 501 through 504, and 510, of the Americans with Disabilities Act of 1990 (42 U.S.C. 12201–12204 and 12210), as such sections related to employment.

Section 794a. Remedies and Attorney Fees

(a) (1) The remedies, procedures, and rights set forth in section 717 of the Civil Rights Act of 1964 (42 U.S.C. 2000e-16), including the application of sections 706(f) through 706 (k) [42 U.S.C. 2000e-5(f) through k)] shall be available, with respect to any complaint under section 791 of this title, to any employee or applicant for employment aggrieved by the final disposition of such complaint, or by the failure to take final action on such complaint. In fashioning an equitable or affirmative action remedy under such section, a court may take into account the reasonableness of the cost of any necessary work place accommodation, and the availability of alternative therefor or other appropriate relief in order to achieve an equitable and appropriate remedy.

(2) The remedies, procedures, and rights set forth in title VI of the Civil Rights Act of 1964 (42 U.S.C. 2000d et seq) shall be available to any person aggrieved by any act or failure to act by any recipient of Federal assistance or Federal provider of such assistant under section 794 of this title.

(b) In any action or proceeding to enforce or charge a violation of a provision of this subchapter, the court, in its discretion, may allow the prevailing party, other than the United States, a reasonable attorney's fee as part of the costs.

Source: Section 504, Rehabilitation Act of 1973 (29 U.S.C. § 701). Available online at https://www.dol.gov/oasam/regs/statutes/sec504.htm

Education for All Handicapped Children Act (1975)

In 1975, after more than two decades of pressure from parents, people with disabilities, and their allies, the U.S. Congress passed "an act to amend the education of the handicapped act to provide educational assistance to all handicapped children, and for other purposes." Congress named this new act the Education for All Handicapped Children Act. The act, as amended, has remained in effect since 1975. Congress amended and renamed the act in 1989–1990. President George H. W. Bush signed the new Individuals with Disabilities Education Act (IDEA) into law on October 30, 1990. Congress amended the IDEA in 1997 and 2004, but the basic intent of the original 1975 law remains intact—equal access to public education for children with disabilities. This right to public education is commonly referred to as "mainstreaming." Following is an excerpt from the original 1975 Education for All Handicapped Children Act:

An Act

To amend the Education of the Handicapped Act to provide educational assistance to all handicapped children, and for other purposes.

Be it enacted by the Senate and House of Representatives of the United States of America in Congress assembled, that this Act may be cited as the "Education for All Handicapped Children Act of 1975.

Extension of Existing Law . . .

Statement of Findings and Purpose

SEC. 3. (a) Section 601 of the Act (20 U.S.C. 1401) is amended by inserting " (a) " immediately before "This title" and by adding at the end thereof the following new subsections: "(b) The Congress finds that—

"(1) there are more than eight million handicapped children in the United States today;

"(2) the special educational needs of such children are not being fully met;

"(3) more than half of the handicapped children in the United States do not receive appropriate educational services which would enable them to have full equality of opportunity;

"(4) one million of the handicapped children in the United States are excluded entirely from the public school system and will not go through the educational process with their peers;

"(5) there are many handicapped children throughout the United States participating in regular school programs whose handicaps prevent them from having a successful educational experience because their handicaps are undetected;

"(6) because of the lack of adequate services within the public school system, families are often forced to find services outside the public school system, often at great distance from their residence and at their own expense;

"(7) developments in the training of teachers and in diagnostic and instructional procedures and methods have advanced to the point that, given appropriate funding, State and local educational agencies can and will provide effective special education and related services to meet the needs of handicapped children;

"(8) State and local educational agencies have a responsibility to provide education for all handicapped children, but present financial resources are inadequate to meet the special educational needs of handicapped children; and

"(9) it is in the national interest that the Federal Government assist State and local efforts to provide programs to meet the educational needs of handicapped children in order to assure equal protection of the law.

"(c) I t is the purpose of this Act to assure that all handicapped children have available to them, within the time periods specified in section 612(2) (B), a free appropriate public education which emphasizes special education and related services designed to meet their unique needs, to assure that the rights of handicapped children and their parents or guardians are protected, to assist States and localities to provide for the education of all handicapped children, and to assess and assure the effectiveness of efforts to educate handicapped children.

"(b) The heading for section 601 of the Act is to read as follows:

"Short Title; Statement of Findings and Purpose."
Definitions
20 USC 1401

SEC. 4. (a) Section 602 of the Act (20 U.S.C. 1402) is amended (1) in paragraph (1) thereof, by striking out "crippled" and inserting in lieu thereof "orthopedically impaired," and by inserting immediately after "impaired children" the following: ", or children with specific learning disabilities,"; (2) in paragraph (5) thereof, by inserting immediately after "instructional materials," the following: "telecommunications, sensory, and other technological aids and devices,"; (3) in the last sentence of paragraph (15) thereof, by inserting immediately after "environmental" the following: ", cultural, or economic"; and (4) by adding at the end thereof the following new paragraphs:

"(16) The term 'special education' means specially designed instruction, at no cost to parents or guardians, to meet the unique needs of a handicapped child, including classroom instruction, instruction in physical education, home instruction, and instruction in hospitals and institutions.

"(17) The term 'related services' means transportation, and such developmental, corrective, and other supportive services (including speech pathology and audiology, psychological services, physical and occupational therapy, recreation, and medical and counseling services, except that such medical services shall be for diagnostic and evaluation purposes only) as may be required to assist a handicapped child to benefit from special education, and includes the early identification and assessment of handicapping conditions in children.

"(18) The term 'free appropriate public education' means special education and related services which (A) have been provided at public expense, under public supervision and direction, and without charge, (B) meet the standards of the State educational agency, (C) include an appropriate preschool, elementary, or secondary school education in the State involved, and (D) are provided in conformity with the individualized education program required under section 614(a)(5).

"(19) The term 'individualized education program' means a written statement for each handicapped child developed in any meeting by a representative of the local educational agency or an intermediate educational unit who shall be qualified to provide, or supervise the provision of, specially designed instruction to meet the unique needs of handicapped children, the teacher, the parents or guardian of such child, and, whenever appropriate, such child, which statement shall include (A) a statement of the present levels of educational performance of such child, (B) a statement of annual goals, including short-term instructional objectives, (C) a statement of the specific educational services to be provided to such child, and the extent to which such child will be able to participate in regular educational programs, (D) the projected date for initiation and anticipated duration of such services, and (E) appropriate objective criteria and evaluation procedures and schedules for determining, on at least an annual basis, whether instructional objectives are being achieved.

"(20) The term 'excess costs' means those costs which are in excess of the average annual per student expenditure in a local educational agency during the preceding school year for an elementary or secondary school student, as may be appropriate, and which shall be computed after deducting (A) amounts received under this part or under title I or title VII of the Elementary and Secondary Education Act of 1965, and (B) any State or local funds expended for programs which would qualify for assistance under this part or under such titles.

"(21) The term 'native language' has the meaning given that term by section 703(a) (2) of the Bilingual Education Act (20 U.S.C. 880b-l(a)(2)).

"(22) The term 'intermediate educational unit' means any public authority, other than a local educational agency, which is under the general supervision of a State educational agency, which is established by State law for the purpose of providing free public education on a regional basis, and which provides special education and related services to handicapped children within that State."

Source: Public Law 94, 142, 89 Stat. 776, November 29, 1975. Available online at https://www.govtrack.us/congress/bills/94/s6/text/enr

Americans with Disabilities Act (1990)

Following decades of organizing and struggle by people with disabilities and their allies, and the implementation by the U.S. Congress of more than 50 other laws designed to protect the rights of people with disabilities in everything from education to air travel and telecommunications, President George H. W. Bush signed the Americans with Disabilities Act (ADA) into law on July 26, 1990. Similar to the 1964 Civil Rights Act, the ADA provided legal enfranchisement to a wide range of disabled Americans. In the following excerpt from the bill that became the ADA, note the number of disabled people in the United States in 1990—43 million, or 20 percent of the U.S. population. The large number of Americans defined as disabled under the ADA is a direct result of the broad definition of "disability" adopted by the U.S. Congress, a definition that is rooted in the social model of disability advocated by disability rights activists. Following is an excerpt of the ADA:

SEC. 2. FINDINGS AND PURPOSES. (a) FINDINGS— The Congress finds that—(1) some 43,000,000 Americans have one or more physical or mental disabilities, and this number is increasing as the population as a whole is growing older; (2) historically, society has tended to isolate and segregate individuals with disabilities, and, despite some improvements, such forms of discrimination against individuals with disabilities continue to be a serious and pervasive social problem; (3) discrimination against individuals with disabilities persists in such critical areas as employment, housing, public accommodations, education, transportation, communication, recreation, institutionalization, health services, voting, and access to public services; (4) unlike individuals who have experienced discrimination on the basis of race, color, sex, national origin, religion, or age, individuals who have experienced discrimination on the basis of disability have often had no legal recourse to redress such discrimination; (5) individuals with disabilities continually encounter various forms of discrimination, including outright intentional exclusion, the discriminatory effects of architectural, transportation, and communication barriers, overprotective rules and policies, failure to make modifications to existing facilities and practices, exclusionary qualification standards and criteria, segregation, and relegation to lesser services, programs, activities, benefits, jobs, or other opportunities; (6) census data, national polls, and other studies have documented that people with disabilities, as a group, occupy an inferior status in our society, and are severely disadvantaged socially, vocationally, economically, and educationally; (7) individuals with disabilities are a discrete and insular minority who have been faced with restrictions and limitations, subjected to a history of purposeful unequal treatment, and relegated to a position of political powerlessness in our society, based on characteristics that are beyond the control of such individuals and resulting from stereotypic assumptions not truly indicative of the individual ability of such individuals to participate in, and contribute to, society; (8) the Nation's proper goals regarding individuals with disabilities are to assure equality of opportunity, full participation, independent living, and economic self-sufficiency for such individuals; and (9) the continuing existence of unfair and unnecessary discrimination and prejudice denies people with disabilities the opportunity to compete on an equal basis and to pursue those opportunities for which our free society is justifiably famous, and costs the United States billions of dollars in unnecessary expenses resulting from dependency and nonproductivity. (b) PURPOSE—It is the purpose of this Act—(1) to provide a clear and comprehensive national mandate for the elimination of discrimination against individuals with disabilities; (2) to provide clear, strong, consistent, enforceable standards addressing discrimination against individuals with disabilities; (3) to ensure that the Federal Government plays a central role in enforcing the standards established in this Act on behalf of individuals with disabilities; and (4) to invoke the sweep of congressional authority, including the power to enforce the fourteenth amendment and to regulate commerce, in order to address the major areas of discrimination faced day-to-day by people with disabilities.

SEC. 3. DEFINITIONS. As used in this Act: (1) AUXILIARY AIDS AND SERVICES—The term "auxiliary aids and services" includes—(A) qualified interpreters or other effective methods of making aurally delivered materials available to individuals with hearing impairments; (B) qualified readers, taped texts, or other effective methods of making visually delivered materials available to individuals with visual impairments; (C) acquisition or modification of equipment or devices; and (D) other similar services and actions. (2) DISABILITY—The term "disability" means, with respect to an individual—(A) a physical or mental impairment that substantially limits one or more of the major life activities of such individual; (B) a record of such an impairment; or (C) being regarded as having such an impairment. (3) STATE—The term "State" means each of the several States, the District of Columbia, the Commonwealth of Puerto Rico, Guam, American Samoa, the Virgin Islands, the Trust Territory of the Pacific Islands, and the Commonwealth of the Northern Mariana Islands.

Source: Public Law 101–336, 42 U.S.C. § 12101, July 26, 1990. Available online at https://www.congress.gov/bill/101st-congress/senate-bill/933/text

Olmstead v. L. C. (1999)

Often referred to as "the Olmstead Decision," *Olmstead v. L. C.* is a U.S. Supreme Court case that involved two women, Lois Curtis and Elaine Wilson, who had mental and developmental disabilities. Following treatment in the state-run Georgia Regional Hospital, mental health professionals stated that both Curtis and Wilson were ready to move to a community-based program. Despite this recommendation, the women remained in the hospital for several years after their initial treatment. They filed suit under the ADA for release from the hospital. On June 22, 1999, the U.S. Supreme Court held in *Olmstead v. L.C.* that unjustified segregation of persons with disabilities constitutes discrimination in violation of title II of the ADA. The Court held that public entities must provide community-based services to persons with disabilities when "(1) such services are appropriate; (2) the affected persons do not oppose community-based treatment; and (3) community-based services can be reasonably accommodated, taking into account the resources available to the public entity and the needs of others who are receiving disability services from the entity." The Supreme Court explained that its holding "reflects two evident judgments." First, "institutional placement of persons who can handle and benefit from community settings perpetuates unwarranted assumptions that persons so isolated are incapable of or unworthy of participating in community life." And second, "confinement in an institution severely diminishes the everyday life activities of individuals, including family relations, social contacts, work options, economic independence, educational advancement, and cultural enrichment." The following document is an excerpt from the ruling of the Supreme Court in the Olmstead case:

In the Americans with Disabilities Act of 1990 (ADA), Congress described the isolation and segregation of individuals with disabilities as a serious and pervasive form of discrimination. 42 U. S. C. §§ 12101(a)(2), (5). Title II of the ADA, which proscribes discrimination in the provision of public services, specifies, *inter alia,* that no qualified individual with a disability shall, "by reason of such disability," be excluded from participation in, or be denied the benefits of, a public entity's services, programs, or activities. § 12132.

Congress instructed the Attorney General to issue regulations implementing Title II's discrimination proscription. See § 12134(a). One such regulation, known as the "integration regulation," requires a "public entity [to] administer . . . programs . . . in the most integrated setting appropriate to the needs of qualified individuals with disabilities." 28 CFR § 35.130(d). A further prescription, here called the "reasonable-modifications regulation," requires public entities to "make reasonable modifications" to avoid "discrimination on the basis of disability," but does not require measures that would

"fundamentally alter" the nature of the entity's programs. §
35.130(b)(7).

Respondents L. C. and E. W. are mentally retarded women;
L. C. has also been diagnosed with schizophrenia, and E. W.,
with a personality disorder. Both women were voluntarily
admitted to Georgia Regional Hospital at Atlanta (GRH),
where they were confined for treatment in a psychiatric unit.
Although their treatment professionals eventually concluded
that each of the women could be cared for appropriately in
a community-based program, the women remained institutionalized at GRH. Seeking placement in community care,
L. C. filed this suit against petitioner state officials (collectively, the State) under 42 U. S. C. § 1983 and Title II. She
alleged that the State violated Title II in failing to place her
in a community-based program once her treating professionals
determined that such placement was appropriate. E. W. intervened, stating an identical claim. The District Court granted
partial summary judgment for the women, ordering their placement in an appropriate community-based treatment program.

The court rejected the State's argument that inadequate
funding, not discrimination against L. C. and E. W. "by reason
of [their] disabilit[ies]," accounted for their retention at GRH.
Under Title II, the court concluded, unnecessary institutional
segregation constitutes discrimination *per se,* which cannot be
justified by a lack of funding. The court also rejected the State's
defense that requiring immediate transfers in such cases would
"fundamentally alter" the State's programs. The Eleventh Circuit affirmed the District Court's judgment, but remanded
for reassessment of the State's cost-based defense. The District
Court had left virtually no room for such a defense. The appeals court read the statute and regulations to allow the defense, but only in tightly limited circumstances. Accordingly,
the Eleventh Circuit instructed the District Court to consider,
as a key factor, whether the additional cost for treatment of L.
C. and E. W. in community-based care would be unreasonable
given the demands of the State's mental health budget.

Held: The judgment is affirmed in part and vacated in part, and the case is remanded.

138 F.3d 893, affirmed in part, vacated in part, and remanded.

JUSTICE GINSBURG delivered the opinion of the Court with respect to Parts I, II, and III-A, concluding that, under Title II of the ADA, States are required to place persons with mental disabilities in community settings rather than in institutions when the State's treatment professionals have determined that community placement is appropriate, the transfer from institutional care to a less restrictive setting is not opposed by the affected individual, and the placement can be reasonably accommodated, taking into account the resources available to the State and the needs of others with mental disabilities. Pp. 596–603.

(a) The integration and reasonable-modifications regulations issued by the Attorney General rest on two key determinations: (1) Unjustified placement or retention of persons in institutions severely limits their exposure to the outside community, and therefore constitutes a form of discrimination based on disability prohibited by Title II, and (2) qualifying their obligation to avoid unjustified isolation of individuals with disabilities, States can resist modifications that would fundamentally alter the nature of their services and programs. The Eleventh Circuit essentially upheld the Attorney General's construction of the ADA. This Court affirms the Court of Appeals decision in substantial part.

Pp. 596–597.

(b) Undue institutionalization qualifies as discrimination "by reason of . . . disability." The Department of Justice has consistently advocated that it does. . . .

Source: *Olmstead v. L. C.* 527 U.S. 581 (1999).

Paul K. Longmore, "Why I Burned My Book" (1989; Published 2003)

Paul K. Longmore, (July 10, 1946–August 9, 2010) was a professor of history, an author, and well-known disability rights activist who taught at San Francisco State University and directed its Institute on Disability. Shortly after Longmore died in 2010, the institute was renamed the Paul K. Longmore Institute on Disability. Longmore had wide-ranging interests both as an academic and as an activist. He wrote and spoke out on everything from the portrayal of people with disabilities in television and film to disability rights protests to physician-assisted suicide and unrestricted access to health care. Longmore was instrumental in creating the Disability History Association, an international professional organization for academics interested in disability history. In 1989, as part of a keynote address given at "On the Move '89," the Sixth Annual Conference for People with Disabilities (YWCA, Riverside, California, May 20, 1989), Longmore recounted why he burned his first book, *The Invention of George Washington*, in protest of Social Security administration rules that prevented people with disabilities from participating in gainful employment and earning meaningful wages. This moment, and the story it engendered, have become part of disability rights culture. Among other qualities, Longmore possessed an unparalleled ability to convey complex issues in ways that most people could understand, and more importantly in ways that often provoked action. Longmore is, by most accounts, considered one of the most influential disability rights leaders and disabled academics of the late 20th century. Following is an excerpt of Longmore's important keynote address, which was published more than a decade after he delivered it:

One afternoon in 1992, I sat in a large wood-paneled seminar room in Stanford University's History Corner. One of the doctoral students gave an interesting talk on mid-twentieth-century U.S. welfare policies, following which the group of faculty and graduate students discussed the history of American welfare. As I listened, it struck me that no one seemed to have much sense of what it was really like to "be on welfare." I wondered if I were the only person there who had actually had that experience. It has often occurred to me that the same lack of direct experience has hobbled the study of disability in general and disability policy in particular, though few scholars in these fields seem aware of that limitation.

My own interest in disability policy and its history grew partly out of the impact of public policies on me personally. The ways in which policy construed "disability" severely constricted my life and work. That direct encounter with the implementation of disability policies not only spurred me to investigate their origins and historical development; it provided me with a perspective other scholars commonly lack.

At the same time, I found that in order to have any hope of building a career as a professional historian and college teacher, indeed, in order to do any kind of work at all, I was inexorably drawn into disability rights advocacy regarding those same policies. Personal inclination made me a historian. Personal encounter with public policies made me an activist.

In October 1988, I organized a demonstration in Los Angeles to protest so-called work disincentives in federal disability related welfare policies. The account that follows expands on a speech I made a few months later in which I recounted both that protest and the experience that led up to it. . . .

I want to tell you why I burned my book. A deed as shocking as burning a book demands an explanation. It seems particularly mystifying and therefore, all the more disturbing when the perpetrator as avowedly devoted his life to books. In order to account for that act, I will have to tell you a good deal about myself. I must say, though, that I feel uncomfortable having to disclose so much about my personal life. I would prefer to keep it private. I would rather write biography than autobiography. But it seems to me that some of us are going to have to talk frankly about what it is really like for us as disabled people if

we ever hope to break down the barriers of prejudice and discrimination that "cripple" our lives.

I—and most disabled Americans—have been exhorted that
if we work hard and "overcome" our disabilities, we can achieve
our dreams. We have heard that pledge repeatedly from counselors and educators and "experts," and from our government
too. We have seen it incarnated by disabled heroes on television, those plucky "overcomers" who supposedly inspire us
with their refusal to let their disabilities limit them. We are
instructed that if we too adopt an indomitable spirit and a
cheerful attitude, we can transcend our disabilities and fulfill
our dreams.

It is a lie. The truth is that the major obstacles we must overcome are pervasive social prejudice, systematic segregation, and
institutionalized discrimination. Government social-service
policies, in particular, have forced millions of us to the margins
of society. Those policies have made the American Dream inaccessible to many disabled citizens.

In saying these things, I risk getting myself labeled as a mal-
adjusted disabled person, a succumber to self-pity, a whining
bitter cripple who blames nondisabled people for his own failure to cope with his condition. That charge—or the fear that
we might provoke it—has intimidated many of us into silence.
As I said, some of us are going to have to risk telling the truth.

The truth is I am a model "rehabilitant." I am, from one perspective, a disabled overachiever, a "supercrip." That shouldn't
surprise anyone. I had polio. The rehabilitation system drilled
people who had polio in overcoming and then held us up as
legendary exemplars of healthy adjustment to disability. American culture has lionized us for our alleged refusal to accept
limitations.

So what did I do? I earned my B.A., M.A., and Ph.D. in
American history, intending to become a college teacher. And
when I published my first book, one reviewer remarked that it
drew on "a truly astounding amount of research." Of course
it did. Would a postpolio supercrip do anything less? How

characters to how characteristically disabled of me to undertake so grandiose a project.

Still, I don't want to reduce my work to "overcoming." At the core of my efforts, I pursued a rather simple personal dream: I wanted to write about American history and to teach it to college students. . . .

One undergraduate professor told me that because of my disability no college would ever hire me as a teacher. I guess he thought he was helping me face the hard facts. . . .

A couple of years later as I was completing my master's degree, the chair of the history department told me he thought I would do well in doctoral studies, because, he said, "You're not bitter like most cripples." But he also informed me matter-of-factly that because of my disability no college would ever hire me as a teacher. . . .

. . . At the end of my first year [at the Claremont Graduate School], I applied for a fellowship, but the departmental committee turned me down. . . . They explained that because of my disability no college would ever hire me as a teacher. In other words, they didn't want to squander the department's money on me. . . . I said, I want to teach, and I'm going to teach whether you help me or not. They said they felt sure I would succeed, because "we really admire your courage."

The committee's decision to deny me a fellowship because of my disability was an act of discrimination, but it was not an illegal act. In 1972, there was no Americans with Disabilities Act. There was no section 504. . . .

For several years through the mid-1970s, I hunted for money to pay for my graduate education. I applied for student fellowships. I got none. I asked about financial aid from disability related charities like the Easter Seal Society. They said they didn't provide that kind of help. I even managed, after a considerable campaign, to become a contestant on the TV game show *Tic Tac Dough*. I lost. . . .

If the struggle to find ways to pay for my graduate studies slowed my progress [toward the PhD], and even greater financial dilemma threatened to stop me altogether. My disability incurs enormous expenses. I have no use of my arms, limited use of my right hand, and, because of a severe spinal curvature I use a ventilator a great deal of the time. As a result, I employ aides in my home to do the housekeeping and to assist me with tasks like showering, shaving, dressing, and eating. As of October 1988, at the time I burned my book, the wages paid to my personal assistants, plus the rental of my ventilators, exceeded $20,000 a year. (By the turn of the century, those costs topped $45,000 a year.) Disability-related living and work expenses have posed the fundamental problem of my adult life. The plain fact is, I am unlikely ever to earn enough in an academic career to cover such costs.

My situation is not unusual. Enormous numbers of Americans with major disabilities grapple with high disability-related expenses. They too could work, at least part-time, but could never earn enough to pay for the services and devices they need. . . .

Necessity has forced many of us to maintain eligibility for federal Supplemental Security Income (SSI) or Social Security Disability Income (SSDI) or both. . . .

SSI and SSDI eligibility make us eligible for other, more essential assistance. For instance, throughout my adult life I have paid my personal assistants through California's In-Home Support Services program. Medi-Cal (the California version of Medicaid) has paid for my ventilators. Without this financial aid, I would have had to spend my adult life in some sort of nursing home. At far greater cost to taxpayers, I might add. In most states, people with disabilities like mine have found themselves in a far more horrendous situation: they get little or no aid for independent living. They are shackled to their families or imprisoned in nursing homes. They are denied access to life and to work. Independent living has enabled me to work productively.

To catch is that for most of my adult life, in order to maintain eligibility for this government aid, I had to refrain from work. . . . If you worked and earned more than [a preset amount], the government would cut off all financial aid to you.

All through the 1970s and much of the 1980s, the all-or-nothing $300-a-month earnings threshold blocked me from getting teaching experience. [If I had worked], I would have jeopardized the financial aid that paid for my in-home assistance and my ventilator, the aid that enabled me to live independently and, in fact, to work. . . .

Year after year in graduate school, I fretted about how I could make myself marketable as a college teacher and how I would get by financially if I ever did get a job. Semester after semester, they considered quitting the Ph.D. program. Why beat my head against a stone wall? What was the point? In virtually every semester of graduate school, there came a moment when I had to sit down and decide once again that I would hang in there for one more term. . . .

I have spent much of my life seeking ways to elude social stigma and outwit discrimination. I have wanted to escape the roles of dependent cripple or inspirational overcomer. I . . . have tried to work productively and to fashion for myself an alternative social identity. . . . I have claimed as my right "an honest pride." Yet for my entire adult life, many government policies have been deliberately designed to prevent me, not just from pursuing my profession, but from attaining the socially respected place in society that goes with honest work. Millions of other Americans with disabilities find their attempts at productivity and pride blocked by these same segregationist work penalties and the social prejudice those policies express. . . .

The Social Security Administration of course claimed that allowing us to work while we received assistance with our disability-related living and medical expenses would cost the government billions of dollars. A national pilot project launched in 1980 proved just the opposite. The government and society got millions back from disabled people who at last bec[a]me workers and taxpayers. . . . Finally in 1986, Congress . . . ordered [the] permanent elimination of most work disincentives from SSI. The new rule, Section 1619 would permit recipients to earn up to a threshold amount equivalent to the cash value of all the assistance they received plus the amount of their "impairment-related work expenses."

For twenty years, I had wondered and worried how I would ever fulfill my dream of teaching and writing American history. I had finally finished my Ph.D. in 1984 but still could not take even a part-time teaching position without jeopardizing the financial aid that paid for ventilators and in-home assistance. With the arrival of Section 1619, the work penalties that had blocked me were at last gone. Or so I thought.

In March of 1988, I learned that although Section 1619 would permit me to earn a living as a college teacher, the reformed rules would not allow research fellowships or publishing royalties. The Social Security Administration would continue to regard such income as "unearned," like royalties from oil well stocks. . . .

I would have to turn [a prestigious] fellowship down. More problematic, in October [1988] the University of California Press would publish my book, *The Invention of George Washington*. I needed the first book to make myself attractive in the college-teaching job market. UC Press expected the book to sell pretty well. That was the problem. Even if it yielded only modest royalties, that money would not fit the Section 1619 definition of "earned" income. So I could lose some or all of the assistance I depended on to work and live and, literally, to breathe.

Don't ask me how the policy makers decided that earnings from a book it took me ten years to write would be "unearned." They live in the Alice-Through-the-Looking Glass realm, where significantly disabled people who work are not really disabled after all.

I wrote President Reagan and other top federal officials to describe my situation. Scholarly careers I explained are rarely lucrative. . . . If I cannot apply for and accept research fellowships or publish books, I said, I cannot advance in my profession. If

I lose the government aid that pays for my in-home assistance and ventilators, I cannot live independently *or* work.

President Reagan . . . forwarded my letters to the Commissioner of Social Security, Doreas Hardy. . . .

Finally on August 26, 1988, Commissioner Hardy notified me that SSA would regard any income I obtained from research fellowships or book royalties as "unearned" and that this would adversely affect eligibility for SSI.

When I read the commissioner's preemptory warning that SSA would punish me if I received any royalties from my book, something in me reached a breaking point. Years of finding myself trapped and thwarted by this system, years of feeling demeaned and degraded by it, came to a head. I said to myself, "I've had enough." I decided in that moment that when my book came out in October I would burn it in protest. . . .

My planned protest got enthusiastic support from the Southern California disability community. Leaders of the California Council of the Blind, the Greater Los Angeles Council on Deafness, several independent-living centers, local chapters of the California Association of the Physically Handicapped, Able Advocates of Santa Barbara, and ADAPT of Southern California endorsed the demonstration.

On October 18, some forty people gathered in front of the federal building on Los Angeles Street in downtown L.A. There were adults with disabilities who were trying to work, or who wanted to and could work, but were thwarted by work penalties. There were college students with disabilities who wondered if they would be prevented from following the careers they dreamed of pursuing when they graduated. There were parents of disabled children who wanted those youngsters to have a useful and fulfilling future. There were teachers and counselors who labored to help people with disabilities get an education or job training. They were paid with government funds to do this, but government policies baffled their efforts. We all came together to demand an end to work and marriage penalties. . . .

I somberly watch the fire consumed my book. I had planned the protest. I had rehearsed how to burn the book. I had even thought about what sort of expression I should have on my face. But I could never have prepared for the emotional effect on me of the act itself. I was burning my own book, a book I had spent ten years of my life laboring over. A book that had earned me my Ph.D. in history, a book I felt proud of, and, in fact, loved. It was a moment of agony.

Everyone in the crowd looked on quietly, soberly. Several wept when confronted with my own reaction, their emotional response surprised me. . . .

The demonstration ended. The protesters dispersed. An LAPD officer approached the three or four of us who were cleaning up. He asked me my name. He wrote it down. I asked if there was a problem. He said he just wanted the information for the record. . . .

Subsequent events gave hope that the book burning might have the political impact we sought. . . .

In January 1989, the new Congress convened in Washington. It took up the Social Security Work Incentives Act, a bill first introduced in the previous session. The proposed legislation aimed to eliminate the major work penalties in Social Security Disability Insurance. . . . When disability rights advocates alerted Congressmen . . . about the book burning and our demands, they decided to add to their bill an amendment that would address the SSI work penalties we had protested. The new provision would classify publishing royalties, speaking honoraria, and research grants and fellowships as "earned" income for purposes of reckoning the income threshold under Section 1619.

In February 1989, I learned that the Social Security Administration was vigorously opposing the entire bill. . . . The few changes SSA would agree to got folded into the Omnibus Budget Reconciliation Act. That legislation allowed honoraria and publishing royalties [but not grants or fellowships to be counted as "earned" income]. . . .

As for me, well, my book, *The Invention of George Washington*, never earned the kind of royalties I had both hoped and feared it would draw. So, fortunately or unfortunately, it never put me in danger of losing the assistance I needed. On the other hand, it did help me finally get a tenure-track teaching position. . . .

I do not tell you this to brag about my achievements or to boast about my tenacity and perseverance or to exhort other disabled people to try harder. . . . I could never have succeeded without the removal of work penalties. What tore them out of my way was the *political* tenacity and perseverance of our disability community. I got this far because of the achievements of the disability rights movement. . . .

The core of what I said in my statement just before I burned my book in October 1988 unfortunately remains true today:

"We, like other Americans, should have the right to work productively. Work and marriage penalties. . ., far more than our disabilities, thwart our efforts and our lives. We demand an end to these discriminatory government policies."

"We are here today, not just for ourselves, but on behalf of millions of Americans with disabilities. My book represents, not just my work, but the work that we all want to do and could do. The burning of a copy of my book symbolizes what the government does to us and our talents and our efforts. It repeatedly turns our dreams to ashes. We find that outrageous, and we will no longer quietly endure that outrage."

"We, like all Americans, have talents to use, work to do, our contributions to make to our communities and country. We want the chance to work and marry without jeopardizing our lives. We want access to opportunity. We want access to work. We want access to the American Dream."

Source: Longmore, Paul K. 2003. "Why I Burned My Book," in *Why I Burned My Book and Other Essays on Disability*. Philadelphia: Temple University Press, 230–259. Used by permission of Temple University Press.

ADA Amendments Act (2008)

The ADA Amendments Act of 2008 (Public Law 110–325, ADAAA) is an act of Congress, which became effective on January 1, 2009. Like other antidiscrimination laws, the ADA of 1990 required that an individual bear the burden of bringing a discrimination lawsuit against the alleged offender. In most cases in the years following the passage of the ADA, the courts ruled in favor of the defendants—that is they ruled against the disabled plaintiff who was claiming discrimination. The result of these court rulings was a significant narrowing of the definition of "disability" under the ADA. Put simply, in most cases, the courts ruled that an individual was not "disabled" (or not "disabled" enough) and therefore could not bring a discrimination suit based on disability under the ADA. In 2008, the U.S. Congress passed the ADA Amendments Act in an effort to undo earlier court rulings and reestablish the original intent of the ADA, which was to define "disability" broadly to include a wide range of American citizens. In the following excerpt taken from the House Bill that became the ADAAA note the specific reference to court rulings that narrowed the definition of "disability" under the original ADA:

AN ACT

To restore the intent and protections of the Americans with Disabilities Act of 1990.

Be it enacted by the Senate and House of Representatives of the United States of America in Congress assembled,

Section 1. Short Title

This Act may be cited as the "ADA Amendments Act of 2008."

Sec. 2. Findings and Purposes

(a) Findings

—-Congress finds that—

(1) in enacting the Americans with Disabilities Act of 1990 (ADA), Congress intended that the Act "provide a clear

and comprehensive national mandate for the elimination of discrimination against individuals with disabilities" and provide broad coverage;

(2) in enacting the ADA, Congress recognized that physical and mental disabilities in no way diminish a person's right to fully participate in all aspects of society, but that people with physical or mental disabilities are frequently precluded from doing so because of prejudice, antiquated attitudes, or the failure to remove societal and institutional barriers;

(3) while Congress expected that the definition of disability under the ADA would be interpreted consistently with how courts had applied the definition of handicap under the Rehabilitation Act of 1973, that expectation has not been fulfilled;

(4) the holdings of the Supreme Court in Sutton v. United Airlines, Inc., 527 U.S. 471 (1999) and its companion cases, and in Toyota Motor Manufacturing, Kentucky, Inc. v. Williams, 534 U.S. 184 (2002) have narrowed the broad scope of protection intended to be afforded by the ADA, thus eliminating protection for many individuals whom Congress intended to protect; and

(5) as a result of these Supreme Court cases, lower courts have incorrectly found in individual cases that people with a range of substantially limiting impairments are not people with disabilities.

(b) Purposes
—The purposes of this Act are—

(1) to carry out the ADA's objectives of providing "a clear and comprehensive national mandate for the elimination of discrimination" and "clear, strong, consistent, enforceable standards addressing discrimination" by reinstating a broad scope of protection to be available under the ADA;

(2) to reject the requirement enunciated by the Supreme Court in Sutton v. United Airlines, Inc., 527 U.S. 471 (1999) and its companion cases that whether an impairment substantially limits a major life activity is to be determined with reference to the ameliorative effects of mitigating measures;

(3) to reject the Supreme Court's reasoning in Sutton v. United Airlines, Inc., 527 U.S. 471 (1999) with regard to coverage under the third prong of the definition of disability and to reinstate the reasoning of the Supreme Court in School Board of Nassau County v. Arline, 480 U.S. 273 (1987) which set forth a broad view of the third prong of the definition of handicap under the Rehabilitation Act of 1973;

(4) to reject the standards enunciated by the Supreme Court in Toyota Motor Manufacturing, Kentucky, Inc. v. Williams, 534 U.S. 184 (2002), that the terms "substantially" and "major" in the definition of disability under the ADA "need to be interpreted strictly to create a demanding standard for qualifying as disabled," and that to be substantially limited in performing a major life activity under the ADA "an individual must have an impairment that prevents or severely restricts the individual from doing activities that are of central importance to most people's daily lives"; and

(5) to provide a new definition of "substantially limits" to indicate that Congress intends to depart from the strict and demanding standard applied by the Supreme Court in Toyota Motor Manufacturing, Kentucky, Inc. v. Williams and by numerous lower courts.

Sec. 3. Codified Findings

Section 2(a) of the Americans with Disabilities Act of 1990 (42 U.S.C. 12101) is amended—(1) by amending paragraph (1) to read as follows:

"(1) physical or mental disabilities in no way diminish a person's right to fully participate in all aspects of society, yet many people with physical or mental disabilities have been precluded from doing so because of discrimination; others who have a record of a disability or are regarded as having a disability also have been subjected to discrimination;"; and

(2) by striking paragraph (7).

Source: *Public Law 110–325.* Available online at https://www .congress.gov/bill/110th-congress/house-bill/3195/text

Teaching the Black Disabled Experience (2015)

Following is an excerpt from an article that appeared in a special issue of *Disability Studies Quarterly* in 2015. The special issue focused on teaching disability studies. This particular article is excerpted and included as a document, because it focuses on teaching the "black disabled experience." For too long, Americans thought about disability in isolation. They did not think about it "intersectionally." They did not think about how the lives of disabled people are shaped by the interactions among race, sex, sexuality, gender, religion, class, and disability. When people thought about disability, they often assumed the "white, male, wheelchair user" as the archetypical disabled person. This limited way of thinking about disability was so pervasive that, for a long time, disability studies—the study of disabled people in history, society, and culture—was, in practice, really only "white, middle-class" disability studies. This idea began to change in the early 21st century. The article excerpted here, which includes a course outline, is an example of the ways in which disability studies scholars are becoming more sophisticated in their thinking about disability:

Introduction

This collection of writing has grown from the work of the National Black Disability Coalition (NBDC), led by Jane Dunhamn and Leroy Moore. The NBDC was founded to advance knowledge about Black disability, both in the US and throughout the African Diaspora. The organization's mission statement is, in part, "to create a space for inquiry within universities that brings together faculty and students . . . to consider Black disability issues within broad-based social, cultural and historical contexts." Elaborating on this mission, in a speech at Temple University in March 2015, coalition co-chair Jane Dunham stated that, among our most important tasks, is to put out a call to action to Black students with disabilities, so that they can lead the next wave of change. This collection of writings is offered in the spirit of that call, and includes a collaboratively-authored Black disability studies (hereafter Black DS) syllabus, as well as reflections from members of the Coalition on their experiences of teaching and learning in Black DS classrooms.

It is not our intention to give a definitive picture of what Black DS pedagogy "is," but rather to suggest some of the things it *may* be, and become, as it grows. In addition to furthering the goals laid out in the mission statement of the Black DS Coalition, we also wish to give educators and students a sense of how they might begin to incorporate some of the principles of Black DS, and disability justice more broadly, into the learning spaces they inhabit.

Throughout this collection of writings, we advocate for Black DS to be taken, *not* as a marginalized special-topic course, but rather as a crucial part of all disability studies courses and pedagogies, as well as all Black and Africana Studies courses. We recognize that, like disability itself, Black DS cannot simply be "added and stirred" into existing pedagogies; rather, the inclusion of Black DS is a paradigm-shifting change. The pieces included in this collection are enactments of an ongoing conversation—a conversation that we hope the readers of *Disability Studies Quarterly* will join thoughtfully. . . .

The pilot syllabus, presented at the end, is the collaborative effort of many NBDC members. This syllabus can be adapted for use in a wide variety of classrooms, not only those formally designated as "Black DS" pedagogical spaces. Our purpose is to invite more students and instructors into active discussion and engagement with these ideas, so that the meaning of what "Black DS pedagogy" is can continue to grow.

Who Shall Introduce the Subject?
Jane Dunhamn, Director, National Black Disability Coalition

The past two years of Black disability studies (Black DS) exploration have proven to be rewarding and overwhelming. I would like to thank the Black DS Committee. From the beginning, the journey of discovery took us home. It was the historic Shiloh Baptist Church that offered us space and fed us well. Our organizer, Deacon Jerome Harris simply asked Rev. Armstrong to host us, and resoundingly, his response was yes! When we met in June 2013, there were many people in the audience who were new to the concepts of disability studies and queer studies. This is, again, testimony that when we come together we grow. That is not to say it is always without struggle.

The most difficult and formidable challenge to Black DS are the two intersections that gave rise to the need for this area of work. The first is, how can Black DS be incorporated into disability studies with authenticity and the commitment to include community action, much as with the model of Black/Africana Studies? In other words, who is competent to introduce the subject from an Afro-disability perspective? The second is, how can Black DS be incorporated into Black/Africana Studies, where there has been little to no knowledge of disability studies? In other words, who is competent to introduce the subject from a disability-Afro perspective? . . .

Course Outline: Black Disabled Experience
Black Disability Studies Committee of the National Black Disability Coalition

The intent of this course is to provide students with an introduction to the intersections of race and disability from a critical social justice perspective. The course is to also provide a guide to scholarly institutions for future fields of study and professional advancement.

Learning Objectives

The course in Black Disabled Experience is to develop critical intellectual skills in the arts, culture, sociology and history of people from the disabled Black community in the United States and the African Diaspora.

1. To create a more accurate and complex understanding of Black people with disabilities and the evolution of Black disabled people in historical contexts of the United States and the Diaspora, including the U.S. civil rights movement and disability rights movement, Black arts/music and Black history.
2. To invite students to reflect on how an appreciation of Black disability relates to the professional, social and personal aspects of their lives.
3. To have the opportunity to learn from Black disabled people and family members.
4. Use the knowledge and skills of Black Disability Studies to effect social change.

Course Outline

Arts
1. Black Music and Disability from Blues to Hip Hop
2. Entertainment Industry: Black Disabled Bodies
3. Black Disabled Images and Media

History
1. Slavery and Disability
2. Talented Tenth and Black Disability

3. Black Civil Rights Activism and Disability Rights and Activism

4. Black Nationalism, Black Power and Disability

5. Black Disabled Activism in the Motherland

6. Black Experience in Dominant Culture Disability

Sociology/Culture

1. Black Family and Disability: Raising Black Disabled Children

2. Black Church and Disability

3. Masculinity and Feminism through the Lens of Black Disabled Men and Women

4. Juvenile Justice Systems, Incarceration & Institutionalization in Disability

   a. "Labeling" and the school to prison pipeline; why minorities are overrepresented in special education.

5. Disability Stigma and Black Leadership

6. Discrimination and Disparities in Disability Service System

Core Competencies

I. Critical Analysis

- Define Black Disabled Experience in a Disability Justice context.

- Discuss the intersections (or lack of) between Black disabled philosophy and dominant culture disability philosophy.

- Define Black Disability centeredness and explain the need for Black Disability Studies discipline.

- Discuss the role of gender in the Black disabled experience.

- Discuss the differences between the role of the mainstream Black intellectual and the Black disabled intellectual.

- Discuss how the concept of race has affected the development of the Black disabled experience in literature and the arts.

- How do we defend the validity of a Black Disabled personality? Discuss how research analysis would aid in the scholarly investigation of a topic in Black Disability Studies social science/behavioral curriculum.

II. Discipline Knowledge

- Discuss how the intersections between race, gender, and class issues in the Black disability experience differ from those in mainstream disciplines.
- Discuss the role sexism and class has played in the discipline.
- Discuss the history of the Black disabled experience in poetry, novels, essays, autobiographies, and narratives.
- Discuss the literary works of major (influential) Black disabled figures.
- Discuss the characteristics of the Black church and its relationship to Black disabled people.
- Discuss the politics of Black popular culture, especially of Black disabled music, the mass media and cinema.
- Discuss the political, economic, and cultural development of the Black Disability Movement.

III. Effective Communication

- The ability to argue Black disability issues orally and to write about them persuasively.
- Development of listening skills.
- Respect for the opinion of others.

IV. Understanding Human and Cultural Diversity

- Ability to work as allies/consultants for Black disability issues and to assist leaders, stakeholders and policymakers in developing Black Disability Studies curricula.
- Assist community organizations in understanding the psychological, sociological, economical, and health issues that relate to the Black disabled experience.

- Lead dialogue inside and outside the academy on recent Black disabled issues and studies.
- Ability to discuss characteristics of a Eurocentric world view of disability.

Readings

(Note: Films and potential speakers are still under discussion)
Arts Readings

a. The Songs of Blind Folk: African American Musicians and the Culture of Blindness; Terry Rowden

b. The Life of M.F. Grim; Percy Carey and Ronald Wimberly

c. Blues People: Negro Music in White America; Leroi Jones

d. Truly Blessed; Teddy Pendergrass

e. Brother Ray: Ray Charles' Own Story; Ray Charles

f. The Illest: Disability as Metaphor in Hip-Hop Music; Moya Bailey

g. When I Move, You Move: Thoughts on the Fusion of Hip-Hop and Disability Activism: Rebecca A. Adelman

h. Krip Hop Nation Is More Than Music; Leroy Moore

History Readings

a. Killing the Black Body; Dorothy E. Roberts

b. Porgy; Dubose Heyward

c. First Waco Horror: Lynching of Jesse Washington and the Rise of the NAACP; Patricia Bernstein

d. Freak Show: Presenting Human Oddities for Amusement and Profit; Robert Bogdan

e. Disability and Difference in Global Contexts: Enabling Transformative Body Politic; Nirmala Erevelles

f. Female, Black and Able: Representations of Sojourner Truth and Theories of Embodiment; Meredith Minister

Sociology/Culture Readings

a. Crippin' Jim Crow: Disability and the School-to-Prison Pipeline; Nirmala Erevelles (In the recently released *Disability Incarcerated: Imprisonment and Disability in the US and Canada,* co-edited by Liat Ben-Moshe, Chris Chapman, and Allison C. Carey)

b. Case Studies of Minority Student Placement in Special Education; Beth Harry, Janette Klingner, Elizabeth Cramer, and Keith Sturges

c. Why Are So Many Minority Students in Special Education? Understanding Race and Disability in Schools; Beth Harry and Janette Klingner

d. Lomax's Matrix: Disability, Solidarity and Black Power of 504; Susan Schweik

e. African American Slavery and Disability: Bodies, Poverty and Power in Antebellum South; Dea H. Boster

f. Blackness and Disability: Critical Examinations and Cultural Interventions; Christopher Bell

g. Sick from Freedom: African American Illness and Suffering during the Civil War and Reconstruction; Jim Downs

h. The Mark of Slavery: The Stigma of Disability, Race and Gender in Antebellum America; Jenifer Barclay

i. Harriet Tubman: A Biography; James A. McGowan and William C Kashatus

j. The Hidden Reassure of Black ASL; Carolyn McCaskill

k. Unspeakable: The Story of Junius Wilson; Susan Burch and Hannah Joyner

l. Black and Deaf in America: We Are Different; Ernest Hairston and Linwood Smith

m. Black Deaf Students: A Model of Educational Success; Carolyn Williamson

n. Roar of Silence: Trial & Triumph Through Deafness; Kenneth Walker and Bob Schaller

o. Still I Rise: The Enduring Legacy of Black Deaf Arkansans before and after Integration; Glenn B. Anderson

p. The Immortal Life of Henrietta Lacks; Rebecca Skloot . . .

Source: Dunhamn, Jane, et. al., 2015. "Developing and Reflecting on a Black Disability Studies Pedagogy: Work from the National Black Disability Coalition," *Disability Studies Quarterly* 35, 2. Available online at http://dsq-sds.org/article/view/4637/3933. Used by permission of the authors.

Introduction

Following is a list of resources that will help to provide more insight into disability and the lived experiences of people with disabilities in American history, culture, and society. While no list can ever be comprehensive or exhaustive, the materials gathered here represent the most widely cited and utilized resources among disability researchers interested in studying disability in the United States. There are a few resources that are not directly related to the United States, but they are nevertheless included because they offer valuable context and points of comparison for the experiences of people with disabilities living in the United States. The list of resources is broken down into five sections: academic peer-reviewed journals, reference works, edited books, monographs (single-authored books), and Internet resources.

Academic Peer-Reviewed Journals

Canadian Journal of Disability Studies (2012–Current)

The *Canadian Journal of Disability Studies* (*CJDS*) publishes peer-reviewed articles that advance research in disability studies primarily in Canada. All documents are open-access. It is free and open to the public. The journal publishes articles that use a wide range of methodologies and perspectives, and those

---

[Makeshift paper signs with new accessibility symbols fastened to a pole] Accessibility signs hung during the Women's March on New York City, January 20, 2018. (Erin Alexis Randolph/Dreamstime.com)

that rely on collaborative and cross-disciplinary work, community engagement, and other approaches to research. This journal will be of interest not only to people involved in disability studies but other academics as well. This journal can be found at http://cjds.uwaterloo.ca/index.php/cjds.

Disability and Society (1994–Current)

Formerly known as *Disability, Handicap & Society* (1986–1993)

An international journal that provides a focus for debate about issues such as human rights, discrimination, definitions, policy, and practices specifically as they relate to disabled people. This journal publishes articles that have a wide range of perspectives, including the importance of the voices and experiences of the disabled people. There is also a current issues section that is intended to give people a platform to write in a less formal or academic way about things that concern them. People are encouraged to write about controversial topics. This journal can be found at http://www.tandfonline.com/loi/cdso20.

Disability Studies Quarterly (1986–Current)

The oldest and most well-respected disability studies journal in North America. *Disability Studies Quarterly* (*DSQ*) is an open-access journal. It is made available for free on the Internet to anyone who has an Internet connection. It can be found at http://dsq-sds.org. It publishes peer-reviewed articles in a number of fields, including cultural and literary studies, English, history, sociology, education, media studies, and philosophy, as well as book, film, and media reviews, personal narratives, reflections, and memoirs, and some conference proceedings.

Journal of Disability Policy Studies (1990–Current)

Journal of Disability Policy Studies (*DPS*) addresses issues in ethics, policy, and law related to individuals with disabilities. The journal has many different features. Two interesting features include "From My Perspective," which discusses issues confronting a particular disability discipline or area, and "Point/

Counterpoint," which addresses timely ethical issues affecting individuals with disabilities. This journal is part of the Committee on Publication Ethics. *DPS* can be found at http://journals.sagepub.com/home/dps.

Journal of Literary and Cultural Disability Studies (2007–Current)

This journal focuses on cultural and literary representations of disability. It publishes a wide variety of articles that are informed by disability theory and by experiences of disability. It is essential for scholars whose work concentrates on the portrayal of disability in literature. With an editorial board of 50 international scholars, it is edited by Dr. David Bolt, director of the Centre for Culture & Disability Studies, Liverpool Hope University. *Journal of Literary and Cultural Disability Studies* can be found online at http://online.liverpooluniversitypress.co.uk/loi/jlcds.

Review of Disability Studies: An International Journal (2004–Current)

The *Review of Disability Studies* (*RDS*) is a peer-reviewed academic journal that is targeted toward any person interested in disability studies. It covers a range of disciplines within disability studies as well as creative works expressing ideas in the area of disability. The sections in the journal include (1) Research and Essays, (2) Topical Forums, (3) Creative Works, (4) Best Practices, (5) Multi-Media Review, (6) Notes from the Field, and (7) Dissertation Abstracts. The journal is published four times a year, and each issue runs about 50 pages. The journal can be found at http://www.rdsjournal.org/index.php/journal/index.

Reference Works

Burch, Susan. 2009. *Encyclopedia of American Disability History.* New York: Facts on File.

> Burch and many other contributors offer an overview of experiences of a wide range of people living with disabilities

from colonial times to the early 21st century. This encyclopedia is organized into three volumes with 12 thematic essays. This encyclopedia is most effective for readers who are focusing on one topic. There are many cross-references that are linked to other resources that can give the reader more insight into the topic of his or her choosing.

Heller, Tamar, Sarah Parker Harris, Carol Gill, and Robert Parry Gould, eds. 2018. *Disability in American Life: An Encyclopedia of Policies, Concepts, and Controversies.* Santa Barbara, CA: ABC-CLIO.

A foundational introduction to disability for a wide audience—from those who are intimately connected with disability to those interested in scientific or medical understandings of disability to disabled people themselves—this collection covers all aspects of disability critical to the U.S. context. Topics include characteristics of disability; disability concepts; models and theories; important historical developments and milestones for people with disabilities; prominent individuals, organizations, and agencies; notable policies and services; and intersections of disability policy with other policy.

Edited Books

Barsch, Sebastian, Anne Klein, and Pieter Verstraete. 2013. *The Imperfect Historian: Disability Histories in Europe.* Frankfurt am Main: Peter Lang.

This book won the Disability History Association's 2014 Outstanding Publication Award, Best Book. The editors assembled a collection of historical essays that speak to the innovative methodological approaches for doing disability history, as well as new and inspiring case studies. This book has four parts: challenging methodologies, power and identity, traveling knowledge, and emerging geographies. These essays contribute greatly to the ongoing discussion of how and why disability came to be seen as a problem for human societies. Especially notable are the book's interdisciplinary methodologies and its wide-ranging geographic focus.

Ben-Moshe, Liat, Chris Chapman, and Allison Carey, eds. 2014. *Disability Incarcerated: Imprisonment and Disability in the United States and Canada*. New York: Palgrave Macmillan.
  This book has a foreword written by Angela Davis, renowned African American political activist whose work focuses on abolishing the prison-industrial complex. With 14 chapters, this book takes an interdisciplinary approach to thinking about disability and incarceration that broadens our understanding of both concepts. Using insights from sociology, history, and cultural studies, the book covers a wide range of geographical, temporal, and disciplinary areas.

Burch, Susan, and Alison Kafer. 2010. *Deaf and Disability Studies: Interdisciplinary Perspectives*. Washington, DC: Gallaudet University Press.
  This is a collection of 14 essays on deaf people, deaf culture, deaf history, and deaf identity. These essays approach these topics from different points of view, including those of deaf and disabled people. The book is divided into three sections: The first section explores deaf identity in different contexts, such as the history of activism that was shaped by Deaf elites in the United States from 1890 to 1920. The second section explores alliances and activism and showcases activism organized across different disabilities. The final section, Boundaries and Overlaps, addresses the relationships among the academic fields of deaf studies and disability studies.

Burch, Susan, and Michael Rembis. 2014. *Disability Histories*. Urbana: University of Illinois Press.
  Susan Burch and Michael Rembis present 18 essays that integrate a critical analysis of gender, race, historical context, geographic location, and other factors to enrich and

challenge the traditional modes of interpretation still dominating the field of disability history. There are four critical areas discussed in this collection: family, community, and daily life; cultural histories; the relationship between disabled people and the medical field; and issues of citizenship, belonging, and normalcy.

Connor, David J., Beth A. Ferri, and Subini Annamma. 2016. *DisCrit: Disability Studies and Critical Race Theory in Education*. New York: Teachers College Press.

This volume brings together major figures in Disability Studies in Education and critical race theory to explore some of today's most important educational issues. In this volume, the authors take a critical look at achievement gaps from both historical and contemporary perspectives along with the overrepresentation of minority students in special education and the school-to-prison pipeline. The inclusion and exclusion of disabled students in school activities and society are also discussed.

Davis, Lennard J. 2017. *The Disability Studies Reader*, 5th ed. New York: Routledge, Taylor & Francis Group.

In its fifth edition in 2017, *The Disability Studies Reader* has, since the 1990s, been one of the most widely used introductory texts in disability studies. This fifth edition addresses the "post-identity" theoretical landscape in disability studies by emphasizing questions of interdependency and independence; the human–animal relationship; and issues around social construction and the materiality of gender, the body, and sexuality. Parts of this edition explore the biases of medical and scientific experiments and explode the binary of the sound and diseased mind. This edition not only addresses visible physical disabilities, but it also investigates disabilities that cannot be seen. Since the editor changes the material included in the book with each new edition, it would be wise to read all five editions of the book. This would be a great way of tracing one strand of North American disability studies scholarship.

Foss, Chris, Jonathan W. Gray, and Zach Whalen. 2016. *Disability in Comic Books and Graphic Narratives*. New York: Palgrave Macmillan.

This book invites readers to consider both canonical and alternative graphic representations of disability. It has chapters on everything from lesser-known characters like Cyborg and Helen Killer to huge stars like Batgirl and Batman. It offers a broad spectrum of represented disabilities as well, including amputation, autism, blindness, deafness, depression, Huntington's disease, multiple sclerosis, obsessive-compulsive disorder, and much more. Some essays show how comics continue to implicate themselves in the objectification and marginalization of persons with disabilities, perpetuating stale stereotypes and stigmas. In contrast, other essays stress how comics and graphic novels can transform our understanding of disability in truly profound ways.

Gerber, David A. 2012. *Disabled Veterans in History*. Ann Arbor: The University of Michigan Press.

Disabled Veterans in History explores the long-neglected history of those who have sustained lasting injuries or chronic illnesses while serving in the military. This book covers a wide range geographically, including countries in Europe and North America as well as chronologically from the ancient world to the present. The book, which was in its second edition in 2012, has 15 chapters and a comprehensive introduction that will be useful to anyone interested in disabled veterans of any time period.

Gill, Michael Carl, and Cathy J. Schlund-Vials. 2014. *Disability, Human Rights and the Limits of Humanitarianism*. London: Routledge.

This collection of 13 new and original essays offers important critiques of contemporary human rights discourse, policies, and programs using a global critical disability studies perspective. Contemporary human rights discourses problematically co-opt disabled bodies as "evidence" of harms done under capitalism, war, and other forms of conflict, while humanitarian nongovernmental organizations often use disabled bodies to generate resources for their humanitarian projects. As a result, disabled people and their experiences are often objectified to achieve other means, but disabled people are rarely empowered to improve their own lot in life. This general theme undergirds all of the chapters in this book, which focus on multiple topics in various locations throughout the world.

Grech, Shaun, and Karen Soldatic. 2016. *Disability in the Global South: The Critical Handbook*. Cham: Springer International Publishing.

This first-of-its-kind volume contains 37 chapters that span the breadth of disability research and practice specifically focusing on the global South. The authors adopt a critical and interdisciplinary approach to challenge and shift commonly held social understandings of disability, such as the social model of disability and dominant understandings of charity. This highly anticipated volume challenges established discourses, epistemologies, and practices in prominent areas such as global health, disability studies, and international development. It shows the importance of studying the global South—places like India, South Asia, Southeast Asia, Africa, and Central and South America—and also considering its relationship with the global North.

Hall, Kim Q. 2011. *Feminist Disability Studies*. Bloomington: Indiana University Press.

This book consists of 13 chapters, some of which are reprinted and others are new and original work. All of the chapters explore the intersection of feminist theory and disability studies. They use cultural and literary studies to question the nature of embodiment and the meaning of disability, to consider how policies play out on those who have been labeled disabled, and to explore how society defines normal functionality or appearance when people raise questions about mental and physical ability.

Hirschmann, Nancy J., and Beth Linker. 2015. *Civil Disabilities: Citizenship, Membership, and Belonging*. Philadelphia: University of Pennsylvania Press.

    Civil Disabilities challenges traditional understandings of the term "citizenship." It urges readers to rethink commonly held ideas about citizenship in an effort to secure a rightful place for disabled persons in society. The book's 11 essays—all from leading scholars in a diversity of fields— offer critical perspectives on current citizenship studies, which still largely assume an ableist world. This volume makes a strong case for reimagining definitions of citizenship that are more consistent, inclusive, and just, in both theory and practice. By placing disability at the center of its analysis, *Civil Disabilities* offers readers a powerful critique of traditional notions of citizenship and helps to transform our understanding of the place of disabled people in our society.

Howe, Blake, Stephanie Jensen-Moulton, Neil William Lerner, and Joseph Nathan Straus. 2016. *The Oxford Handbook of Music and Disability Studies*. New York: Oxford University Press.

    The Oxford handbook series is meant to provide readers with a clear understanding of the state of a particular field, as well as insights into new veins of research. This handbook consists of a comprehensive assessment of the state of current research in the area of disability studies and music. Containing 42 chapters, this massive book spans a wide chronological and geographical range, from biblical, medieval, and early modern through the canonical classics of the 19th and 20th centuries. It explores

20th-century modernist styles and contemporary musical theater and popular genres. Also contained within this volume are topics as varied as post–Civil War America, Ghana, and the South Pacific, as well as many other interesting times and places. This book is essential for anyone interested in the critical study of music and disability.

LeFrançois, Brenda A., Robert J. Menzies, and Geoffrey Reaume. 2013. *Mad Matters: A Critical Reader in Canadian Mad Studies*. Toronto: Canadian Scholars' Press Inc.

In 1981, Toronto activist Mel Starkman wrote: "An important new movement is sweeping through the western world. . . . The 'mad', the oppressed, the ex-inmates of society's asylums are coming together and speaking for themselves." *Mad Matters* is the first Canadian book to bring together the writings of this movement, which is usually called the Mad People's Liberation movement, or Mad Pride movement. The movement and its corresponding academic field of mad studies have grown in the years since Starkman made that statement in 1981. This book presents diverse critical voices that convey the lived experiences of psychiatrized people. Together, the chapters challenge dominant understandings of "mental illness." The connections between mad activism and other liberation struggles are stressed throughout the book, making it an important contribution to the literature on human rights and anti-oppression.

Longmore, Paul K., and Lauri Umansky. 2001. *The New Disability History: American Perspectives*. New York: New York University Press.

When it was published in 2001, this volume opened up disability's "hidden history." This book contains 14 chapters that explore a broad range of topics within U.S. disability history. In this book, a North Carolina Youth finds his identity; a deaf Southerner is challenged in Civil War–era New York; Deaf community leaders ardently defend sign language in early 20th-century America; and Helen Keller, as well as the long-forgotten American Blind People's Higher Education and General Improvement Association both struggle in their own ways to shape public and private roles for blind Americans. This book brings together empirical evidence with the interdisciplinary tools and insights of disability studies. It explores the complex meanings of disability as an identity and a cultural signifier in American history. This book is called the "new disability history," because it was the first substantive sustained attempt to move the study of disability away from the medical or health-related fields and approach it specifically from the discipline of history.

McRuer, Robert, and Anna Mollow. 2012. *Sex and Disability*. Durham, NC: Duke University Press.

This collection of 17 essays combines two terms that most people do not consider together: sex and disability. Most disability studies scholars do not discuss sex in much detail. This collection tackles the idea that sex and disability are intimately related concepts and that disabled people can be seen as both subjects and objects of a range of erotic desires and practices through different perspectives such as literary analysis, ethnography, and autobiography.

Mitchell, David R., and Valerie Karr. 2014. *Crises, Conflict and Disability: Ensuring Equality*. Abingdon, Oxon: Routledge, Taylor & Francis Group.

People with disabilities are among the most adversely affected during conflict situations or when natural disasters strike. They experience higher death rates and have fewer resources available to them. This book focuses on an urgent issue in the international field of emergency planning. This book's 27 chapters discuss how to meet the needs of people with disabilities in crises and conflict situations all around the world. This book is an important reference for all those people working in or researching disability and inclusion, and emergency and disaster planning and relief, in both developed and developing countries.

Rembis, Michael. 2016. *Disabling Domesticity*. New York: Palgrave Macmillan.

Bringing together a range of authors from the multidisciplinary field of disability studies, this book uses disability and the experiences of disabled people living in the United States and Canada to explore and analyze dynamic sites of human interaction in both historical and contemporary contexts to provide readers with new ways of envisioning home, care, and family. Contributors to *Disabling Domesticity* focus on the varied domestic sites where intimate, and interdependent, human relations are formed and maintained. Analyzing domesticity through the lens of disability forces readers to think in new ways about family and household forms, care work, an ethic of care, reproductive labor, gendered and generational conflicts and cooperation, ageing, dependence, and local and global economies and political systems, in part by bringing the notion of interdependence, which undergirds all of the chapters in this book, into the foreground.

Rembis, Michael, Catherine Kudlick, and Kim E. Nielsen, eds. 2018. *The Oxford Handbook of Disability History*. New York: Oxford University Press.

This is the first volume of its kind to represent disability history outside institutions, healers, and treatments and in its global scale, from ancient Greece to British West Africa. There are 27 chapters, written by 30 experts from across the historical discipline. This volume captures the diversity and liveliness of this emerging subdiscipline within the historical profession. This collection offers new and valuable insights into the rich and varied lives of disabled people across time and place.

Soldatic, Karen, Hannah Morgan, and Alan Roulstone. 2014. *Disability, Spaces and Places of Policy Exclusion*. Abingdon, Oxon; New York: Routledge.

> Geographies of disability have become a key research priority for many disability scholars and geographers. This collection of 10 essays written by leading international disability researchers seeks to expand the current geographical frame operating within the realm of disability. Divided into two parts, the first section explores key concepts within the field of disability geographies, and their relationship to new policy regimes. The second section provides an in-depth examination of disabled people's experience of changing landscapes within the onset of emerging disability policy regimes.

Spandler, Helen, Jill Anderson, and Bob Sapey. 2016. *Madness, Distress and the Politics of Disablement*. Bristol: Policy Press.

> Along with *Mad Matters* (see earlier in the chapter), this book represents the cutting-edge of the new field of mad studies. It brings together academics and activists, many of whom are identified as mad, to explore the challenges of applying disability theory and policy, including the social model of disability, to madness and distress. This book has chapters that explore the relationships among madness, distress, and disability in various countries within Europe and North America, as well as Australia and India. Especially noteworthy is this book's sophisticated and eminently useful critique of the social model of disability. This book will appeal to policy makers, practitioners, activists, and academics.

Monographs

Baynton, Douglas C. 2016. *Defectives in the Land: Disability and Immigration in the Age of Eugenics*. Chicago: University of Chicago Press.

> In this important book, Baynton brings together decades of his own research into eugenics and immigration in the

United States. *Defectives in the Land* combines a cultural
and intellectual history of key terms associated with disability and poignant examples of immigrants' experiences
with immigration officials to forge a powerful analysis of
the importance of disability in U.S. immigration history.
The book is divided into four chapters with a short introduction and conclusion. Each of the chapters uses a single
word related to disability as its title: *Defective, Handicapped, Dependent,* and *Ugly.* As its title indicates, *Defectives in the Land* explores disability and immigration "in
the age of eugenics," from about the time Congress passed
the Chinese Exclusion Act in 1882 through the passage
of the Johnson-Reed Immigration Act in 1924. The book
focuses on European immigration to the East Coast of the
United States, primarily Ellis Island in New York harbor.

Bogdan, Robert. 1988. *Freak Show: Presenting Human Oddities
for Amusement and Profit.* Chicago: University of Chicago Press.
Freak Show sparked one of the first scholarly debates
within disability history. Beginning with the earliest min-
strel performances and P. T. Barnum's American Museum,
the book traces disabled performers through most of the
19th century to the end of vaudeville in the early 20th
century, with a coda devoted to late-20th-century carni-
val performers. According to Bogdan, freak shows were
part of a wider culture characterized by geographic and
intellectual exploration, the display of modern curiosi-
ties, and a growing commercialization of leisure. Freaks
and freak shows were "socially constructed," to the point
that some performers found opportunity and camara-
derie in what others saw as humiliating abuse. Bogdan's
research revealed how, in many cases, people with disabilities participated, sometimes willingly, in their own
"enfreakment"—that is, they actively cultivated careers
by creating, with the input and oversight of freak show
organizers and promoters, both a public persona and an

onstage presence, much like any other entertainer. Bogdan argued that, like many mainstream performers, those who made lucrative careers from their disabilities also found that they sometimes paid a heavy personal price. Through his detailed research on American freak shows, Bogdan showed that they consisted of much more than simply an unreflective display of "human oddities," and he made the then (1988) controversial claim that freak shows provided some disabled people with community, identity, and an important source of independence and upward social mobility.

Boster, Dea H. 2013. *African American Slavery and Disability: Bodies, Property, and Power in the Antebellum South, 1800–1860*. New York: Routledge.
This volume uncovers histories of disability in African American slavery from primary records, analyzing how concepts of race, disability, and power converged in the United States in the first half of the 19th century. Slaves with physical and mental impairments often faced unique limitations and conditions in their diagnosis, treatment, and evaluation as property. Being physically "unfit" sometimes allowed slaves to escape bondage and oppression.

Charlton, James I. 2004. *Nothing about Us without Us: Disability Oppression and Empowerment*. Berkeley: University of California Press.
James Charlton's book is the first work in disability studies to provide a theoretical overview of disability oppression that shows its similarities to, and differences from, racism, sexism, and colonialism. Charlton's Marxist materialist analysis relies on interviews he conducted over a 10-year period with disability rights activists throughout the "Third World," Europe, and the United States. His book is one of the first to mark the growing worldwide resistance to disability oppression.

Dolmage, Jay. 2014. *Disability Rhetoric*. Syracuse, NY: Syracuse University Press.

Disability Rhetoric views rhetorical theory and history through the lens of disability studies. Dolmage argues that communication has always been concerned with the meaning of the body and that bodily difference is always rhetorical. He outlines the development of a new theory that considers a greater range of bodies while also affirming the idea that all communication is embodied and that the body plays a central role in expression.

Edwards, R. A. R. 2016. *Words Made Flesh: Nineteenth-Century Deaf Education and the Growth of Deaf Culture*. New York: New York University Press.

Words Made Flesh explores the educational battles of the 19th century from both hearing and deaf points of view. During the early 19th century, schools for the deaf appeared in the United States, making it possible to create a deaf community by bringing deaf people together. A Deaf culture emerged within the schools. Just as the Deaf community began to grow, a powerful movement for oral education arose in the 1850s. Advocates of oralism, as it was called, argued that deaf people should stop signing and start speaking and reading lips in hopes that their Deaf language and culture would vanish.

Ellcessor, Elizabeth. 2016. *Restricted Access: Media, Disability, and the Politics of Participation*. New York: New York University Press.

Restricted Access investigates digital media accessibility. It argues for the necessity of conceptualizing access in a way that will enable greater participation in all forms of mediated culture. Drawing on disability and cultural studies, the book uses issues of regulation, use, content, form, and experience to examine contemporary digital media.

Through interviews with policy makers and accessibility professionals, popular culture, and archival material, as well as an ethnographic study of Internet use by people with disabilities, *Restricted Access* interrogates the assumptions that undergird contemporary technologies and participatory cultures.

Ellis, Katie. 2015. *Disability and Popular Culture: Focusing Passion, Creating Community and Expressing Defiance*. Farnham: Ashgate.

Drawing on disability studies theories, *Disability and Popular Culture* examines disabilities across a number of internationally recognized texts and objects from popular culture, including film, television, magazines and advertising campaigns, children's toys, music videos, sports, and online spaces, to investigate the representation of disability and disabled people. *Disability and Popular Culture* celebrates and complicates the increasing visibility of disability in popular culture. It argues that popular culture has the power to focus passion, create community, and express defiance in the context of disability and social change.

Elman, Julie Passanante. 2014. *Chronic Youth: Disability, Sexuality, and U.S. Media Cultures of Rehabilitation*. New York: New York University Press.

Chronic Youth examines television, popular novels, science journalism, new media, and public policy to show how teenagers became a cultural pivot for shifting notions of able-bodiedness, heteronormativity, and neoliberalism in the late 20th century. Highlighting the "troubled teen" as a site of pop cultural, medical, and governmental intervention, *Chronic Youth* traces the teenager as a figure through which broad threats to the normative order have been negotiated and contained.

Erevelles, Nirmala. 2011. *Disability and Difference in Global Contexts: Enabling a Transformative Body Politic*. New York: Palgrave Macmillan.

> *Disability and Difference in Global Contexts* explores the possibilities and limitations of rethinking disability using historical materialism. The book engages with social theory, cultural studies, social and education policy, feminist ethics, and theories of citizenship.

Garland-Thomson, Rosemarie. 1997. *Extraordinary Bodies: Figuring Physical Disability in American Culture and Literature*. New York: Columbia University Press.

> The first major critical study to examine literary and cultural representations of physical disability, *Extraordinary Bodies* shifts disability from a property of bodies to a product of cultural rules about what bodies should be or do. *Extraordinary Bodies* examines disabled figures in sentimental novels such as Harriet Beecher Stowe's *Uncle Tom's Cabin* and Rebecca Harding Davis's *Life in the Iron Mills*, African American novels by Toni Morrison and Audre Lorde, and the popular cultural ritual of the freak show. *Extraordinary Bodies* is one of the first books in the humanities in disability. It considers disability as a minority discourse, rather than a medical one, ultimately revising oppressive narratives of disability and revealing liberatory ones.

Goodley, Dan. 2014. *Dis/Ability Studies: Theorising Disablism and Ableism*. Abingdon, Oxon; New York: Routledge.

> This book draws from a range of interdisciplinary areas. It takes on important issues in critical disability theory and pushes them into new theoretical territory. *Dis/Ability Studies* argues that we are entering a time of disability studies, when both categories of disability and ability require expansion as a response to the global politics of neoliberal capitalism. The book is divided into two parts:

The first part traces the dual processes of ableism and disablism and argues that one cannot exist without the other, and the second part applies this new analytical framework to a range of topics. This book will appeal to students and researchers of disability across a range of disciplines. It is advanced reading and may not be easily accessible to beginners in the field of disability studies.

Goodley, Dan. 2017. *Disability Studies: An Interdisciplinary Introduction*, 2nd ed. Los Angeles: Sage.

This introduction to disability studies gives a clear, engaging, and thought-provoking overview of the field. It is an excellent resource for newcomers to the field of disability studies. The book discusses the need for a global focus in disability studies and disability politics. It introduces key debates in the field and highlights the intersections of disability studies with feminism, queer, and postcolonial theory. The book is separated into chapters on sociology, critical psychology, discourse analysis, psychoanalysis, and education. Each chapter engages with important areas of analysis such as the individual, society, community, and education to explore the realities of oppression experienced by disabled people and to develop the possibilities for addressing it.

Hampton. Jameel. 2015. *Disability and the Welfare State in Britain: Changes in Perception and Policy, 1948–1979*. Chicago: University of Chicago Press.

Disability and the Welfare State in Britain traces the long history of welfare in England. It provides historical contexts for the attempts made since the mid-1970s to reverse the exclusion of millions of disabled people from social welfare programs. This is the first book to set disability in the context of the history of the welfare state in Britain. It shows how policy and perceptions were slow to change and offers a close analysis of key groups and moments. When paired with *Telethons* (see Longmore in this section) it provides an excellent comparative analysis of disability and the formation of 20th-century welfare states.

Hamraie, Aimi. 2017. *Building Access: Universal Design and the Politics of Disability*. Minneapolis: University of Minnesota Press.
  Building Access investigates 20th-century strategies for designing the world with disability in mind. One important area of focus is universal design, which purports to create a built environment for everyone, not only the average citizen. What does this mean? Who counts as "everyone?" Blending technoscience studies and design history with critical disability, race, and feminist theories, *Building Access* interrogates the historical, cultural, and theoretical contexts for these questions, offering a critical history of universal design.

Jack, Jordynn. 2014. *Autism and Gender: From Refrigerator Mothers to Computer Geeks*. Chicago: University of Illinois Press.
  Autism and Gender focuses on the ways gender influences popular discussion and understanding of autism's causes and effects. She identifies gendered theories like the "refrigerator mother" theory and the "extreme male brain." Her analysis reveals how people employ such highly gendered theories to craft rhetorical narratives around stock "autistic" characters, like the computer geek.

Jennings, Audra. 2016. *Out of the Horrors of War: Disability Politics in World War II America*. Philadelphia: University of Pennsylvania Press.
  The first half of the 20th century brought the issue of disability into national focus. This book explores the history of disability activism, concentrating on the American Federation of the Physically Handicapped (AFPH), to address federal disability policy. The AFPH brought thousands of

disabled citizens and veterans into the national political arena, demanding equal access to economic security and full citizenship. *Out of the Horrors of War* argues that the disability rights movement is firmly rooted in the politics of World War II. This book extends the study of the disability rights movement into the 1940s and traces how its terms of inclusion influenced the movement for decades after, leading up to the passage of Americans with Disabilities Act of 1990.

Kafer, Alison. 2013. *Feminist, Queer, Crip*. Bloomington: Indiana University Press.

Kafer rejects the idea of disability as a pre-determined limit. Instead, she imagines a different future for disability and disabled bodies. She challenges the ways in which ideas about the future and time have been used in the service of compulsory able-bodiedness and able-mindedness. She juxtaposes theories, movements, and identities that are typically discussed in isolation and envisions new possibilities for "crip" or disabled futures and feminist/queer/crip alliances. *Feminist, Queer, Crip* goes against the urge to normalize disability and promotes a political framework for a more just world.

Kinder, John M. 2015. *Paying with Their Bodies: American War and the Problem of the Disabled Veteran*. Chicago: University of Chicago Press.

Paying with Their Bodies traces the complicated and intertwined histories of war and disability in modern America. Focusing mostly on World War I, Kinder argues that disabled veterans have long been at the center of two competing visions of American war: one that highlights the relative safety of U.S. military intervention overseas and the other associating American war with injury, mutilation, and suffering. *Paying with Their Bodies* will force readers to think in new ways about war and its painful costs.

Longmore, Paul K. 2016. *Telethons: Spectacle, Disability, and the Business of Charity*. New York: Oxford University Press.

During the second half of the 20th century, the telethon helped to define American popular culture. Millions of people watched weekend-long variety shows that raised billions of dollars for disability-related charities. Based on over two decades of research, *Telethons* explores the complexity underneath the TV spectacles. Disabled children turned out to be an ideal tool for promoting corporate interests, privatized health care, and class status. Telethon organizers and hosts used disabled children to give the public a message that people with disabilities were helpless, passive, apolitical members of American society. Longmore's posthumously published book shows how telethons helped major corporations increase their bottom lines, while filling in gaps in the strange public–private hybrid U.S. health insurance system.

McRuer, Robert. 2006. *Crip Theory: Cultural Signs of Queerness and Disability*. New York: New York University Press.

Crip Theory focuses on disability and queerness in contemporary cultures. Both disability studies and queer theory are concerned with how bodies, pleasures, and identities are represented as normal or as abject. *Crip Theory* was one of the first books to use these two interdisciplinary fields to inform our understanding of disability. McRuer's analysis is also informed by feminist theory, African American and Latino/a cultural theories, composition studies, film and television studies, and theories of globalization and counter-globalization. One of the key contributions of this book to the field of disability studies is its articulation of the idea of "compulsory able-bodiedness," or the idea that social and cultural pressures compel humans to achieve an essentially unattainable level of "normality," which in turn is rooted in unrealistic and often-unattainable expressions or representations of "normal" sexuality, gender, and ability.

Minich, Julie Avril. 2014. *Accessible Citizenships: Disability, Nation, and the Cultural Politics of Greater Mexico.* Philadelphia: Temple University Press.

Accessible Citizenships examines Chicana/o cultural representations in the southwestern United States that conceptualize political community through images of disability. Working against the assumption that disability is a metaphor for social decay or political crisis, Minich analyzes post-1980 literature, film, and visual art in which representations of nonnormative bodies work to expand our understanding of what it means to belong to a political community. This book illustrates how the work of queer writers gestures toward less exclusionary forms of citizenship and nationalism. Minich argues that the corporeal images used to depict national belonging have important consequences for how the rights and benefits of citizenship are understood and distributed.

Mitchell, David T., and Sharon Snyder. 2000. *Narrative Prosthesis: Disability and the Dependencies of Discourse.* Ann Arbor: University of Michigan Press.

Narrative Prosthesis develops a narrative theory of the pervasive use of disability as a device of characterization in literature and film. It argues that, while other marginalized identities have suffered cultural exclusion due to a dearth of images reflecting their experience, the marginality of disabled people has occurred in the midst of the perpetual circulation of images of disability in print and visual media. The book's six chapters offer comparative readings of key texts in the history of disability representation, including the tin soldier and lame Oedipus, Montaigne's "infinities of forms" and Nietzsche's "higher men," the performance history of Shakespeare's *Richard III*, Melville's Captain Ahab, the small town grotesques of Sherwood Anderson's *Winesburg, Ohio*, and Katherine Dunn's self-induced freaks in *Geek Love*.

Nakamura, Karen. 2013. *A Disability of the Soul: An Ethnography of Schizophrenia and Mental Illness in Contemporary Japan.* Ithaca, NY: Cornell University Press.

Nakamura explores how the members of the Bethel House community in northern Japan struggle with their lives, their illnesses, and the meaning of community. Bethel House, located in a small fishing village in northern Japan, was founded in 1984 as an intentional community for people with schizophrenia and other psychiatric disabilities. As part of its community approach, Bethel House started its own businesses. The idea was to create employment and socialization opportunities for its residents and to change public attitudes toward people living with mental "illness." The business ended up providing a significant boost to the distressed local economy. Told through engaging historical narrative, insightful ethnographic vignettes, and compelling life stories, Nakamura's account of Bethel House depicts its achievements and setbacks, its promises and limitations. It is important for people in the United States to think about how this community approach is either similar to or different from the treatment of "mentally ill" people in the United States.

Nielsen, Kim E. 2012. *A Disability History of the United States.* Boston: Beacon Press.

This book draws on primary source documents and social histories to retell American history through the eyes, words, and other expressions of the disabled and non-disabled people who lived it. A leader in the fields of disability history and disability studies, Nielsen argues that to understand disability history is not to focus only on a series of individual triumphs or tragedies, but rather to examine mass movements and pivotal daily events through the experiences of different historical actors. The first disability history textbook, *A Disability History of the United States* illustrates how concepts of disability have deeply shaped the American experience—from deciding who was allowed to immigrate to establishing labor laws and justifying slavery and gender discrimination.

Puar, Jasbir K. 2017. *The Right to Maim: Debility, Capacity, Disability.* Durham, NC: Duke University Press.

In *The Right to Maim*, Puar brings her work on the liberal state, sexuality, and biopolitics to bear on our understanding of disability. Drawing on an array of theoretical and methodological frameworks, Puar uses the concept of "debility"—bodily injury and social exclusion brought on by economic and political factors—to disrupt the category of disability. Although the ultimate aim of the book is to focus on Israel's treatment of Palestinians, *The Right to Maim* contains early chapters that are directly relevant to the disability rights movement in the United States and to the creation of disability as a political identity.

Reagan, Leslie J. 2010. *Dangerous Pregnancies: Mothers, Disabilities, and Abortion in America.* Berkeley: University of California Press.

This book tells the story of the German measles epidemic in the mid-20th-century United States and how it created national anxiety about dying, disabled, and "dangerous" babies. This anxiety ultimately worked its way into abortion politics, produced new science, and helped create two of the most enduring social movements of the late 20th century—the reproductive rights and the disabilities rights movements. One of the most important things that this book does is it shows how mothers and physicians worked together to create dominant ideas about and understandings of German measles in the mid-20th century. Scientific knowledge about the disease and its consequences both for mothers and for their babies was not known at the time. Doctors and parents were discovering and learning these things together. *Dangerous Pregnancies* does an excellent job of showing this interactive process, which could include heart-wrenching decisions about if and when to terminate a pregnancy.

Rembis, Michael A. 2011. *Defining Deviance: Sex, Science, and Delinquent Girls, 1890–1960.* Urbana: University of Illinois Press.

Defining Deviance analyzes how reformers in the late 19th and early 20th centuries perceived delinquent girls and their often-troubled lives. It uses Illinois as a case study to show how implementation of involuntary commitment laws in the United States reflected eugenic thinking about juvenile delinquency. Much more than an institutional history, *Defining Deviance* examines the cases of young women to reveal the centrality of sex, class, gender, and disability in the formation of scientific and social reform. This study provides new insights into the treatment of young women whom the dominant society perceived as threats to the sexual and eugenic purity of modern America.

Rose, Sarah F. 2017. *No Right to Be Idle: The Invention of Disability, 1850–1930.* Chapel Hill: University of North Carolina Press.

During the late 19th century and early 20th century, people with disabilities came to be labeled as "unproductive citizens" in America. Rose explains that a combination of public policies, shifting family structures, and economic changes effectively barred workers with disabilities from mainstream workplaces and simultaneously cast disabled people as morally questionable dependents in need of permanent rehabilitation to achieve "self-care" and "self-support." Rose integrates disability history and labor history. She shows how people with disabilities lost access to paid work and the status of "worker."

Samuels, Ellen J. 2014. *Fantasies of Identification: Disability, Gender, Race*. New York: New York University Press.

In *Fantasies of Identification*, Samuels traces the cultural processes through which embodied social identities became fixed, verifiable, and visible. Through modern science bodies understood as black, white, or Indian; able-bodied or disabled; and male or female, got defined as biologically distinct and scientifically verifiable marked bodies. *Fantasies of Identification* examines how this process of marking bodies has circulated among cultural representations, law, science, and policy to become one of the most powerfully institutionalized ideologies of modern U.S. society. The idea that one would need "documentation" to "prove" their disability, gender status, race, or other marker of identity is not something that has always existed in U.S. society, neither have the categories that require documentation. Samuels traces the history of the creation of these twinned processes from the 19th century to the end of the 20th century.

Schweik, Susan M. 2009. *The Ugly Laws: Disability in Public*. New York: New York University Press.

The Ugly Laws traces the history of municipal laws targeting "unsightly beggars" who sprang up in cities across America during the late 19th and early 20th centuries. Part of broader social and political movements to control poor and disabled people, these "ugly laws" have become a site of significant interest in disability studies, law, and the arts because they provide insights into the crucial intersection of evolving and unstable concepts of race, nation, sex, class, and gender.

Through her cultural and textual analysis, Schweik uncovers the history behind the laws, giving readers a deeper understanding of the urban industrial context within which they were created. In addition to situating the laws within their historical context, Schweik contemplates the legacies of the laws for disabled people living in the 20th century.

Shakespeare, Tom. 2014. *Disability Rights and Wrongs Revisited.* London; New York: Routledge.

From the 1970s to the early 21st century, the field of disability studies grew out of and often reflected the political activism of disabled people. Shakespeare argues that disability research needs a firmer, less ephemeral, conceptual and empirical footing. Using what he calls a "critical realist" approach, *Disability Rights and Wrongs Revisited* promotes a multilayered, interdisciplinary, engaged, and nuanced approach to disability. Key topics include dichotomies, identity, bioethics, and relationships. This is an invaluable resource for researchers and students in disability studies and sociology, as well as professionals, policy makers, and activists. Although Shakespeare is based in the United Kingdom, his work is critical for people studying disability in the United States, because his "critical realist" approach challenges both the social model of disability and U.S. ideas about the social construction of disability. Put simply, Shakespeare argues that impairment is "real" in the sense that it is rooted in the materiality of the body and in that it has significant effects on disabled people's daily lives. Therefore theorists and researchers must take the existence of impairment seriously and consider it in their work.

Shapiro, Joseph P. 1994. *No Pity: People with Disabilities Forging a New Civil Rights Movement.* New York: Times Books.

Written by a journalist, *No Pity* is a chronicle of the ways that both society and self-perceptions have changed for

disabled people. Published only four years after the enactment of the Americans with Disabilities Act (ADA), *No
Pity* focuses on the concerns of people who are deaf, blind,
autistic, or mentally disabled, and examines the impact
of technology on disabled people, the need for nursing
home reform, and the potential for backlash against the
ADA as the public becomes aware of the costs of implementing disability laws. Shapiro interviewed hundreds
of people for his book, and his conversations with them
bring *No Pity* to life.

Siebers, Tobin. 2011. *Disability Theory*. Ann Arbor: University
of Michigan Press.

Disability Theory revolutionized disability theory by providing evidence of the value and utility of a disability studies approach to social and cultural analysis that transforms
basic ideas about identity, ideology, language, politics, social oppression, and the body. At the same time, the book
advances the emerging field of disability studies by putting its core issues into contact with important thinkers
in cultural studies, literary theory, queer theory, gender
studies, and critical race theory. This book is critical for
understanding disability studies in the United States. It
puts forth Siebers ideas about "complex embodiment"
and masquerade, both of which have been used exten-
sively by subsequent theorists.

Taylor, Steven. 2009. *Acts of Conscience: World War II, Mental
Institutions, and Religious Objectors*. Syracuse, NY: Syracuse
University Press.

In the mid- to late 1940s, a group of young men who
were among the 12,000 conscientious objectors or COs
who chose to perform civilian public service as an alternative to fighting in World War II challenged the psychiatric establishment by putting a public spotlight on the
brutal conditions inside America's mental hospitals and

training schools for people with psychiatric and intellectual disabilities. After the war, COs led a reform to change public attitudes and to improve the training and status of institutional staff that was primarily waged through the media, in magazines and books. The reform efforts had a significant impact on federal legislation in the late 1940s and early 1950s. *Acts of Conscience* is important for people interested in the history of psychiatry, the history of institutions, disability history, and mad people's history.

Wexler, Alice. 2016. *Autism in a Decentered World*. New York: Routledge.

Autism in a Decentered World will be of particular interest to researchers and scholars within the fields of disability studies, art education, and art therapy. It is the first book to integrate a discussion of philosophical and scientific explanations of autism with commentary on "real-world" efforts to provide support and social and creative outlets for people living on the autism spectrum. Autistic people are empirically and scientifically generalized as living in a fragmented, alternate reality, without a coherent continuous self. In Part I of this book, recent neuropsychological research and its implications for existing theories of autism, selfhood, and identity are presented, challenging common assumptions about the formation and structure of the autistic self and autism's relationship to neurotypicality. In Part II, the book explores the ways in which artists diagnosed with autism have constructed their identities through participation within art communities and cultures, and how the concept of self as a "story" can be utilized to better understand neurological difference and typical cognition.

Williamson, Bess. 2018. *Accessible America: A History of Disability and Design*. New York: New York University Press.

Accessible America explores the important role that disabled people and their allies played in the history of design in the

United States from World War II to the present. As Williamson shows, disability culture and politics both mirrored and shaped in important ways changes made to the built environment and normal everyday products consumed by millions of Americans. Initially prodded by disabled veterans of World War II seeking prosthetics, automobiles, and accessible houses, the federal government became involved in funding technological advancements, through the G.I. Bill, and in creating design standards. Local communities such as the University of Illinois and the University of California, Berkeley, were centers of design innovation because they had active disabled populations. These local efforts to improve access led to the creation of state and national projects and standards. By the end of the 20th century, disability art, culture, and politics infused the design world and influenced the personal touches that many disabled people applied to the built environment and the technology and products they consumed.

Wilson, Daniel J. 2007. *Living with Polio: The Epidemic and Its Survivors*. Chicago: University of Chicago Press.
Living with Polio is one of the first books to focus primarily on the personal stories of the men and women who had acute polio and lived with its disabling consequences. Writing primarily from memoirs produced by 100 polio survivors—men and women who had been diagnosed with polio and went through rehabilitation in the United States during the years between 1930 and 1960—Wilson follows every physical and emotional stage of the disease. This book is important because it highlights the voices of polio survivors. Although the book gestures toward some of the important legacies enacted by polio survivors, like improvements in public education for disabled people, or access to jobs and housing, it focuses mostly on survivors' experiences as young people in the hospital and in rehabilitation. Nevertheless, this is an important and powerful

book that shows the importance of incorporating the voices and experiences of disabled people themselves into their own histories.

Internet Resources

Archives and Deaf Collections, Gallaudet University. https://www.gallaudet.edu/archives-and-deaf-collections. Accessed July 14, 2017.

The Gallaudet University Library Archives and Deaf Collections works to build, maintain, and organize the world's largest collection of materials related to the Deaf community. It is also the home to Gallaudet University's institutional records and the records of the Gallaudet family. Founded in 1857, Gallaudet University was originally a grammar school for both deaf and blind children. By its second year, it had 14 deaf students and 7 blind students. The school offered college-level classes for the first time during the 1863–1864 academic year. Gallaudet became the first school offering postsecondary education to deaf and hard-of-hearing students. It remains the only higher education institution in the world in which all programs and services are specifically designed for deaf and hard-of-hearing students. In 1954, Congress amended the charter of the school, changing its name to Gallaudet College, which had been the official name of the collegiate department since 1894. In 1986, Congress again changed the charter, renaming the school Gallaudet University.

Center for Inclusive Design and Environmental Access. http://idea.ap.buffalo.edu. Accessed July 14, 2017.

The Center for Inclusive Design and Environmental Access at the University at Buffalo is dedicated to making environments and products more usable, safer, and healthier in response to the needs of an increasingly diverse population. The Center has been in operation since the mid-1980s and is an international leader in transportation research and research on the built environment and product design. It is also a world leader in universal design.

Deaf People and World War II. http://www.rit.edu/ntid/ccs/deafww2/. Accessed July 14, 2017.
This site is the result of several years of gathering materials about Deaf people's experiences related to World War II. The site focuses on three areas of the world involved in this conflict. Deaf North American, Deaf European, and Deaf Asian people's lives are examined before, during, and after the war. There are videotape clips and full testimonies, articles, transcripts, artwork, books, and links to other related sites.

Disability History Museum. http://www.disabilitymuseum.org/dhm/index.html. Accessed July 14, 2017.
The Disability History Museum is a virtual online platform that aims to provide a wide array of resources to help deepen visitors' understanding of human variation and difference, and to expand their appreciation of how vital the role of disabled people in history. The site's mission is to foster a deeper understanding of how changing cultural values, notions of identity, laws, and policies have shaped and influenced the experiences of disabled people, their families, and their communities over time.

The Disability Rights and Independent Living Movement. http://bancroft.berkeley.edu/collections/drilm/. Accessed July 14, 2017.
The Disability Rights and Independent Living Movement Project was launched to capture the history of the movement by people with disabilities to win legally defined civil rights and control over their own lives. A rich collection of personal papers and the records of key disability

organizations, as well as oral histories, are available through the Bancroft library at University of California, Berkeley. The collection is an in-depth research resource for the study of a social movement that has changed the social, cultural, and legal landscape of the United States.

Disability Rights Education and Defense Fund. https://dredf .org. Accessed July 14, 2017.

The Disability Rights Education and Defense Fund (DREDF) was founded in 1979 and is the leading national civil rights law and policy center directed by individuals with disabilities and parents who have children with disabilities. Its mission is to advance the civil and human rights of people with disabilities through legal advocacy, training, education, public policy, and legislation. It trains and educates people with disabilities about their rights under state and federal disability rights laws and represents clients in disability rights litigation. DREDF also designs and carries out strategies that strengthen public policy and federal and state laws, such as the Handicapped Children's Protection Act, the Civil Rights Restoration Act, and the landmark 1990 Americans with Disabilities Act.

EveryBody: An Artifact History of Disability in America. https://everybody.si.edu. Accessed July 14, 2017.

This website, which is part of the Smithsonian Institute's American History Museum in Washington, D.C., is dedicated to raising awareness and sensitivity about disability through a look at the history of disability in the United States. To that end, they have designed this website to be accessible to all users.

The Icarus Project. http://theicarusproject.net. Accessed July 14, 2017.

The Icarus Project is a support network and education project by and for people who experience the world in ways that are often diagnosed as mental illness. It advances social justice by fostering mutual-aid practices that reconnect healing and collective liberation. It transforms people through transforming the world around them. Its publications include tangible ways in which people in emotional distress can be helped through a simple and practical checklist, and provides political education on social justice and mental health issues.

Image Archive on the American Eugenics Movement. http://www.eugenicsarchive.org/eugenics/. Accessed July 14, 2017.
 This site offers the unfiltered story of American eugenics told primarily through materials from the Eugenics Record Office at Cold Spring Harbor, which was the center of American eugenics research from 1910 to 1940. In this archive, there are numerous reports, articles, charts, and pedigrees that were considered scientific "facts" in their day.

Madness Radio. http://www.madnessradio.net. Accessed July 14, 2017.
 Madness Radio focuses on personal experiences with "madness" and extreme states of consciousness from beyond conventional perspectives and mainstream treatments. They also feature authors, advocates, and researchers on madness-related topics, including civil rights, science, policy reform, holistic health, history, and art.

Making Historical Sign Language Materials Accessible. http://hsldb.georgetown.edu/index.php. Accessed July 14, 2017.
 Making Historical Sign Language Materials Accessible is an ongoing project to build a comprehensive platform to store and access not only early forms of American Sign Language, but to link these with data from other languages both historical and modern to expand the ability of researchers to do effective comparative analyses.

MindFreedom International. http://www.mindfreedom.org. Accessed July 14, 2017.

   MindFreedom International is a nonprofit organization that unites 100 sponsor and affiliate grassroots groups with thousands of individual members to win human rights and alternatives for people labeled with psychiatric disabilities. Its goals are to win human rights campaigns in mental health; challenge abuse by the psychiatric drug industry; support the self-determination of psychiatric survivors and mental health consumers; and promote safe, humane, and effective options in mental health.

Museum of Disability History. http://museumofdisability.org. Accessed July 14, 2017.

   The Museum of disability History is a project of People Inc. and is chartered by the New York State Department of Education Board of Regents. It is one of only two bricks-and-mortar disability history museums in the world—the other is in São Paulo, Brazil. In addition to its collections and exhibits located in Buffalo, New York, the museum has an extensive virtual presence, with its online museum, archive, library database, and K–12 curricular materials.

Patient No More: People with Disabilities Securing Civil Rights. http://longmoreinstitute.sfsu.edu/patient-no-more. Accessed July 14, 2017.

   The Paul K. Longmore Institute on Disability at San Francisco State University created "Patient No More," an exhibit situated at the crossroads of disability history, the arts, education, and social justice. The exhibit uses innovative research, provocative discussions, and influential cultural events to connect the Bay Area's vibrant disability communities with the faculty and students of San Francisco State University and the rest of the world through its online presence.

Wordgathering: A Journal of Disability Poetry and Literature. http://www.wordgathering.com/index.html. Accessed July 14, 2017.

> *Wordgathering* is an online quarterly journal of disability poetry, literature, and art dedicated to providing a venue where the work of writers with disabilities can be found and to building up a core of work for those interested in disability literature.

World Institute on Disability. https://wid.org. Accessed July 14, 2017.

> World Institute on Disability's (WID's) mission in communities and nations worldwide is to eliminate barriers to full social integration and increase employment, economic security, and healthcare for people with disabilities. WID creates innovative programs and tools; conducts research, public education, training and advocacy campaigns; and provides technical assistance.

7 Chronology

Introduction

From the early 19th century to the mid-20th century, people with disabilities in the United States were increasingly institutionalized and removed from society. Whether motivated by a Christian desire to provide relief, charity, and salvation to the nation's poor and less fortunate souls, an increasingly medicalized urge to treat and cure "defective" citizens, or an economically driven need to control "unruly" and ostensibly ungovernable populations, a number of individuals and groups in the early decades of the 19th century began to form "special" schools for deaf, blind, and what would in the 21st century be called developmentally or intellectually disabled children, as well as asylums for the insane. Although an individual's experience was greatly influenced by his or her gender, race, age, class, and veteran status, many disabled people found themselves entangled in this growing web of institutions, which by the end of the 19th century became primarily custodial. Influenced by the rise of eugenics and later genetics, as well as evolutionary thought, and the popular notion of social Darwinism, schools, asylums, and hospitals that were once meant to educate, treat, and cure disabled people, enabling them to return to society, had become wretched, dirty, deplorably overcrowded, and underfunded human warehouses.

[Two adult males wearing T-shirts and shorts, their prosthetic legs visible] Athletes with disabilities running in the 2014 Boston Marathon. (Marcio Silva/Dreamstime.com)

281

By the early decades of the 20th century, people with disabilities and their allies began to speak out against the inhumane conditions within which many disabled people were forced to live. These individual efforts became catalyzed in the 1930s with an increasing national awareness of polio and the social dislocation of a significant number of working Americans during the Great Depression, and during the 1940s with the revelations of Nazi atrocities abroad and the deplorable conditions of institutions at home, which were made public by Conscientious Objectors to World War II who served their country by working in asylums and hospitals throughout the nation during the war. Although institutionalized populations continued to rise during the 1950s, some parents of disabled children and others began to advocate for change, forming groups like the National Association for Retarded Children. The African American civil rights movement and the student movements of the 1960s provided the final push for disability activists who became more organized and publicly vocal by the late 1960s and early 1970s.

Since then, people with disabilities, with the help of their families and other allies, have fought to gain their release from various institutional settings and to secure their rights. The Disability Rights movement, the Mad People's Liberation or Mad Pride movement, the Independent Living movement, and the Self-Advocacy movement have been successful in gaining the legal enfranchisement and community integration of people with all types of disabilities. More work remains to be done, however. People with disabilities, especially those experiencing intellectual, developmental, mental, or emotional disabilities, remain disproportionately under- or uneducated, and under- or unemployed, and isolated from the community, with many of them living in group homes or other institutionalized residential settings, living homeless on the streets, or experiencing disproportionate levels of incarceration in the nation's jails and prisons.

The following timeline, which has been drawn from a number of different sources, offers a detailed journey through this interesting and important history. No timeline is comprehensive. This timeline stops in 2008 with the passage of the Americans with Disabilities Act Amendments Act. It is up to readers like you to fill in gaps in the timeline and extended it beyond 2008. Good luck!

Timeline

1751   A group of Quakers and other community leaders in Philadelphia, Benjamin Franklin among them, petition the Pennsylvania colonial assembly to build a hospital that would include facilities designed to cure the "insane."

1756   The Pennsylvania Hospital opens. "Lunatics" are kept in dank, gloomy, foul-smelling cells, with little light and no heat; they are watched over by "keepers" who used whips, chains, handcuffs, ankle-irons, and "Madd-shirts" and beat them regularly. Visiting the hospital and viewing the "lunatics" become a popular Sunday outing for Philadelphians.

1760   Pennsylvania hospital administrators construct an iron wall to keep the curious at bay.

1762   Unable to keep visitors away, the hospital begins charging admission of four pence to view the "lunatics."

1762   The colonies' first medical school is established at College of Philadelphia. Benjamin Rush is one of its first faculty.

1773   The colonies' only hospital dedicated exclusively to the care of insane patients opens in Williamsburg, Virginia, but remains little used until the 1790s.

1776   At the time of the American Revolution, fewer than 5 percent of American doctors have degrees and only about 10 percent have any formal training at all.

1776   Stephen Hopkins, a man believed to be living with what would later become known as cerebral palsy, is one of the signers of the Declaration of Independence. Hopkins is known for saying, "my hands may tremble, my heart does not."

1783   Benjamin Rush, member of the Continental Congress, signer of the Declaration of Independence, and America's first "Mad Doctor," arrives at Pennsylvania Hospital.

1790s   The first medical societies are formed, and the first periodical medical journal is published.

1796   Pennsylvania Hospital builds a new wing for its mad residents at the request of Benjamin Rush.

1798   U.S. president John Adams signs an act for the relief of sick and disabled seamen on July 16.

1812   Benjamin Rush publishes *Medical Inquiries and Observations upon the Diseases of the Mind*, the first psychiatric text published in the United States.

1813   Benjamin Rush dies.

1815   Thomas H. Gallaudet departs America for Europe to seek new methods to educate deaf people.

1816   Gallaudet returns to America with Laurent Clerc, a deaf Frenchmen and innovator in deaf education.

1817   Philadelphia Quakers open America's first "moral treatment" asylum.

1817   The social elite of Boston, under the leadership of members of the Congregational Church, open their own "moral treatment" asylum, known as Charlestown Asylum, later known as the McLean Hospital.

1817   The Connecticut Asylum for the Education and Instruction of Deaf and Dumb persons is founded in Hartford, Connecticut.

1821   Quaker Thomas Eddy oversees the opening of Bloomingdale Asylum in New York City on the site of what is now Columbia University.

1822   The American School for the Deaf adds vocational training to its curriculum.

1824   The Hartford Retreat for the insane opens in Connecticut.

1829   Louis Braille, a Frenchman, invents the raised point alphabet, enabling visually impaired and blind people to read.

1832   The Perkins School for the Blind in Boston admits its first two students, the sisters Sophia and Abbey Carter.

1833   The first public moral treatment asylum opens in Worcester, Massachusetts.

1835   Richard Lawrence attempts to assassinate President Andrew Jackson. Lawrence is determined to be "afflicted" with "astromania" and found not guilty by reason of insanity.

1840   In the United States, 2,561 mentally ill patients are being cared for in 18 mental hospitals.

1840   The first attempt to record and classify psychiatric data is made by the U.S. census.

1840   Entrepreneur and entertainer P. T. Barnum purchases the American Museum in New York City and begins to exhibit "freaks" as a form of entertainment.

1840   The U.S. census reports that "insanity" among "Negroes" living in the North is 11 times greater than in the South. Although clearly biased, this figured is used by pro-slavery Southerners to justify the continued existence of slavery.

1841   There are 16 moral treatment asylums in America, both public and private.

1841   Quaker physician Thomas Kirkbride becomes the head of the new Pennsylvania Hospital for the Insane.

1841   Dorothea Dix begins her campaign for asylum reform in Massachusetts.

1843   The New York State Lunatic Asylum in Utica opens under the leadership of Superintendent Amariah Brigham.

1844   Thirteen asylum superintendents form the Association of Medical Superintendents of American Institutions for the Insane (AMSAII)

1846   *American Annals of the Deaf* begins publication at the American School for the Deaf in Hartford, Connecticut.

1848   Dorothea Dix takes her campaign for asylum reform to Washington, D.C. Dix proposes selling 5 million acres of federal land to endow the building of public asylums.

1848   Samuel Gridley Howe opens the Perkins Institution, the first residential school for children with intellectual disabilities.

1849   The first "sheltered workshop" for blind people is developed at the Perkins Institution in Massachusetts.

1849   "Blind" Tom plays his first public performance.

1850   The U.S. census counts 15,610 mentally ill people in a population of 21 million.

1851   Thomas H. Gallaudet dies on September 10.

1854   The New England Gallaudet Association of the Deaf is founded in Montpelier, Vermont.

1855   In his study of "insanity" in Massachusetts, Edward Jarvis finds that "insanity" is 64 times more common among the financially destitute.

1860   The braille system of communication is introduced to America and taught at the St. Louis School for the Blind.

1860–1880   "Insanity" among "Negroes" rises fivefold nationwide.

1861–1865   The U.S. Civil War produces hundreds of thousands of casualties, with 30,000 amputees.

1864   The Columbia Institution for the Deaf and Dumb and Blind opens in Washington, D.C., becoming the first college for people with disabilities in the United States. Its name is later changed to Gallaudet College and Gallaudet University.

1868   Elizabeth Packard publishes *The Prisoner's Hidden Life; or, Insane Asylums Unveiled*, the story of her involuntary commitment to the Jacksonville State Asylum in Illinois.

1869   The first wheelchair patent is registered with the U.S. Patent Office.

1870   Approximately 45,000 "insane" persons are being treated in institutions throughout the country.

1872   Alexander Graham Bell opens a school dedicated to oralism in the education of deaf people in Boston.

1878   Joel W. Smith introduces modified braille to the American Association of Instructors of the Blind.

1880   The National Convention of Deaf Mutes meets in Cincinnati, Ohio, forming the nucleus of what will become the National Association of the Deaf (NAD). The first major issue taken on by the NAD is the rise of oralism and the suppression of American Sign Language.

1880   Approximately 74,000 mental patients are being treated in 139 hospitals in the United States.

1880   The U.S. census codifies seven types of "insanity": mania, melancholia, monomania (obsession or paranoia), paresis (general or partial paralysis), dementia, dipsomania (alcoholism), and epilepsy.

1880   The U.S. census counts 91,997 mental ill people in a population of 50 million: 1 in every 554 Americans.

1880   The National Association for the Protection of the Insane and the Prevention of Insanity is formed.

1881   The idea of "moral insanity" becomes an issue in the trial of Charles J. Guiteau, who assassinated President Garfield on July 2, 1881. Guiteau is convicted and condemned to death.

1882   The U.S. Congress passes a law barring "lunatics, idiots, and persons likely to be a public charge" from entering the country.

1883   In England, Sir Francis Galton, a cousin of Charles Darwin, names his science of controlled human breeding, "eugenics."

1886   On March 21, the *New York Times* publishes "A Burden from Abroad," in which it attributes the increasing number of "insane" people in asylums to "the shipment of insane men and women to this country from Europe." This article and others like it are at least partly reflective of growing nativist, anti-immigrant, and eugenic sentiment in the United States.

1887   Women are admitted to the National Deaf-Mute College (Gallaudet University).

1887   Helen Keller, a deaf blind seven-year-old living in Tuscumbia, Alabama, meets her new tutor, Anne Sullivan.

1887   Elizabeth Cochrane, known popularly as Nelly Bly, one of America's first woman reporters, feigns insanity to be admitted to Blackwell Island Asylum, where she spends 10 days doing research for the *New York World*. Cochrane quickly discovers that patients are treated poorly and that once admitted, it is difficult for patients to be released from the asylum.

1892   Asylum superintendents change the name of their association from AMSAII to the American Medico-Psychological Association.

1892   American writer Charlotte Perkins Gilman publishes her short story "The Yellow Wallpaper," in the *New England Magazine*. Considered an important work of early feminist literature, Gilman's story offers a critique of treatments considered effective for women's physical and mental ill health.

1894   The National Deaf-Mute College is renamed Gallaudet College.

1896   Connecticut becomes the first state to prohibit "defectives" from marrying.

1904   Nearly 200,000 "insane" individuals are being cared for in 328 institutions nationwide (public and private). This amounts to 1 mentally ill or institutionalized person for every 530 Americans.

1904   The Station for Experimental Evolution opens at Cold Spring Harbor, New York. Funded by the Carnegie Foundation and directed by Charles B. Davenport, the Station becomes the center of eugenic research in the United States and the world.

Davenport earns an annual salary of $3,500, making him one of the highest-paid scientists in the country.

1907   Indiana becomes the first state to pass a compulsory sterilization law. Over the next 20 years, 30 state legislatures approve sterilization bills.

1908   Clifford Beers publishes *A Mind That Found Itself*, his own account of the time he spent in mental institutions. His work would become influential in the foundation of the mental hygiene movement in the United States.

1909   The National Committee for Mental Hygiene is founded. The committee originally serves as a clearinghouse for information on nervous and mental diseases.

1909   Renowned European psychiatrist Sigmund Freud delivers five lectures over five days at Clark University in Massachusetts. Renowned child psychologist and president of Clark University, G. Stanley Hall invites Freud as part of a commemoration of Clark's 20th anniversary. This is Freud's one and only visit to America. Popularized versions of Freud's theories would dominate psychiatry for the next 50 years.

1910   Davenport opens the Eugenics Record Office in Cold Spring Harbor, New York. It is directed by Harry H. Laughlin, and funded by Mary Harriman, widow of the railroad magnate who had died in 1909. Harriman contributes $500,000 over the next eight years; John D. Rockefeller, Jr., adds more funds.

1912   Henry Goddard publishes *The Kallikak Family: A Study in the Heredity of Feeble-Mindedness*.

1915   More than 20 states have marriage restriction laws.

1915   In England, the term "shell shock" enters the mental health lexicon with the publication of a paper on the subject in *Lancet* by Capt. C. S. Myers, a specialist in psychological medicine. It is debated whether shell shock is caused by brain injury or psychological forces.

1915   The film *The Black Stork* is released, documenting Dr. Harry Haiselden's decision to let a disabled infant die.

1916   In Europe, 40 percent of casualties from World War I are from "shell-shock."

1916   Henry Cotton, superintendent of the Trenton State Hospital in New Jersey, begins removing his patients' teeth as a cure for insanity. Soon, Cotton begins removing patients' tonsils, colon, gall bladder, appendix, fallopian tubes, uterus, cervix, ovaries, and seminal vesicles, all as a cure for insanity. A 1924 study reveals that 43 percent of Cotton's patients had died, and that he had killed more than 100 people with his intestinal surgeries alone.

1916   Former New York state commissioner on lunacy Stephen Smith publishes *Who Is Insane?*, in which he argues that although the "nature" of insanity remains "illusive," its prevention and treatment must rely on "scientific principles."

1917   The National Committee for Mental Hygiene begins publishing its journal, *Mental Hygiene.*

1918   The Smith-Sear Veterans Vocational Rehabilitation Act establishes a federal vocational rehabilitation program for veterans.

1920   Congress passes the Fess–Smith Civilian Vocational Rehabilitation Act.

1921   About 7,499 U.S. veterans are receiving hospital care for neuropsychiatric disorders.

1921   The American Foundation for the Blind is founded.

1923   The amount of money spent on service-connected disability awards to World War I veterans for neuropsychiatric disorders equals $28,256.

1925–1929   American psychiatrist Harry Stack Sullivan treats schizophrenics at the Sheppard Pratt Hospital near Baltimore, Maryland, with his own form of psychoanalysis that focuses on interpersonal relationships, rather than intrapsychic conflict (Freud). Sullivan develops and promotes the notion that cultural forces, most notably loneliness, create mental illness.

1926   The American Eugenics Society is founded. John D. Rockefeller contributes $10,000, and George Eastman of Eastman Kodak contributes $20,000. Yale professor Irving Fisher becomes the organization's first president.

1927   In an 8–1 majority, the U.S, Supreme Court upholds the Constitutionality of forced sterilization in *Buck v. Bell.*

1927   Philip Drinker and Louis Shaw develop the iron lung, a chamber that provides artificial respiration for polio patients being treated for respiratory muscular paralysis.

1927   Franklin Delano Roosevelt helps to establish the Warm Springs Foundation in Warm Springs, Georgia.

1927   In the textbook *Mental Hygiene*, Daniel Wolford La Rue advises students, "*Eugenics* aims to get children better born. We are coming to see that we cannot keep people healthy-minded unless they are well born" (La Rue, 1927, 10).

1928   The American Psychiatric Association (APA) joins with 21 other organizations in writing the Standard Classified Nomenclature of Diseases.

1929   Seeing Eye establishes the first guide dog school in the United States.

1929   About 272,527 Americans are in mental hospitals.

1930s   Patients in New York state hospitals die at a rate five times that of the general population.

1930s–1940s   Psychiatrists who recognize "institutionalization" syndrome argue that prolonged institutionalization can deprive patients of individual interests and social contacts, as well as their own individuality. Patients may become passive and unmotivated. The first attempts are made to treat mental patients outside the institution.

1930   Schizophrenia accounts for 22 percent of all first-time psychiatric hospital admissions.

1931   About 11,342 U.S. veterans are receiving hospital care for neuropsychiatric disorders.

1932 The amount of money spent on service-connected disability awards to World War I veterans for neuropsychiatric disorders equals $67,916.

1932 The film *Freaks* (Todd Browning), featuring disabled performers, is released.

1933 Franklin Delano Roosevelt (elected 1932), the first U.S. President with a significant disability, is sworn into office.

1933 Every U.S. state has some form of marriage restriction.

1934 The National Committee for Mental Hygiene publishes *State Hospitals in the Depression: A Survey of the Effects of the Economic Crisis on the Operation of Institutions for the Mentally Ill in the United States*. One hundred and four of 181 hospitals surveyed responded. Among other things, the survey finds that the number of patients in mental hospitals has increased from 272,252 in 1929 to 318,948 in 1933.

1934 Jacobus tenBroek, 23 years old and blind since age 14, joins with Dr. Newel Perry and others to form the California Council of the Blind, which later becomes the National Federation of the Blind of California.

1935 The League of the Physically Handicapped is formed to advocate for jobs for disabled people during the Great Depression.

1935 Actor Peter Lorre plays Dr. Gogol in *Mad Love*, the story of an insane surgeon whose obsession with an actress leads him to replace her wounded pianist's hands with the hands of a knife murderer that still have the urge to throw knives.

1936 Walter Freeman and James Watts become the first physicians to perform a prefrontal lobotomy in the United States.

1936 About 566,000 Americans are housed in institutions or asylums, up from 45,000 in 1870.

1936–1941 About 37,000 American mental patients are forced to endure metrazol-induced convulsive "therapy," many of them against their will.

1937 A *Fortune* magazine poll finds that 66 percent of Americans favor sterilizing "defectives."

1937   Herbert A. Everest and Harry C. Jennings patent the design for a folding wheelchair capable of fitting in a car trunk. They go on to form Everest & Jennings (E&J), the largest wheelchair manufacture in the United States.

1937   Albert Deutsch publishes *The Mentally Ill in America: A History of Their Care and Treatment from Colonial Times.* The book is well researched and thorough and earns him a reputation as an expert in the field.

1938   Benjamin Malzberg of the New York State Psychiatric Institute reports "positive" results of insulin-coma therapy on schizophrenics.

1938   President Franklin Delano Roosevelt creates the March of Dimes to help fight polio.

1939   The New York State Psychiatric Institute finds that 43 percent of patients treated with metrazol-induced convulsive therapy suffer from spinal fractures. The therapy, which induced an explosive seizure, was also known to fracture other bones; break and loosen teeth; dislocate shoulders; tear muscles; and cause hemorrhaging in the lungs, kidneys, spleen, and brain.

1939   Seventy percent of American hospitals report using metrazol-induced convulsive therapy.

1939   The U.S. Public Health Service publishes *A Study of Public Mental Hospitals in the United States, 1937–1939.* The survey reports on the hospitalization of various patients for 1938, including mental disease, 447,321; mental deficiency, 94,284; epilepsy, 21,026; and others, 6,634. The average daily population of "mentally diseased" patients in 1938 is 376,787, and per capita expenditure for all state hospitals in 1938 is $291.27 or about 80 cents per day.

1940   About 419,374 patients are being treated in 181 mental hospitals.

1940   The American Federation of the Physically Handicapped is formed. It is the first cross-disability political organization to call for an end to employment discrimination and a National Employ the Physically Handicapped Week.

1940   Electroshock therapy is introduced to U.S. hospitals. During the 1940s and 1950s, well over 1 million Americans endure electroshock.

1941   A U.S. Public Health survey finds that 5 percent of patients treated with insulin-coma therapy die from the procedure; the rest live with irreparable brain damage.

1941   McLean doctors John Talbot and Kenneth Tillotson begin using hypothermia as a treatment for mental illness.

1942–1945   Approximately 1.6 million men are rejected for military service during World War II because of psychiatric and neurological problems, which amounts to 12 percent of the 20 million men evaluated. This rejection rate is 7.6 times higher than the rejection rate in World War I. There were also 1.1 million admissions to military hospitals for psychiatric disorders over the course of the war. About 438,000 men are discharged from the military for psychiatric reasons during the war, a rate of discharge five times greater than the rate of discharge during World War I.

1942   Physicians at New York City's Bellevue Hospital begin a study in which they subject 98 children between the ages of 4 and 11 to electroshock twice daily for 20 days.

1943   William Menninger, an outspoken member of the Topeka Psychoanalytic Society, is appointed chief military psychiatrist.

1943   "Little Moron" books become popular with their "jokes" at the expense of Little Moron and his low IQ.

1943   In April, the U.S. Army initiates its program of "forward psychiatric treatment" during its Tunisian campaign.

1943   Dr. Leo Kanner of Johns Hopkins University first uses the term "early infantile autism."

1944   Almost half of the 67,000 beds in U.S. Veterans Administration hospitals are occupied by World War I veterans with neuropsychiatric disorders.

1944   Ingrid Bergman earns an Academy Award for her performance in *Gaslight*, the story of a woman attempting to maintain her recovery from a nervous breakdown.

1945   President Harry Truman enacts Public Law 176, creating an annual National Employ the Physically Handicapped Week.

1945   About 45,127 Americans are sterilized; about 21,311 are patients in state mental hospitals.

1945   Rochester State Hospital in New York reports that its patients are receiving electroshock three times a week.

1946   Albert Q. Maisel publishes a scathing indictment of state mental hospitals in *Life* magazine based on the reports of Conscientious Objectors to World War II who served in state mental hospitals during the war.

1946   The U.S. Army Pictorial Services releases *Let There Be Light*, the final entry in a trilogy of films produced for the U.S. government by John Huston. It is a documentary film that follows 75 U.S. soldiers who have sustained debilitating emotional trauma and depression. A series of scenes chronicle their entry into a psychiatric hospital, their treatment, and eventual recovery. Considered too controversial, the film was not made widely available until the 1970s.

1946   The U.S. Congress passes the Mental Health Act, leading to the creation of the National Institute of Mental Health (NIMH) in 1949.

1946   In May, the formation of the National Mental Health Foundation is announced. The organization is the successor to the Mental Hygiene Program, a reform organization founded by Conscientious Objectors to World War II who served in the hospitals during the war. U.S. Supreme Court justice Owen J. Roberts would serve as national chairman for the new organization.

1946   Walter Freeman performs his first transorbital lobotomy. After rendering the patient unconscious with electroshock,

Freeman inserts an ice pick through the bony orbit in the eye socket, driving the pick seven centimeters into the patient's brain. Freeman then moves the pick vigorously back and forth, damaging the brain's frontal lobes.

1947   Frank L. Wright, Jr., publishes the book *Out of Sight, Out of Mind*. It is based on the reports of Conscientious Objectors to World War II who served in mental hospitals during the war. It is reportedly based on more than 2,000 eyewitness reports of conditions and treatment at 46 mental hospitals located throughout the United States. The institutions are not named, but the states in which they were located include Connecticut, Delaware, Illinois, Indiana, Iowa, Maryland, Michigan, New Jersey, New York, Ohio, Pennsylvania, Rhode Island, Vermont, Virginia, Washington, and Wisconsin.

1948   Timothy J. Nugent establishes the disabled students program at the University of Illinois, Galesburg. It is later moved to University of Illinois, Urbana–Champaign, where it becomes a national model for educating disabled students.

1948   Mental patients at the Rockland State Hospital in New York City form We Are Not Alone (WANA), a patient self-help group.

1949   The first annual wheelchair basketball tournament is held at the University of Illinois, Galesburg.

1949   Paul Hoch, director of the Department of Experimental Psychiatry at the New York State Psychiatric Institute, begins a study in which he gives LSD and mescaline to mentally ill patients in an effort to exacerbate their psychosis. Hoch's study and others like it begin 50 years of NIMH funded system-exacerbation experiments that do not end until 1998.

1949   The NIMH is established. It is one of the first four NIH institutes.

1950s   Walter Freeman begins performing lobotomies on children.

1950   The National Mental Health Foundation, the National Committee for Mental Hygiene, and the Psychiatric Foundation (a fund-raising arm of the APA) merge to form the National Association for Mental Health. The October 1950 issue of *Mental Hygiene* announces the new organization as the National Association of Mental Health, Inc., the Voluntary Promotional Agency of the Mental Hygiene Movement, founded by Clifford W. Beers.

1950   More than 500,000 patients are treated in mental hospitals throughout the United States. Total expenditures reach $500 million annually, less than $2 per day, per patient.

1951   Howard Rusk opens the Institute of Rehabilitation Medicine at New York University Medical Center.

1951   *Life* magazine publishes "Scandal Results in Real Reforms," by Albert Q. Maisel, in which he argues that the exposés written during the mid-1940s led at least in part to state increases in funds for mental hospital renovation and construction and the hiring of additional physicians, professionals, and attendants. Spending on mental hospitals increases 100 percent, and the number of mental hospital employees rises from 79,740 to more than 100,000. There is also a shift in the philosophy governing most mental hospitals away from custodial care to intensive treatment and release. This move makes the beginning of "de-institutionalization" in the United States

1952   The first edition of psychiatry's *Diagnostic and Statistical Manual of Mental Disorders* (*DSM-I*) covers 62 discrete diagnoses.

1953   Federal spending on mental health research equals $10.9 million.

1953   Los Angeles County provides in-home attendant care to adult polio survivors as an alternative to the more expensive hospitalization.

1953   Actress Vivien Leigh (Scarlett O'Hara, *Gone with the Wind*) is hospitalized for the treatment of mental illness.

1953   Medical experiments are conducted on 100 boys at the Fernald School for developmentally disabled children in Waverley, Massachusetts. They are subjected to radioactive elements in their food to determine the effect of these elements.

1954   Mary Switzer, director of the Office of Vocational Rehabilitation, authorizes the distribution of federal funds to more than 100 universities for rehabilitation-related programs.

1954   Pharmaceutical company Smith, Kline & French introduces chlorpromazine into the U.S. market, selling it as Thorazine. From 1954 through 1964, 50 million Americans will use Thorazine. The company's revenues skyrocket from $53 million in 1953 to $347 million in 1970, with $116 million coming from the sale of Thorazine alone.

1955   New York City's Bellevue Hospital's Lauretta Bender reports that she has put a toddler, not yet three years old, through a 20-day electroshock treatment.

1955   More than 20,000 Americans have been lobotomized. More than 60 percent of all lobotomies are performed on patients in state mental hospitals.

1955   The U.S. Congress passes the Mental Health Study Act, creating the Joint Commission on Mental Illness and Mental Health. The commission's final report, *Action for Mental Health*, provides the background for President John F. Kennedy's special message to Congress on mental health.

1956   Congress appropriates $12 million for research in the clinical and basic aspects of psychopharmacology. The Psychopharmacology Service Center is established. The Health Amendments Act authorizes the support of community services for the mentally ill, such as halfway houses, daycare, and aftercare under Title V.

1957   The first National Wheelchair Games in the United States are held at Adelphi College in Garden City, New York.

1957   Little People of America is founded in Reno, Nevada, to advocate on behalf of little people or dwarfs.

1957   In *The Three Faces of Eve* (20th Century Fox Film Corporation), Eve White's (Joanne Woodward) multiple-personality disorder is cured with psychoanalytic therapy.

1958   The *Rehabilitation Gazette* (formerly the *Toomeyville Gazette*) is published. It is a grassroots publication that promotes disability rights, independent living, and cross-disability organizing. It features articles written by disabled people on all aspects of the disability experience.

1958   The first African American to apply for admission to the University of Mississippi, Clennon King, is sent to a state mental hospital.

1959   Horizon Pictures releases *Suddenly, Last Summer*. Nominated for three Academy Awards, it is the story of a wealthy harridan, Violet Venable (Katharine Hepburn), who attempts to bribe Dr. Cukrowicz (Montgomery Clift), a young "psychosurgeon" from a New Orleans mental hospital that is desperately in need of funds, into lobotomizing her niece, Catherine Holly (Elizabeth Taylor). Violet wants the operation performed in order to prevent Catherine from defiling the memory of her son, the poet Sebastian. Catherine has been babbling incessantly about Sebastian's mysterious death that she witnessed while on holiday together in Spain the previous summer.

1959   The first report linking neuroleptics (Thorazine) to irreversible motor dysfunction is issued. One year later, the motor dysfunction is given the name tardive dyskinesia.

1960   The first International Paralympic Games organized by the International Paralympic Committee are held in Rome, Italy.

1961   The *Atlantic* devotes an entire issue to psychiatry in America in which it states that the influence of psychoanalytic theory had been "incalculable."

1961   Federal spending on mental health research increases tenfold to $100.9 million.

1961   Sociologist Erving Goffman publishes *Asylums: Essays on the Social Situation of Mental Patients and Other Inmates*.

1961   The American National Standard Institute publishes "American Standard Specifications for Making Buildings Accessible to and Usable by the Physically Handicapped."

1961   Pulitzer- and Nobel Prize–winning author Ernest Hemingway, who had a history of mental illness, shoots and kills himself in his home.

1962   The President's Committee on Employment of the Physically Handicapped changes its name to the President's Committee on Employment of the Handicapped, reflecting a desire to be inclusive of people with developmental disabilities and mental illness.

1962   A polio survivor who uses a wheelchair and an iron lung, Ed Roberts, sues the University of California at Berkeley for admission. He is successful.

1962   Ken Kesey publishes *One Flew over the Cuckoo's Nest*, a novel set in an Oregon asylum.

1962   Eunice Kennedy Shriver founds the Special Olympics.

1963   Sociologist Erving Goffman publishes *Stigma: Notes on the Management of Spoiled Identity*.

1963   South Carolina becomes the first state to pass an architectural access code.

1963   President John F. Kennedy signs the Community Mental Health Centers Act.

1963   American writer Sylvia Plath publishes her only novel, *The Bell Jar*, a semi-autobiographical account of her own struggles with mental illness. The book was originally published under the pseudonym Victoria Lucas.

1964   Robert H. Weitbrecht invents the "acoustic coupler," a forerunner to the modem. It allows teletypewriters to send messages via standard telephone lines, making it possible for deaf and hard-of-hearing to use the phone.

1965   American troops serving in Vietnam experience "psychiatric breakdown" at a rate of 10.8 per 1,000.

1965   Congress establishes the National Technical Institute for the Deaf at Rochester Institute of Technology in Rochester, New York.

1965   Congress creates the Medicaid and Medicare programs, providing federal subsidies for care in nursing homes, but no such subsides in state mental hospitals. Between 1965 and 1970, the population of institutionalized mental patients decreases by 140,000, with most of those patients going into nursing homes.

1966   "Christmas in Purgatory," by Burton Blatt and Fred Kaplan, documents the appalling conditions in institutions for people with developmental disabilities.

1966   Thomas J. Scheff publishes *Being Mentally Ill: Sociological Theory*.

1966   The first Jerry Lewis Labor Day telethon for the Muscular Dystrophy Association is aired on television.

1967   The National Theater of the Deaf is founded.

1967   American troops serving in Vietnam experience "psychiatric breakdown" at a rate of 9.8 per 1,000.

1968   The federal Architectural Barriers Act requires that all federally owned or leased buildings be accessible to people with physical disabilities.

1968   The APA publishes the first revision of its *Diagnostic and Statistical Manual of Mental Disorders*, known commonly as the *DSM-II*.

1968   The first international Special Olympic Games take place in Chicago, Illinois.

1969   American troops serving in Vietnam experience "psychiatric breakdown" at a rate of 15 per 1,000.

1970s   In the early 1970s, ex-patients and other "mad survivors" begin forming their own civil rights groups. They hold conferences and human rights demonstrations. Some of the groups include Insane Liberation Front, Portland, OR; Mental

Patients' Liberation Project, New York City; and Network against Psychiatric Assault, San Francisco.

1970   American troops serving in Vietnam experience "psychiatric breakdown" at a rate of 24.1 per 1,000.

1970   The Urban Mass Transit Act requires all new mass transit vehicles be lift equipped. Implementation of the act will be delayed 20 years.

1970   Judith Heumann founds Disabled in Action, a disability rights organization, in New York City, after her successful employment discrimination suit against the city's public school system.

1970   Thomas Szasz, MD, publishes his scathing critique of institutional psychiatry, *The Manufacture of Madness*.

1970   *Playboy* magazine offers its first braille edition.

1970   Food and Drug Administration (FDA) approves the use of lithium based on NIMH research.

1970   Ed Roberts, John Hessler, Hale Zukas, and others form the disabled students program at the University of California, Berkeley.

1970   More than 19 million prescriptions are written annually for neuroleptics (Thorazine, Haldol, Prolixin), despite the appearance of severe and often permanent side effects, including brain damage and permanent motor dysfunction. Fifty percent of "mentally retarded" children in the United States are being prescribed neuroleptics, as are elderly residents of nursing homes, and juvenile delinquents—the latter referring to them as "zombie juice."

1971   The Soteria Project begins in Santa Clara, California. Led by Loren Mosher, a Harvard-trained physician and director of the Center for Schizophrenia Studies at the NIMH, the Soteria Project sought to provide mental patients with "love and food and understanding, not drugs" in a residential setting staffed by nonprofessional personnel. The Soteria project was quite successful, so much so that an additional house was opened a few years later. The NIMH Clinical Projects Research Review Committee persuaded the NIMH to replace Mosher and cut funding to the project, leading to its eventual demise by the end of the 1970s. Mosher and other critics of the traditional medical model of mental health were shunned by the psychiatric community and much of the American public.

1971   The U.S. District Court for the Middle District of Alabama decides in *Wyatt v. Stickney* that people in residential state schools and institutions have a constitutional right to "receive such individual treatment as (would) give them a realistic opportunity to be cured or to improve his or her mental condition." People with developmental disabilities were no longer going to be locked away in institutions without treatment or education.

1971   The Caption Center is founded at WGBH public television in Boston. It provides captioned programming for deaf viewers.

1972   The U.S. District Court for the District of Columbia in *Mills v. Board of Education* rules that the District of Columbia cannot exclude disabled children from the public schools.

1972   U.S. District Court for the Eastern District of Pennsylvania in *PARC v. Pennsylvania* strikes down various state laws used to exclude disabled children from public schools.

1972   The Center for Independent Living at University of California, Berkeley, is created. It is recognized as the first center for independent living in the United States.

1972   U.S. federal government provides Social Security income to disabled people. The number of patients in mental hospitals drops by 15.4 percent, the largest decrease ever.

1972   Sixty-one percent of medical evacuations out of Vietnam are "psychiatric cases," most of which involve heroin addiction.

1972   The Judge David L. Bazelon Center for Mental Health Law is founded in Washington, D.C., to provide legal representation to advocate for the rights of people with mental illness.

1972   Paralyzed Veterans of America, the National Paraplegia Foundation, and Richard Heddinger file suit to force the Washington Metropolitan Area Transit Authority to incorporate access into their design for a new, multibillion-dollar subway system in Washington, D.C. Their victory becomes a landmark in the struggle for accessible public mass transit.

1972   Parents of residents at the Willowbrook State School on Staten Island, New York, file suit to end the appalling conditions at that institution. A televised investigation of the institution by reporter Geraldo Rivera causes public outrage. Thousands of institution residents will be moved into community-based living arrangements. The case is *New York ARC v. Rockefeller*.

1972   Demonstrations are held by disabled activists in New York City, Washington, D.C., and elsewhere to protest President Nixon's veto of the Rehabilitation Act.

1973   The board of directors of the APA votes to remove homosexuality from its *Diagnostic and Statistical Manual of Mental Disorders*. The vote is ratified by APA members in 1974.

1973   The first handicap parking stickers are introduced in Washington, D.C.

1973   The Federal-Aid Highway Act authorizes federal funds for the construction of curb cuts.

1973   Congress passes the Rehabilitation Act over two vetoes by President Nixon. It contains Section 504, which bans discrimination.

1974   Thomas Szasz, M.D., publishes *The Myth of Mental Illness* in which he argues that mental illness is a myth, metaphor, and ideology, not an objective medical condition.

1974   The first U.S. National Wheelchair Basketball tournament and the first National Wheelchair Marathon are both held.

1974   Susan Sygall, Deborah Kaplan, Kitty Cone, Corbett O'Toole, Susan Schapiro, and other women found the Disabled Women's Coalition at the University of California, Berkeley, to run support groups, retreats, publish feminist writings, and lecture on women and disability.

1974   The first convention of People First, a self-advocacy organization, is held in Salem, Oregon. People First will become the largest U.S. organization composed of and led by people with developmental disabilities.

1975   Congress passes the Education for All Handicapped Children Act (Public Law 94–142), establishing the right of children with disabilities to a public school education.

1975   The American Coalition of Citizens with Disabilities is founded.

1975   The U.S. Supreme Court rules in *O'Connor v. Donaldson* that people cannot be institutionalized against their will in a psychiatric hospital unless they are determined to be a threat to themselves or to others.

1976   Disabled in Action pickets the United Cerebral Palsy telethon in New York City, calling telethons "demeaning and paternalistic shows which celebrate and encourage pity."

1977   Known as the "504 sit-ins," disability rights activists in 10 cities stage demonstrations and occupations of the federal Department of Health Education and Welfare (HEW) to force the Carter administration to issue regulations for the implementation of Section 504 of the Rehabilitation Act of 1973. The demonstration in San Francisco lasts nearly one month, with HEW secretary Joseph Califano signing the regulations on April 28.

1978   It is estimated that more than 100,000 Americans have been misdiagnosed with "schizophrenia."

1978   Disability rights activists in Denver stage a sit-in demonstration, blocking several Denver Regional Transit Authority buses, to protest the complete inaccessibility of that city's mass transit system.

1978 Title VII of the Rehabilitation Act Amendments of 1978 establishes the first federal funding for Centers for Independent Living and creates the National Council of the Handicapped under the U.S. Department of Education.

1979 Boston judge Joseph Tauro hands down the controversial landmark decision that forced treatment is a violation of patients' constitutional rights, but that the use of neuroleptics constitutes sound medical practice. In the future, medical practitioners need only to obtain permission from the court to force patients into treatment.

1979 A World Health Organization (WHO) study of outcomes of persons diagnosed with "schizophrenia" in poor countries versus those in rich countries reveals that while about two-thirds of "schizophrenics" fare well and are able to live in society in poor countries, two-thirds of "schizophrenics" in rich countries, like the United States, fare poorly and remain chronically mentally ill.

1979 The U.S. Olympic Committee organizes its Handicapped in Sports Committee.

1979 The U.S. Supreme Court in *Southeastern Community College v. Davis* rules that under Section 504 of the Rehabilitation Act of 1973, programs receiving federal funds must make "reasonable modifications" to enable participation of otherwise-qualified disabled individuals.

1979 Marilyn Hamilton, Jim Okamoto, and Don Helan produce their Quickie lightweight, folding wheelchair, revolutionizing manual wheelchair design.

1979 The Disability Rights Education and Defense Fund (DREDF) is founded in Berkeley, California, becoming the nation's preeminent disability rights legal advocacy center and participating in much of the landmark litigation and lobbying of the 1980s and 1990s.

1979   The National Alliance for the Mentally Ill is founded in Madison, Wisconsin, by parents of persons with mental illness.

1979   Self-Help for Hard of Hearing People is founded in Bethesda, Maryland, by Howard "Rocky" Stone.

1980s   The State University of New York Health Science Center in Syracuse finds that 90,000 Americans develop "irreversible TD [tardive dyskinesia] each year" during the 1980s.

1980s   By the 1980s more than 85 percent of "schizophrenics" are on high-potency neuroleptics (Haldol and Prolixin), equivalent to 1,500 milligrams of Thorazine—a dosage 15 times more powerful than the dosage initially recommended by European doctors and 5 times more powerful than the dosage deemed dangerous by British doctors. High-dose patients are known to suffer more from a number of side effects, including depression, anxiety, motor retardation, emotional withdrawal, and akathisia (severe blunting of emotions), as well as dystonia (severe and sustained muscle spasms). High dosages of Prolixin are linked to increased risk of suicide, and even moderately high doses of Haldol are linked to the onset of extremely violent behavior.

1980–1983   Sears Roebuck and Company begins selling decoders for closed captioning for television.

1980–1983   Corbett O'Toole creates and leads the National Disabled Women's Educational Equity Project based at the DREDF. It conducts the first national survey on disability and gender.

1980–1983   The National Disabled Women's Educational Equity Project hosts the first National Conference on Disabled Women's Educational Equity in Bethesda, Maryland.

1980–1983   Harilyn Russo creates the Networking Project on Disabled Women and Girls at the YWCA in New York City. She produces a book and film entitled *Loud, Proud and Female*.

1980   The APA publishes a revised edition of its *Diagnostic and Statistical Manual of Mental Disorders*, known commonly as the *DSM-III*. Post-traumatic stress disorder is added as a response to anti–Vietnam War activists, the activist group Vietnam Veterans against the War, and Chaim F. Shatan, who first identified what is referred to as post–Vietnam Syndrome.

1980   A census of U.S. state mental hospitals sets the inpatient population at 132,164, down from 559,000 in 1955.

1980   It is estimated that from 1960 through 1980, as many as 100,000 Americans died from neuroleptic malignant syndrome (an acute reaction experienced when some patients begin taking neuroleptics) and that 80,000 of these deaths could have been avoided if physicians had been educated to recognize the signs of neuroleptic malignant syndrome.

1980   Congress passes the Civil Rights of Institutionalized Persons Act, authorizing the U.S. Justice Department to file civil suits on behalf of residents of institutions whose rights are being violated.

1980   The first issue of "The Disability Rag and Resource" is published in Louisville, Kentucky.

1981   Congress passes the Telecommunications for the Disabled Act, mandating telephone access for deaf and hard-of-hearing people at important public places, such as hospitals and police stations, and that all coin-operated phones be hearing aid compatible by January 1985.

1981   John Hinckley attempts to assassinate President Ronald Reagan and is found not guilty by reason of insanity. Hinckley's acquittal led to Congress passing the Insanity Defense Reform Act of 1984, which made it much more difficult to get a not-guilty-by-reason-of-insanity verdict.

1981   The National Council on Independent Living is formed to advocate on behalf of Centers for Independent Living and the Independent Living Movement.

1982   A review of Manhattan State Hospital's patient records reveals that 80 percent of patients diagnosed with "schizophrenia" had never exhibited the symptoms necessary for the diagnosis.

1982   A study of 1,023 African Americans determined to be "schizophrenic" reveals that 64 percent had never displayed the symptoms necessary for diagnosis under APA guidelines.

1983   Ed Roberts, Judy Heumann, and Joan Leon found the World Institute on Disability in Oakland, California.

1983   American Disabled for Accessible Public Transit is organized at the Atlantis Community Headquarters in Denver, Colorado.

1983   The National Council on the Handicapped issues a call for Congress to "act forthwith to include persons with disabilities in the Civil Rights Act of 1964 and other civil and voting rights legislation and regulations."

1984   The NIMH undertakes its Epidemiological Catchment Area Study to determine the prevalence of mental illness in the United States. The study reveals that approximately 30–40 million Americans in any given six-month period will manifest signs of a diagnosable mental disorder and that over the course of a lifetime, one in five Americans will experience a mental illness.

1984   George Murray becomes the first wheelchair athlete to be featured on a Wheaties cereal box.

1985   A review of the case histories of 89 patients diagnosed with "schizophrenia" at the Manhattan State Hospital reveals that only 16, based on their initial symptoms, should have been diagnosed as "schizophrenic."

1985   The National Association of Psychiatric Survivors is founded.

1985   Fifty percent of people with a serious mental illness are receiving no treatment.

1986   The Society for Disability Studies, a professional academic organization, is founded.

1986   Congress passes the Air Carrier Access Act, prohibiting airlines from refusing service to people because they are disabled, and from charging them more for airfare than non-disabled travelers.

1987   A study finds that doctors ignore the appearance of akathisia (severe blunting of emotions) in 75 percent of patients using neuroleptics.

1988   The number of patients in American public mental hospitals is 80 percent fewer than the historic highs of the mid-1950s.

1988   Students at Gallaudet University in Washington, D.C., organize the "Deaf President Now" protest. I. King Jordan becomes the university's first deaf president.

1988   The anti-depressant Prozac is introduced into the American market. It is one of the new selective serotonin reuptake inhibitor anti-depressants.

1988   Congress passes the Fair Housing Amendments Act, which adds people with disabilities to those groups protected by federal fair housing legislation. It establishes minimum standards of accessibility for newly constructed multiple dwelling housing.

1989   *Mouth: The Voice of Disability Rights* magazine begins publication.

1990s   During the early 1990s, neuroscientists begin using fMRI or functional magnetic resonance imagining to observe brain activity.

1990   U.S. president George H. W. Bush announces the opening of "The Decade of the Brain."

1990   ADAPT organizes the Wheels of Justice campaign in Washington, D.C., bringing hundreds of disabled people to the nation's capitol in support of the Americans with Disabilities Act (ADA). Activists occupy the Capitol rotunda and are arrested when they refuse to leave.

1990   U.S. president George H. W. Bush signs the landmark ADA into law.

1990   With the passage of the ADA, ADAPT changes its name and its focus to American Disabled for Attendant Programs Today.

1990   The new antipsychotic drug, clozapine, is brought to the U.S. market by Sandoz. The drug, which is marketed as Clozaril, was first tested as an antipsychotic in the 1960s. In the 1990s, Sandoz sells clozapine and a necessary blood test performed by its affiliate, Caremark, to patients at a price of $9,000 per year.

1990   The historic Education for all Handicapped Children Act is amended and renamed the Individuals with Disabilities Education Act.

1990   The NAMHC (National Advisory Mental Health Council) report to Congress, *National Plan for Research on Child and Adolescent Mental Disorders*, is submitted.

1991   The NAMHC submits two reports to Congress: *Caring for People with Severe Mental Disorders: A National Plan of Research to Improve Services* and *Mental Health in America: A Series of Public Hearings*.

1991   The activist group Jerry's Orphans stages its first protest of the Jerry Lewis Muscular Dystrophy Association telethon.

1992   The WHO releases the results of a second study that confirms the findings of its 1979 study.

1992   A review of the research on violence and mental disorder reveals that, despite common stereotypes and dominant misconceptions concerning the prevalence of violence among the mentally ill, the majority (90 percent) of mentally ill people are *not* violent.

1993   Janssen gains FDA approval to sell risperidone in the United States.

1993   American author Susanna Kaysen publishes her bestselling memoir, *Girl, Interrupted*, based on her experiences of being diagnosed with "borderline personality disorder" as a young woman and spending time in a psychiatric hospital.

1994   Risperidone is approved by the FDA as a treatment for patients with schizophrenia.

1994   APA's fourth edition of its *Diagnostic and Statistical Manual of Mental Disorders* or *DSM-IV* contains over 300 diagnoses, up from 62 in 1952.

1995   The anti-depressant Prozac exceeds $1 billion in sales.

1995   The American Association of People with Disabilities is founded in Washington, D.C.

1995   Sales of the antidepressant Prozac hit $2 billion.

1996   U.S. sales of risperidone top $500 million.

1996   The group Not Dead Yet is formed by disabled activists to oppose Jack Kevorkian and proponents of assisted suicide for people with disabilities.

1996   Eli Lilly releases olanzapine, marketed as Zyprexa, on the U.S. market.

1997   Venture capital groups pour $100 million into for-profit clinical research sites that test the efficacy and safety of antipsychotics.

1998   U.S. sales of olanzapine top $1 billion.

1998   Total sales of antipsychotics in the United States tops $2.3 billion.

1998   Ninety-two percent of all "schizophrenics" in America are routinely taking antipsychotic (neuroleptic) medication.

1999   President Bill Clinton convenes a high-profile summit meeting on the state of the nation's mental health.

1999   The U.S. Supreme Court hands down its landmark decision in the *Olmstead v. L. C.* case.

1999   The U.S. surgeon general reports that "the majority of those with a diagnosable mental disorder [are] not receiving treatment."

1999   The U.S. surgeon general's report on mental health identifies stigma as one of the foremost obstacles to improved mental healthcare, noting that "stigma tragically deprives people of their dignity and interferes with their full participation in society."

2000   Forty-two percent of people with a serious mental illness are receiving *no* treatment.

2000   Big pharmaceutical companies increase their spending on clinical trials from under $1 billion in 1990 to $3.5 billion in 2000.

2001   Forty-six percent of people with a serious mental illness are receiving *no* treatment.

2001   *Harvard Mental Health Newsletter* admits, "Researchers are still in the dark about schizophrenia."

2001   The Commonwealth of Virginia House of Delegates approves a resolution expressing regret for its eugenic practices (primarily forced sterilizations) between 1924 and 1979.

2001   The drug company Merck reaps more than $7 billion in profits.

2001   *A Beautiful Mind* (Universal Pictures), the cinematic portrayal of the life of Nobel Prize recipient John Nash, wins four Academy Awards.

2001   The U.S. Substance Abuse and Mental Health Services Administration convenes a National Mental Health Symposium to Address Discrimination and Stigma, the first-ever national conference devoted exclusively to issues of discrimination and stigma related to mental illnesses.

2001   The World Psychiatric Association (WPA) sponsors the first-ever International Conference on Reducing Stigma and Discrimination because of Schizophrenia.

2002   More than 11 percent of women and 5 percent of men are taking antidepressants, about 25 million people.

2002   More than one in three doctor's office visits by women involve antidepressants, either for a new prescription or for a refill.

2002   President George W. Bush issues his own statement on mental health and publicly supports "mental health parity"— equality in insurance coverage for both physical and mental ailments.

2002   The United States registers early 1.5 million admissions to psychiatric wards of general hospitals or private psychiatric facilities.

2002   Eleven million antidepressant prescriptions are written for American children and adolescents.

2002   The profits from the top 10 drug companies are greater than the combined profits of all of the other 490 *Fortune* 500 companies.

2003   According to the Centers for Disease Control and Prevention, doctors report 21 million office visits for "depression."

2003   The drug company Pfizer reaps more than $12 billion in profits.

2003   More than 103,000 Americans live in "congregated care" facilities, like group homes or board-and-care facilities.

2003   Eighty-three percent of the global market for attention deficit hyperactivity disorder (ADHD) medications is accounted for by the United States, primarily American children.

2004   There are 6.7 million downloads of articles from the *Journal of Neuroscience*, the official journal of the Society for Neuroscience.

2004   What is believed to be the first-ever Disability Pride parade is held in Chicago. Similar demonstrations are held in other cities throughout the country.

2004   The popular magazine *Scientific American* launches a new magazine, *Scientific American Mind*.

2004   The top seven U.S.-based drug companies make more than $34 billion profit from $139 billion in revenues.

2004   California passes Proposition 63, the "millionaires for mental health tax." Citizens with personal income over $1 million are levied an additional tax to help pay for the expansion of public psychiatric services.

2004   About 300,000 Americans with psychiatric diagnoses (other than dementia) are living in nursing homes.

2004   About 33 million Americans are prescribed at least one psychiatric drug in 2004, up from 21 million in 1997.

2004   In a Rice University study of attitudes toward mental illness, respondents are 12 times more likely to ascribe the cause of mental illness to a brain disorder than to a character flaw.

2004   In a WHO study of the global prevalence of mental illness, 26 percent of Americans report that they had suffered from any type of psychiatric disorder the previous year. In contrast, only 5 percent of Nigerians, 8 percent of Italians, 9 percent of Germans, and 12 percent of Mexicans reported having a psychiatric disorder.

2004   More than 1 million U.S. children are taking psychotropic drugs and more than 11 million prescriptions for antidepressants are written for them.

2005   A study shows that more than one-quarter of people with severe mental illness had been the victims of a violent crime in the past year—11 times the rate of the general population.

2005   American sales of the antidepressant Zoloft equal $3.1 billion, exceeding the sales of Tide laundry detergent.

2006   Funding for the NIMH, which was $90 million in 1976, reaches $1.4 billion.

2006   Membership in the Society for Neuroscience reaches 37,000. It had 91 members in 1971.

2006   The return on revenues for the pharmaceutical industry was 20 percent, making it the second-most profitable industry in the United States.

2006   Seventy-two percent of Americans see depression as a health problem.

2006   Worldwide sales of one drug for schizophrenia, Zyprexa, equal $4.7 billion, exceeding the revenue by the apparel company Levi Strauss Co.

2006   More than 1.25 million of the U.S. state and federal prisoners and local jail inmates have mental health problems.

2006   About 227 million antidepressant prescriptions are dispensed in the United States, more than any other class of medication in that year. The United States accounts for 66 percent of the global antidepressant market.

2006   Spending on antidepressants equals $13.5 billion, up from $5.1 billion in 1997. Spending on antipsychotics equals $11.5 billion, up from $1.3 billion in 1997.

2006   Two U.S. government studies of the real-world efficacy (as opposed to that revealed in clinical trials) of both antidepressants and antipsychotics show that most patients taking the drugs do not get better.

2007   One in four people who appear depressed are actually dealing with psychological distress and not a mental illness.

2007   Cable News Network (CNN) reports that one-third of veterans returning from Iraq and Afghanistan experience psychiatric or psychosocial ills.

2007   American Howard Dully publishes *My Lobotomy* (with Charles Fleming). At age 12, in 1960, Dully was one of the youngest of the more than 10,000 "patients" to receive a transorbital or ice pick lobotomy from Dr. Walter Freeman, who invented the procedure as a "cure" for mental illness.

2008   Congress passes the Americans with Disabilities Act Amendments Act to reinstate the original intent of the ADA, which was significantly narrowed by nearly 20 years of court rulings.

Glossary

Introduction

Disability is a sensitive topic for many Americans. People always seem concerned with using the "proper" language when referencing and speaking to people with disabilities. Disability definitions are further complicated by the fact that disability can be defined legally, medically, socially, and culturally. By most accounts disability encompasses a broad range of lived experiences that can be divided into physical, sensory, emotional or psychic, and intellectual or developmental disabilities. Disabled and mad people, as well as self-advocates with developmental disabilities, have reclaimed and redefined certain words, making them their own, which adds further complexity to the definitions of some words. Following is a list of terms, some of them are used in this book, others you might encounter out in the world or in future research. The definitions for these terms will not always correspond precisely to "standard" definitions that a reader might encounter in a dictionary.

Key Terms

Ableism   The systemic and institutionalized exclusion of people with disabilities that results in a society that is created by and for able-bodied people. Ableism can be seen in inaccessible built environments; discrimination against people with disabilities in education, housing, and employment; the segregation of disabled people in nursing homes, group homes, and other settings; and a general ignorance of, unfamiliarity with, lack of interest in, or open hostility toward disabled people and their well-being.

Accommodation   The legally mandated inclusion of disabled people in society through adaptations to the built environment, work routines, or other policies or procedures that enable their full participation. The Americans with Disabilities Act (1990) requires that "reasonable accommodation" be made to ensure that disabled people have the same opportunities to utilize public spaces (including transportation), educational settings, and work settings.

Complex embodiment   Theoretical or conceptual framework; first articulated by disability studies theorist Tobin Siebers in *Disability Theory* (2008); the idea that disability cannot be considered in isolation; the experience of disability is shaped by race, class, gender, religion, and other markers of identity and social position, and by the material realities or embodied nature of impairment. *See also* intersectional.

Crip   Derived from the word "cripple"; reclaimed by disability rights activists and disability studies scholars since the 1980s; denotes a politicized activist stance that rejects the medical model of disability in favor of social or cultural models of disability and the empowerment and politicization of disabled people.

Deaf (as opposed to "small d" deaf)   Big "D" Deaf denotes a distinct deaf culture rooted in the use of sign language. Most Deaf people do not consider themselves disabled, but rather part of a distinct cultural minority that speaks a separate language. They are generally opposed to oralism and cochlear implants.

Disabled people   The term "disabled people" is more common in the United Kingdom. It is used by people who want to identify disability as an important part of their identity and as something that is both political and positive. Similar to being identified as an African American or a big "D" Deaf person, people who identify as disabled consider themselves to be part of a sociopolitical minority and wish to claim their citizenship rights as a member of that group in society. People who use the term "disabled people" find the term "people with disabilities" problematic because it implies that disability is something that exists outside of them and it is something that they have or possess, rather than being part of their identity, part of what makes them a person. Critics claim that the term "people with disabilities" removes disability from the social and political realm. (*See* People with disabilities)

Disablism   Individual acts of discrimination against or hostility toward disabled people; can be the result of living in an ableist society. Most disability rights activists and disability studies scholars prefer to use the term "ableism," which has a broader and more systemic definition.

Impairment   Within the social model; a value-free or neutral form of bodily difference.

Intersectional or intersectionality   Theoretical or conceptual framework; denotes the consideration of multiple identities or subject positions simultaneously; for example, race, class, gender, religion, and disability all combine to contribute to the formation of human experience.

Mad   Reclaimed by mad activists, the mad liberation movement, and mad and disability studies scholars since the 1960s; denotes a politicized activist stance that rejects the medical model of mental illness in favor of social or cultural models of madness and the empowerment and politicization of mad people.

Medical model (of disability and mental illness)   Dominant in Western cultures since the 17th century; relies on Western medicine and its adherents; disability and mental illness are individual embodied deficits that must be corrected, cured, or eliminated in order to make a person whole or normal.

Neuro-atypical or neuroqueer   Used mostly by people living on the autism spectrum; politicized social and cultural identity; rejects the medical model of disability and mental illness; values divergent ways of thinking, processing information, communicating, sensing, emoting, and behaving.

Oralism   A movement begun in the second half of the 19th century and championed by such notable people as Alexander Graham Bell to prohibit deaf people from communicating using sign language in favor of the promotion of speaking and reading lips. The thought among its proponents was that oralism would make deaf people more "normal" and enable them to fit into mainstream society.

People with disabilities   The term "people with disabilities" originated in the United States primarily among participants in the self-advocacy movement who wanted to emphasize the "person" and not the disability. (*See* Disabled people)

Psychiatrized (or psychiatrization)   The process of, or the end result of, being labeled "mentally ill." People who use this term generally reject the medical model of mental illness and prefer instead to see diagnosing mental illness as a social, cultural, and political process.

Sanism   The systemic and institutionalized exclusion of psychiatrized people that results in a society that is created by and for "sane" people. Sanism can be seen in discrimination against people considered "mentally ill" in education, housing, and employment; the segregation of "mentally ill" people in nursing homes, group homes, and other settings; and a general ignorance of, unfamiliarity with, lack of interest in, or open hostility toward "mentally ill" people and their well-being.

Social model (of disability or madness)   Political ideology and academic theory; separates disability from impairment and roots disability in society; impairment (individual body) is not necessarily disabling; ableism and disablism are what disable people. (See Mad)

Universal design   Political ideology and academic theory or method; emerged in the United States in the 1960s; an approach that attempts to make the built environment, products, educational settings and curricula, the Internet/websites, cultural productions, accessible to the broadest range of humans without the need for accommodation. (See Accommodation)

Index

About the Author

Michael Rembis, PhD, is the director of the Center for Disability Studies and an associate professor in the Department of History at the University at Buffalo (SUNY). Rembis has authored or edited many books, articles, and book chapters, including *Defining Deviance: Sex, Science, and Delinquent Girls, 1890–1960* (2011/2013); *Disability Histories*, coedited with Susan Burch (2014); *The Oxford Handbook of Disability History*, coedited with Catherine Kudlick and Kim Nielsen (2018); *Disabling Domesticity* (2016); and *(Dis)Integration: Buffalo Poets, Writers, and Artists 2017*, coedited with colleagues (2017). In 2012, Rembis and coeditor Kim Nielsen launched the *Disability Histories* book series with University of Illinois Press. His research interests include the history of institutionalization, mad people's history, and the history of eugenics. He is currently working on a book entitled *"A Secret Worth Knowing": Living Mad Lives in the Shadow of the Asylum.*

Since completing his PhD in history, Rembis has worked with colleagues throughout the world to expand and solidify the fields of disability history and disability studies. He is a cofounder of the Disability Studies Initiative at the University of Arizona, where he helped to create undergraduate curricula in disability studies. He was a visiting scholar at the University of Notre Dame, where he participated in their Disability Studies Forum. In Buffalo, Rembis was fortunate to benefit from a close collaboration with David Gerber (distinguished professor of history [retired 2012/2014]). They worked together to expand the UB Center for Disability Studies (founded 2009) by creating a formal master's (MA) degree concentration in disability studies (2011) and a graduate certificate in disability studies (2014), as well as the Center's oral history project. Rembis has served on the American Historical Association's Committee on Disability and the board of directors of the Society for Disability Studies (2011–2014). He was elected vice president of the Society for Disability Studies in 2013 and president in 2014. The Organization of American Historians honored Rembis by naming him a Distinguished Lecturer in 2014. In 2015, Rembis was named to the Fulbright Roster of Specialists.